THE FORMATION OF THE
CHINESE PEOPLE

LONDON : HUMPHREY MILFORD

OXFORD UNIVERSITY PRESS

ERRATA

NOTE: The manuscript of this book was completed in the spring of 1923. Immediately after, the author returned to China. It was sent to the press more than two years later, but it was impossible for him to read the proofs of the work. Unexpectedly, the author revisited this country just after the printing of the book had been completed. A number of errata, mostly concerning the Chinese proper names, have been found. Some are of a general nature: for instance, a di-syllabic Chinese proper name may appear in different places differently, as, Yüng Chia, Yüng-Chia, Yüng-chia, Yüngchia, and so forth; they can be easily recognized as the variants of the same term. Those that need specific correction are included here:

Page	Line	Read	For
39	Table 11, last column	78.80	70.02
40	35	$Y = 1.67 X + 15.85$	$Y = 1.98 X + 5.54$
41	Table 13	$Y = 1.67 X + 15.85$	$Y = 167 X + 15.85$
64	10 (from the bottom)	deviation	derivation
68	7	(p. 60)	(p. 103)
70	1	differences (Graph 6)	differences
108–112	Maps 14–18, inclusive, belong to Chapter IV, immediately preceding Map 19, p. 169.		
117		29 E-period	29 C-period
		30 F-period	30 D-period
122	Graphs 69–80	80 Kiangsi	80 Kiangei
123	Graphs 81–86	82 Chekiang	82 Chekiany
		84 Kwangtung	84 Kuxesitung
		86 Kweichow	86 Yuveichow
136	1	Ch'ên	Ch'en
137	2	Wang Shih-chên	Wang Shih-chêg
138	Account 2	"The surname Chu . . . Chus of Tan-yang."	The surname Chu . . . Chus of Tan-yang.
148	10	Kao-tsu	Nao-tsu
157	16	Hsiung-nu	Hiung-nu
160	22	Ch'ên	Chen
167	4 (from the bottom)	surname	name
242	31	Liao	Lias
243	14–15	*History of the Earlier Han Dynasty*	*History of Ch'ien Han Shu*
244	26	Yang-t'u	Hang-tu
256	32	Tungt'ing	Tungting
258	25	Lang-jen	Lang-S'en
262	13 (from the bottom)	Chiang T'ung	Tsiang-tung
263	30	Yüng Ch'u	Yüng Ch'ie
266	Table 76, 3d column	907–1119 A.D.	907–1003 A.D.
267	2	Ch'iangs	Changs
269	11	Han-jen	Hanjer
275	20	Ching K'ang	Chiang K'ang

THE FORMATION OF THE CHINESE PEOPLE

AN ANTHROPOLOGICAL INQUIRY

BY

CHI LI, Ph.D. (Harvard)

LECTURER IN ANTHROPOLOGY IN THE TSING HUA RESEARCH INSTITUTE

CAMBRIDGE

HARVARD UNIVERSITY PRESS

1928

PRINTED AT THE HARVARD UNIVERSITY PRESS
CAMBRIDGE, MASS., U.S.A.

PREFACE

IN preparing this book I have tried to combine the zoölogical and the genetic methods. At present, there are hardly enough facts for a thorough study of this problem; yet, by making use of both the historical material and the anthropometrical data, one sees this problem in a different light and finds a new angle of approach. It is not merely an attempt to make a compromise between the ways of the older school of the Chinese historians, who rely almost entirely on past records for their work, and those of the Western anthropologists, who have frequently over-simplified the problem. The inquiry is designed also to help to smooth away many of the unnecessary difficulties which have persistently confronted both the Chinese historians and the Western anthropologists. No longer, for instance, do we have to look for a Chinese type as an unchangeable physical unit, or invent plausible theories to account for the Chinese origin. I have stated the nature of the problem quite clearly in the first chapter. Here it remains for me to acknowledge my indebtedness to many of my friends and teachers, who have helped me in the course of preparing this book. Professor Roland B. Dixon went over the whole book and made many valuable suggestions; Professor E. A. Hooton did the same thing. To both of them I owe my special gratitude. They have helped me both as teachers and as friends; without their guidance and encouragement the book would not have attained the present form. My friend, Dr. Biraja Guha, was a very unsparing critic of the manuscript; his criticism caused me to rewrite many parts. I wish to record my thanks to him. There are many other friends in Cambridge and at home who have assisted me in one way or another, to all of whom I wish to express my indebtedness. Special mention must be made of Mr. C. W. Bishop, who has shown a great interest in the publication of this book and has made it possible for me to get relieved from some of the pressure of work in order to revise the manuscript, which was completed more than two years ago, but was delayed in being sent to the printer because of lack of revision.

CHI LI

PEKING, January, 1926

CONTENTS

CHAPTER I

THE PROBLEM   3

CHAPTER II

THE PHYSICAL TRAITS OF THE MODERN CHINESE   7

CHAPTER III

THE EVOLUTION OF THE WE–GROUP: SIZE   56

CHAPTER IV

THE EVOLUTION OF THE WE–GROUP: CONSTITUENTS 124

CHAPTER V

MIGRATIONS OF THE WE–GROUP: FIFTEEN HUNDRED YEARS OF THE CHINESE
CENSUS 229

CHAPTER VI

THE SOUTHERN YOU–GROUP 239

CHAPTER VII

THE THREE GREAT NORTHERN INVASIONS PREVIOUS TO 1644 A.D. 262

CHAPTER VIII

INTEGRATION OF THE MODERN CHINESE 273

APPENDIX 285

THE FORMATION OF THE CHINESE
PEOPLE

CHAPTER I

THE PROBLEM

FOR generations Chinese history was studied from only one point of view. But since the rise of the Oriental school in Europe, a different angle has been chosen and consequently a different perspective is presented. These two positions are by all means new to each other — not, indeed, in open conflict, but certainly as far apart as the two polar regions. The advantage seems, when all is considered, to be on the side of the Orientalists, if only because they know something about the history of their own countries in addition to their acquaintance with the Chinese. The Chinese historians, on the other hand, have hitherto seldom transcended the boundary of the Middle Kingdom. Handicapped by their ignorance of other centres of civilization, the Chinese historians, sharing human foibles in common with the Egyptians, the Greeks, and the Romans, have considered their own country as the centre of the world, and the outsiders as barbarians, interesting only in so far as they are in some way related to the Middle Kingdom. Once this view is understood, all Chinese history becomes readable, even to a European. But the Orientalists are, of course, a little irritated at this somewhat unwarranted assumption on the part of the Chinese historian, whereby a set opinion has been developed regarding the Chinese: "They have no historical sense, they are unchanging, and their culture has remained on a dead level for four thousand years," and so on.

It is obvious that both views are equally untenable. There would be no necessity to consider them, if it were not for the fact that they tend to obscure certain anthropological problems. To say, for instance, that the Chinese have been unchanging for several thousands of years would immediately obliterate all problems concerning the physical make-up of the modern Chinese and the ethnographical changes pertaining to them during their quite remarkably long existence. It may help to simplify the task of scientists, but it certainly does not bring the solution of the problem any nearer. Rightly considered, the formation of the modern Chinese cannot be dismissed as a simple affair just because of their apparent physical homogeneity. Physically, they are in no way as homogeneous as they may appear at first glance, and their ethnography is full of ups and downs. The process of this formation is itself an anthropological problem of great magnitude, and it has taken quite a long period of time. If we take the better-known part alone, it is at least a matter of twenty-six centuries. "The Chinese of the present day," says James Legge in his Prolegomena to the translation of Shê-king, "what we call China proper, embracing the eighteen provinces, may be described in general terms as lying between 20° and 40° north latitude and 100° and 121° east longitude, and containing an area of about 1,300,000 square miles. The China of Chow dynasty lay between the 33rd and the 38th parallels of latitude, and the 106th and 119th [meridians] of longitude. The degrees of longitude included in it were thus about two thirds of the present, and of the 20 degrees of latitude, the territory of Chow embraced no more than five." [1]

One question may immediately occur: are *all* the inhabitants who to-day live between 20° and 40° north latitude and 100° and 121° east longitude the descendants of those who occupied the territory between 33° and 38° north latitude and 106° and 119° east longitude twenty-six hundred years ago? The affirmative answer may invariably be inferred from such loose statements as: "What the Chinese are to-day is what their ancestors were four, three, or two thousand years ago." If this were true, the task that I propose to undertake here would amount to an identification of the formative process of the modern Chinese with a simple biological phenomenon of multiple breeding. The problem as to the formation of the modern Chinese would be no more than that of the formation of the Chinese whose life was sung by the bard in the period of the Book of Poetry. This, I contend, is not true. The Chinese have not remained unchanged for four, three, or two thousand years. Nay, not even for one thousand or five hundred years. In the course of their expansion, they have been conquering, conquered, and reconquering, adapting themselves to new environment and reshaping their culture, absorbing new blood wherever they have gone; therefore there is a real problem in regard to the formation of the modern Chinese. Until this problem is solved, it is useless to inquire into the origin of the Chinese, as many have attempted to do.

It is useless, not only because it is a case of putting the cart before the horse, but also because no one knows exactly what the Chinese are, except as to their geographical distribution. They cannot be defined by a study of the etymological derivation of their name, for "etymological research is a scientific investigation only of second or third

[1] *The Chinese Classics*, vol. IV, part I, p. 127.

rank," says an author who has spent valuable time on this task,[1] and its value at its best will always remain philological. To study this problem properly, a consideration of the physical traits of the Chinese seems to be the only rational starting-point. The Chinese head, the Chinese body, the Chinese hand, and the Chinese foot must be studied, in order to establish a firmer concept of the physical status of the Chinese. Without a firm concept of the physical anthropology of the Chinese, it is hard to see how we can search for their origin.

But a starting-point is merely a starting-point: it helps us to establish the type of the Chinese and their affiliation with other varieties, but no more. It defines the man only in repose. The man in action, his dynamic aspect, has to be studied by a method other than biological, which may be called ethnological. The name, however, does not matter. Let us see what it may accomplish.

The Chinese historians, as has been pointed out, have always considered their country the cultural centre of the world. But they are also aware of the existence of other human beings on the fringe. From the very beginning of Chinese history, there are two distinct ethnographical concepts in their mind. The one, to borrow Mr. Sumner's apt phrase here, may be described as the "We-group," the group which the Chinese historians consider as their kind, the civilizers. What they have called the barbarians may be described for our purpose as the "You-group."[2] It must be emphasized here that the line of demarcation between these two groups is by no means always a political one. Political boundary, no doubt, helps to clarify the frontier of the We-group in many cases; but it has not been such a powerful agency of assimilation as it might have been under different circumstances. The coexistence of several distinct ethnical units on the constantly changing political map of China is familiar to any reader of Chinese history. Even now there are at least five distinct ethnical units under the flag of the Chinese Republic.

The grouping is, then, entirely ethnographical. There are distinct ethnographical traits, which, in the minds of Chinese historians, are always associated with the We-group. Any human being possessing

---

[1] This refers to an article by Berthold Laufer on "The Name China," *T'oung-Pao*, XIII, 725. The most recent discussion on the etymology of this word is between Laufer and Paul Pelliot. The article by Pelliot is to be found in Bull. École Française de l'Extrême Orient, IV (1904), 143–150. A summary of earlier discussions on this interesting topic is also found in these two articles.

[2] Mr. Sumner, however, considers this concept peculiar to primitive society. *Folkways* (Ginn & Co., 1911), p. 12.

these traits, no matter what his physical appearance, black-haired or red-haired, is to be classified in the We-group; devoid of these traits, he is a barbarian — of the You-group.

The ethnographical traits associated with the We-group, however, are in no way stereotyped at any time, in spite of Chinese conservatism. Compare, for instance, the manners of the Chinese in the She-king period with those of their descendants under the T'ang dynasty, and again with what one observes at the close of the nineteenth century, when the men wear queues and the women bind their feet. The immensity of the gap needs certainly many years to bridge; and the changing ethnical characters studied in their changing perspective are useful clues in interpreting the formative process of the modern Chinese.

If we confine our inquiry spatially within the eighteen provinces and temporally between the period of the Book of Poetry and the fall of the Ming dynasty (A.D. 1644) we are even then setting ourselves quite a formidable task. But it is not a desperate one, since we need not go into the four dimensions of the problem all at once. I propose to attack the problem on the basis of the two fundamental Chinese historical concepts which I have already explained. On the one hand, we have all the romances and adventures associated with the evolution of the historical We-group in the course of its expansion; on the other hand, the evolution of the You-group within these limits, proceeding side by side with this expansion.

Several salient aspects of the problem are immediately suggested here. What are the routes that the We-group have taken in their course of expansion? What are the characteristics of the historical You-group? What are the relations of the You-group with the We-group — are they exterminated, absorbed, or simply driven southward? All these aspects of the question I propose to study here in a somewhat novel fashion; and I believe that only in this way can we arrive inductively at any substantial knowledge of the Chinese prototype in regard to whose origin there has been so much discussion.

CHAPTER II

THE PHYSICAL TRAITS OF THE MODERN CHINESE

THE starting-point is to be China proper. China proper, defined politically, lies between 20° and 40° north latitude and 99° and 121° east longitude. This immediately excludes from our attention everything outside of this boundary — Manchuria and Tibet, for instance, in spite of their cultural affiliation with China proper in many respects. But within this limit there is reason to draw another line. In China proper there are some inhabitants who have been associated with the making of Chinese history from the very beginning and who acknowledge their association with it. There are others who do not — for instance, the Miaotze and the Manchus, who still call themselves the Miaotze and the Manchus. They are found in most parts of China proper. But with them we shall be concerned only in so far as they are related to the historical Chinese.

We are thus led to a tentative definition of the Chinese.

The Chinese are the people who are found in, or whose origin is traceable to, the land called China proper, and who acknowledge their association with the making of Chinese history from the beginning. This, it must be emphasized, is only a tentative definition. But it is these Chinese whom I propose to study physically in this chapter.

I. THE DATA AND THEIR SOURCES

The first observations on Chinese skulls, so far as we know, were published in 1790, by Blumenbach. Since then von der Hoeven, Sandifort, Aitgen, Lucae, Becker, von Baer, Maggiorani, Welcker, Retzius, Dusseaus, Pruner Bey, Davis, Swaving, de Koning, Hudler have all made casual observations. In 1877 Schaaffhausen began the publication *Anthropologischen Sammlungen Deutschlands*, in which ninety Chinese skulls were described in more or less detail. This was followed by the studies of Flower, Zaborowski, and Broca. Ten Kate, however, was the first anthropologist who made an intensive study of the physical traits of the Mongoloids. In his doctor's dissertation, he made, among other observations, studies of ten Chinese skulls. Then appeared the catalogue of Quatrefages and Hamy and the study of Koganei. But it remained for Haberer to give the direction of all these studies a new twist.   His publication on *Schädel und Skeletteile aus Peking,* although it has been out for twenty years, still remains as the standard reference to Chinese somatology.   Many of the anthropometric means established by him are still used.   In the last twenty years, it seems that the progress of study along this line has been almost nil.   With the exception of some minor work by Mochi and Reicher, we have almost nothing worth mentioning here.   Nor is the state of affairs in any way better with regard to the purely anthropometrical studies, which started much earlier.   The workers in this field can be counted almost on the fingers of two hands — Weisbach, Bréton, Hagen, Koganei, Girard, Legendre, and Stein.   Yet these studies are almost all, without exception, the products of casual diversion; so we have to conclude that there is as yet not a single series of systematic anthropometrical studies on the Chinese.   However, it must not be inferred that these results have no scientific value.[1]

My own observations were made between March 1 and October 1, 1921.   The subjects consist of two classes: (1) Chinese students in the Eastern universities of the United States of America, and (2) Chinese laborers, all from Kwangtung, in Boston.

Instruments Used

Anthropometer—P. Hermann, Zürich.
Spreading caliper—P. Hermann, Zürich.
Sliding compass—Collin, Paris.
Steel tape—Lufkin Rule Co., Saginaw, Mich., U.S.A.
Color scale—P. Hermann, Zürich.

METHODS

(a) *Metrical*

1. *Stature.*   The subject was made to stand erect against a wall, with the heels together and the arms hanging in a natural position.   The vertex of his head was ascertained.   Then he was measured three times in succession by the anthropometer.   Whenever possible, the subject was made to take off his shoes; if not, the stature was corrected by taking off 2 cm.

2. *Auditory height.*   With the subject in the same position, the bottom of the notch between the tragus and the helix of the ear was taken as the anatomical landmark.   The head height was obtained by subtracting the auditory height from the total height.

[1] See the bibliography at the end of this chapter.

3. *Head length.* The distance between the most prominent point of the glabella and the most prominent point on the occiput was measured with the spreading caliper.

4. *Head breadth.* With the same instrument, the maximum transverse diameter was measured.

5. *Minimum frontal diameter.* The shortest horizontal breadth between the two temporal crests on the frontal bone was measured with the spreading caliper.

6. *Bizygomatic diameter.* The greatest distance between the bizygomatic arches measured with the spreading caliper.

7. *Horizontal circumference.* This was measured by passing the steel tape across the occipital point and over the brow-ridges.

8. *Nasion-menton height.* The nasion was first ascertained with the second finger of the right hand, and marked by a pencil point. The distance between the lowest point of the bony chin and the nasion was measured with the sliding compass.

9. *Nasal height.* The distance between the nasion and the nasal septum was measured with the sliding compass.

10. *Nasal breadth.* The greatest breadth of the nasal wings was measured with the sliding compass.

(b) *Descriptive*

Skin color. Von Luschan color scale was used. I have found that the yellow series of the scale is altogether unsatisfactory. In all cases, I have secured only a remotely approximate matching. The yellow series consists of 7 grades, numbered 15 to 21. The other descriptive terms are adapted from Hrdlička, *Anthropometry*, pages 52–88.

TABLE 1

ANTHROPOMETRICAL MEASUREMENTS OF 111 CHINESE

A.		1	2	3	4	5	6	7
B.	Province	Chekiang	Kiangsu	Hupeh	Kiangsu	Chekiang	Kwangtung	Shansi
C.	Sex..................	M.	M.	M.	M.	M.	M.	M.
D.	Age..................	23	23	28	21	24	26	27
E.	Stature...............1688		1662	1744	1672	1638	1740	1673
F.	Head height..........	126	126	125	129	124	131	127
G.	Head length..........	190	194	198	186	192	182	192
H.	Head breadth........	151	155	162	160	157	147	143
I.	Height-length index....	66.32	64.95	63.13	69.35	64.58	71.98	66.15
J.	Length-breadth index ..	79.47	79.7	81.82	86.02	81.77	80.8	76.6
K.	Horizontal circumfer...	...	...	...	...	...	...	...
L.	Minimum frontal diam.	95	105	102	105	105	97	100
M.	Bizygomatic diameter ..	130	143	140	147	148	138	137
N.	Nasion-menton height..	115	123	128	120	116	131	119
O.	Facial index..........	88.5	86.01	91.4	81.6	78.4	94.9	86.9
P.	Nasal height..........	46	54	52	51	49	56	52
Q.	Nasal breadth	35	38	38	42	36	35	38
R.	Nasal index..........	76.09	70.39	73.1	82.35	73.47	62.5	67.3

A.		17	18	19	20	21	22	23
B.	Province	Hunan	Fukien	Kwangtung	Chihli	Kwangtung	Kwangtung	Kwangtung
C.	Sex..................	M.	M.	M.	M.	M.	M.	M.
D.	Age..................	23	23	24	24	56	21	23
E.	Stature..............1578		1635	1664	1656	1604	1650	1662
F.	Head height.........	119	119	131	113	111	116	115
G.	Head length.........	185	178	185	182	184	200	192
H.	Head breadth........	152	155	150	150	147	155	157
I.	Height-length index ...	64.32	66.85	70.81	62.09	60.33	58	59.90
J.	Length-breadth index .	82.2	87.1	81.1	82.4	74.9	77.5	81.2
K.	Horizontal circumfer. .	*	*	*	*	*	*	*
L.	Minimum frontal diam.	105	106	106	108	103	114	104
M.	Bizygomatic diameter	140	142	142	142	135	146	141
N.	Nasion-menton height .	119	117	115	119	124	118	116
O.	Facial index.........	85	82.4	81.0	83.8	91.85	80.82	82.3
P.	Nasal height.........	50	53	51	54	43	47	50
Q.	Nasal breadth........	38	39	39	35	36	44	37
R.	Nasal index..........	76	73.6	76.5	64.8	83.7	93.6	74

TABLE 1 (Continued)

ANTHROPOMETRICAL MEASUREMENTS OF 111 CHINESE

A	8	9	10	11	12	13	14	15	16
B	Hupeh	Kiangsu	Kiangsi	Hunan	Kiangsu	Fukien	Kiangsi	Kiangsi	Kiangsu
C	M.	M.	M.	M.	M.	M.	M.	M.	M.
D	28	23	30	22	25	24	24	24	20
E	1572	1593	1673	1580	1610	1720	1655	1715	1645
F	120	125	132	120	126	120	131	125	114
G	186	186	196	191	182	185	169	177	177
H	158	162	145	147	153	157	167	165	149
I	64.52	67.20	67.35	62.83	69.23	64.86	77.51	70.62	64.41
J	85	87	73.98	76.96	84.1	84.9	98.82	93.22	84.2
K	...	...	...	...	...	...	...	*	*
L	105	108	101	95	106	95	108	120	102
M	135	142	135	132	138	142	154	155	130
N	117	120	122	113	117	118	120	121	119
O	86.7	84.5	90.4	85.6	84.8	83.1	77.9	78.1	88.15
P	56	59	49	47	50	50	51	51	54
Q	38	38	40	35	40	37	39	37	38
R	67.86	64.4	81.6	74.5	80	74	76.47	72.55	70.37

A	24	25	26	27	28	29	30	31	32
B	Kwangtung	Kwangtung	Kwangtung	Kwangtung	Kwangtung	Kwangtung	Kwangtung	Kwangtung	Kwangtung
C	M.	M.	M.	M.	M.	M.	M.	M.	M.
D	19	33	(?)	60	24	33	26	30	27
E	1635	1689	1702	1446	1472	1669	1694	1693	1612
F	121	138	116	134	114	127	130	135	109
G	180	185	192	188	192	183	188	178	184
H	145	154	156	162	156	157	153	158	146
I	67.22	74.50	60.42	71.28	59.38	69.40	69.15	75.84	59.24
J	80.6	83.2	81.25	86.2	81.25	85.8	81.4	88.8	79.35
K	*	*	*	*	*	*	*	*	*
L	105	116	112	109	108	100	112	107	104
M	140	127	144	139	149	141	148	145	138
N	108	98 (?)	112	127	111	109	123	121	112
O	77.14	77.16	77.8	91.4	74.5	77.3	83.11	83.45	81.2
P	46	47	54	55	41	43	49	54	45
Q	36	38	42	40	37	35	40	39	35
R	78.2	80.85	77.8	72.7	90.24	81.4	81.6	72.2	77.8

TABLE 1 (Continued)

A.		33	34	35	36	37	38	39
B.	Province	Kwangtung	Kwangtung	Kwangtung	Kwangtung	Kwangtung	Kwangtung	Chekiang
C.	Sex	M.	M.	M.	M.	M.	M.	M.
D.	Age	27	24	30	21	27	46	25
E.	Stature	1571	1630	1725	1710	1697	1700	1663
F.	Head height	120	120	135	127	130	121	128
G.	Head length	175	196	192	197	186	185	188
H.	Head breadth	146	146	152	153	154	151	162
I.	Height-length index	68.57	61.22	70.31	64.47	69.89	65.41	68.09
J.	Length-breadth index	83.43	74.5	79.2	77.66	82.8	81.62	86.2
K.	Horizontal circumfer.	*	*	*	*	*	*	*
L.	Min. frontal diam.	98	107	113	110	109	105	112
M.	Bizygomatic diam.	134	146	146	141	149	147	146
N.	Nasion-menton height	106	123	119	128	134	124	136
O.	Facial index	79.1	84.25	81.5	90.8	89.9	84.35	93.2
P.	Nasal height	46	52	51	53	61	54	55
Q.	Nasal breadth	34	40	44	39	38	44	34
R.	Nasal index	73.9	76.9	86.3	73.6	62.3	81.5	61.8

A.		49	50	51	52	53	54	55
B.	Province	Kiangsu	Kiangsu	Fukien	(?)	Kwangtung	Chekiang	Nganhui
C.	Sex	M.	M.	M.	M.	M.	M.	M.
D.	Age	19	23	21	23	23	24	27
E.	Stature	1698	1740	1722	1701	1679	1685	1791
F.	Head height	134	133	130	135	126	120	149
G.	Head length	184	184	174	186	192	186	186
H.	Head breadth	156	170	154	152	149	157	156
I.	Height-length index	72.83	72.28	74.71	72.58	65.63	64.52	80.10
J.	Length-breadth index	84.78	92.37	88.51	81.52	77.60	84.4	83.87
K.	Horizontal circumfer.	550	576	557	...	*	*	*
L.	Minimum frontal diam.	107	125	107	105	107	106	96
M.	Bizygomatic diameter	147	157	138	138	140	140	141
N.	Nasion-menton height	122	122	116	118	133	136	129
O.	Facial index	82.99	77.71	84.06	85.51	95	97.14	91.49
P.	Nasal height	58	52	57	53	56	51	57
Q.	Nasal breadth	39	42	37	39	39	42	42
R.	Nasal index	67.24	80.77	64.91	73.58	69.64	82.35	73.68

TABLE 1 (Continued)

A	40	41	42	43	44	45	46	47	48
B	Chekiang	Chekiang	Fukien	Kwangsi	Kwangtung	Chihli	Fukien	Kiangsu	Fukien
C	M.	M.	M.	M.	M.	M.	M.	M.	M.
D	23	22	23	31	22	25	30	23	20
E	1580	1604	1716	1681	1691	1699	1655	1701	1796
F	128	123	129	125	129	126	126	130	138
G	194	195	184	186	188	192	185	185	188
H	151	150	158	150	146	160	147	152	154
I	65.98	70.15	70.11	67.20	68.62	65.63	68.11	70.27	73.4
J	77.84	85.7	85.9	80.65	77.66	83.33	79.46	82.16	81.91
K	*	*	*	*	547	561	542	538	570
L	100	101	105	110	106	106	106	104	112
M	133	138	143	138	134	153	143	135	148
N	117	102	128	124	122	128	115	125	131
O	87.97	73.9	89.5	89.9	91.04	83.66	80.42	92.59	88.51
P	47	48	52	52	55	59	50	56	59
Q	35	34	38	36	37	36	36	39	40
R	74.5	70.8	73.1	69.23	62.27	61.02	72	69.64	67.8

A	56	57	58	59	60	61	62	63	64
B	Chihli	Chekiang	Chihli	Szechuan	Kwangtung	Kiangsi	Chekiang	Nganhui	Hunan
C	M.	M.	M.	M.	M.	M.	M.	M.	M.
D	(?)	24	24	23	26	24	21	22	22
E	1691	1650	1699	1590	1684	1775	1695	1632	1714
F	139	125	128	126	123	136	138	120	125
G	192	184	193	191	187	183	187	191	183
H	164	156	152	163	148	162	150	153	144
I	72.40	67.93	66.32	65.97	65.78	74.32	73.80	62.38	68.68
J	85.42	84.78	78.76	85.34	79.14	88.52	80.21	80.10	79.12
K	...	...	*	567	537	550	545	558	529
L	108	112	107	118	106	112	103	107	104
M	143	144	141	147	138	152	135	143	135
N	127	119	111	132	133	115	118	128	111
O	88.81	82.64	78.72	89.80	96.38	75.66	87.41	89.51	82.22
P	55	54	46	58	58	46	47	51	47
Q	39	39	36	40	36	38	37	40	37
R	70.91	72.22	78.26	68.97	62.07	82.61	78.72	78.43	78.72

TABLE 1 (CONTINUED)

A.		65	66	67	68	69	70	71
B.	Province	Hunan	Chihli	Kiangsi	Kwangtung	Shensi	Kiangsu	Chekiang
C.	Sex.................	M.	M.	M.	M.	M.	M.	M.
D.	Age.................	20	23	26	23	27	23	29
E.	Stature.............1613		1712	1745	1651	1739	1774	1730
F.	Head height..........	114	123	133	121	134	130	122
G.	Head length..........	187	183	194	185	192	183	185
H.	Head breadth........	147	158	159	153	139	157	154
I.	Height-length index....	60.96	67.21	68.56	65.41	69.79	71.04	65.95
J.	Length-breadth index ..	78.61	86.34	81.96	82.71	72.40	85.79	83.24
K.	Horizontal circumfer. ..	528	505	565	548	543	555	543
L.	Minimum frontal diam.	99	117	108	110	101	108	105
M.	Bizygomatic diameter .	138	144	142	143	137	143	143
N.	Nasion-menton height..	118	126	132	124	121	122	113
O.	Facial index..........	85.51	87.50	92.96	86.71	88.32	85.31	79.02
P.	Nasal height..........	50	54	56	52	52	51	51
Q.	Nasal breadth........	36	40	39	37	39	35	42
R.	Nasal index..........	72	74.07	69.94	71.15	75	68.63	82.35

A.		81	82	83	84	85	86	87
B.	Province	Hunan	Hunan	Kiangsu	Kwangtung	Chekiang	Fukien	Szechuan
C.	Sex.................	M.	M.	M.	M.	M.	M.	M.
D.	Age.................	25	24	22	21	22	29	30
E.	Stature.............1612		(?)	1678	1648	1699	1703	1683
F.	Head height..........	127	*	138	135	122	133	118
G.	Head length..........	192	188	180	191	185	190	191
H.	Head breadth........	145	150	163	144	148	150	154
I.	Height-length index....	66.15	*	76.67	70.68	65.95	70	61.78
J.	Length-breadth index ..	75.52	79.79	90.56	75.39	80	78.95	80.63
K.	Horizontal circumfer. ..	560	545	552	552	507	550	557
L.	Minimum frontal diam.	108	110	117	108	104	108	111
M.	Bizygomatic diameter .	134	160	145	137	137	142	148
N.	Nasion-menton height..	119	125	135	117	123	125	120
O.	Facial index..........	88.81	89.29	93.10	85.40	89.78	88.03	81.08
P.	Nasal height..........	56	55	60	50	53	55	52
Q.	Nasal breadth........	35	36	40	37	37	38	39
R.	Nasal index..........	62.50	65.45	66.67	74	69.81	69.09	75

TABLE 1 (Continued)

A......	72	73	74	75	76	77	78	79	80
B......	Nganhui	Fukien	Chekiang	Nganhui	Chekiang	Chekiang	Shantung	Kiangsi	Kiangsu
C......	M.	M.	M.	M.	M.	M.	M.	M.	M.
D......	23	23	22	22	22	24	28	25	26
E......	1740	1696	1667	1696	1628	1710	1806	1755	1658
F......	128	132	128	141	129	127	135	134	129
G......	196	191	187	187	183	193	195	190	188
H......	148	153	149	157	156	155	153	156	157
I......	65.31	69.11	68.45	75.40	70.49	65.80	69.23	70.53	68.62
J......	75.51	80.10	79.68	83.96	85.25	80.31	78.46	82.11	83.51
K......	566	545	540	550	550	556	570	562	560
L......	113	101	110	105	105	106	108	118	112
M......	143	127	140	142	142	147	141	148	142
N......	122	123	123	130	122	133	142	127	136
O......	85.31	89.78	87.86	91.55	85.92	90.48	100.7	85.81	95.77
P......	49	52	52	59	51	56	55	55	56
Q......	40	39	35	43	36	40	38	42	38
R......	81.63	94.23	67.31	72.88	70.59	71.43	69.09	76.36	67.86

A......	88	89	90	91	92	93	94	95	96
B......	Kiangsu	Yunnan	Chekiang	Hunan	Kwangtung	Kwangtung	Kiangsu	Hunan	Chihli
C......	M.	M.	M.	M.	M.	M.	M.	M.	M.
D......	26	28	24	27	22	23	23	25	27
E......	1654	1648	1703	1627	1735	1646	1754	1696	1815
F......	127	117	137	138	135	130	128	123	143
G......	188	192	178	190	190	191	177	203	175
H......	156	154	149	153	154	150	145	155	164
I......	67.55	60.94	76.97	72.63	71.05	68.06	72.36	60.59	81.71
J......	82.98	80.21	83.71	80.53	81.05	78.53	81.92	76.35	93.71
K......	557	560	530	552	560	560	501	581	550
L......	115	106	127	111	111	102	103	111	117
M......	138	136	145	146	142	140	137	145	151
N......	121	127	125	113	123	128	127	118	123
O......	87.68	93.38	86.21	77.40	86.62	91.43	92.70	81.38	81.46
P......	53	62	53	48	52	50	53	49	56
Q......	38	39	41	35	40	43	36	38	41
R......	71.70	62.9	77.36	72.92	76.92	86	67.92	77.55	73.21

TABLE 1 (Continued)

A.		97	98	99	100	101	102	103
B.	Province	Chihli	Shansi	Chekiang	Fukien	Kiangsu	Kiangsu	Kiangsu
C.	Sex..................	M.	M.	M.	M.	M.	M.	M.
D.	Age..................	(?)	24	24	20	36	23	24 (?)
E.	Stature...............	1725	1663	1723	1682	1833	1666	1675
F.	Head height..........	135	141	127	119	141	145	123
G.	Head length..........	188	185	196	182	201	181	179
H.	Head breadth........	151	153	163	153	158	163	147
I.	Height-length index ...	71.81	72.31	64.80	65.38	70.15	80.11	68.7
J.	Length-breadth index ..	80.32	78.46	83.16	84.07	78.61	90.06	82.12
K.	Horizontal circumfer. ..	507	560	572	534	582	550	535
L.	Minimum frontal diam.	112	116	110	127	113	112	98
M.	Bizygomatic diameter .	139	142	146	138	145	144	134
N.	Nasion-menton height..	126	130	128	126	136	130	126
O.	Facial index..........	90.65	91.55	87.67	91.30	93.79	90.28	94.03
P.	Nasal height..........	56	61	53	56	61	53	57
Q.	Nasal breadth........	38	38	39	39	40	34	36
R.	Nasal index..........	67.86	62.30	73.58	69.64	65.57	64.15	63.16

TABLE 1 (Continued)

A......	104	105	106	107	108	109	110	111
B......	(?)	Fukien	Chekiang	Kiangsu	Kiangsu	Hunan	Hunan	Kiangsu
C......	M.	M.	M.	F.	F.	M.	M.	M.
D......	24	26	26	...	...	23	(?)	30
E......	1661	1658	1653	1565	1490	1722	1585	1703
F......	130	126	114	119	127	125	116	130
G.....	191	191	192	173	180	190	186	192
H.....	151	152	142	145	150	150	147	155
I......	68.06	65.97	59.38	68.79	70.56	65.79	62.37	67.71
J......	79.06	79.58	73.96	83.82	83.33	78.45	79.03	80.73
K.....	563	565	545	*	*	547	542	563
L......	107	110	112	99	108	107	107	110
M.....	143	141	141	128	140	138	133	142
N......	112	122	120	106	117	118	119	125
O.....	78.82	86.52	85.11	82.81	83.57	85.51	89.47	88.03
P......	56	52	57	47	47	53	51	58.5
Q......	39	37	40	36	36	34	38	39
R......	69.64	71.15	70.18	76.60	76.60	64.15	74.51	66.81

TABLE 2

ANTHROPOLOGICAL OBSERVATIONS OF 111 CHINESE

a.		**1**	**2**	**3**	**4**	**5**	**6**	**7**
b.	SKIN COLOR	10, 9	14, 9	12, 9	9, 7	12, 7	13, 9	12, 9
c.	HAIR:							
	Col.	Black	Black	Black	Black	Black	Black	Black
	Quan.	...	...	...	...	...	Med.	Med.
	Form	Straight	Straight	Straight	Straight	Straight	Straight	Straight
d.	BEARD:							
	Col.	...	Black	Black	Black	D. Br.	Black	Black
	Quan.	V. Sm.	Sm.	Sm.	Sm.	Sm.	Sm.	Med.
	Form	...	Straight	Straight	Straight	Straight	Straight	Straight
e.	EYE COL.:							
	Iris	Br.	L. Br.	L. Br.	L. Br.	L. Br.	L. Br.	L. Br.
	Sclerotic	...	...	Yellowish	Yellowish	Yellowish	Yellowish	Yellowish
f.	EYEBROWS	Med.	Med.	Med.	Med.	Med.	Med.	Bushy
g.	BROW-RIDGES	...	...	...	...	...	Mod.	Mod.
h.	EYELIDS:							
	Opening	Nar.	Nar.	Med.	Nar.	Nar.	Nar.	...
	Dir.	Sm. Obl.	Sm. Obl.	Sm. Obl.	Obl.	Obl.	Obl. Sm.	Obl.
	Epican.	...	...	...	Pr.	Pr.	Pr.	Abs.
i.	FOREHEAD:							
	Height	Med.	High	Med.	Med.	Med.	Med.	Med.
	Breadth	Med.	Med.	Med.	Broad	Broad	Broad	Med.
	Slope	Sm.	Round	Round	Sm.	Sm.	Sm.	None
j.	NOSE:							
	N. D.	Med.	Med.	Med.	Med.	Sm.	Med.	Sm.
	Sept.	Hori.	Hori.	Hori.	Sm. Up	Hori.	Hori.	Up
k.	MALAR	Med.	Med.	Mod.	Pron.	Med.	Med.	Pron.
l.	PROGNATH.	None	None	None	None	None	None	None
m.	CHIN	Med.	Pron.	Med.	Med.	Med.	Med.	Med.

a.		**15**	**16**	**17**	**18**	**19**	**20**	**21**
b.	SKIN COLOR	9, 9	11, 9	14, 9	15, 9	11. 9	14, 9	14, 9
c.	HAIR:							
	Col.	Black	Black	Black	Black	Black	Black	Black
	Quan.	Med.	Med.	Med.	Med.	Med.	Med.	Med.
	Form	Straight	Straight	Straight	Straight	Straight	Straight	Straight
d.	BEARD:							
	Col.	Sm.	Sm.	Sm.	Sm.	Sm.	...	...
	Quan.	...	...	...	...	...	Sm.	Sm.
	Form	...	...	...	...	...	...	...
e.	EYE COL.:							
	Iris	L. Br.	L. Br.	L. Br.	L. Br.	L. Br.	L. Br.	L. Br.
	Sclerotic	Yellowish	Yellowish	Yellowish	Yellowish	Yellowish	Yellowish	Yellowish
f.	EYEBROWS	Med.	Med.	Bushy	Med.	Bushy	Med.	Med.
g.	BROW-RIDGES	Perc.	Sm.	Mod.	Mod.	...	Mod.	...
h.	EYELIDS:							
	Opening	Nar.	Nar.	Nar.	Nar.	Nar.	Nar.	Nar.
	Dir.	Obl.	Sm. Obl.	Obl.	Obl.	Obl.	Obl.	Obl.
	Epican.	Pr.	Pr.	Pr.	Abs.	Pr.	Pr.	Pr.
i.	FOREHEAD:							
	Height	Med.	Med.	Med.	Med.	Med.	Med.	Med.
	Breadth	Broad	Med.	Broad	Med.	Med.	Broad	Med.
	Slope	Mod. Ro.	Mod. Ro.	Mod. Ro.	Mod. Ro.	Mod. Ro.	Mod. Ro.	Sm. Ro.
j.	NOSE:							
	N. D.	Deep	Med.	Med.	Med.	Med.	Med.	Med.
	Sept.	Hori.	Hori.	Hori.	Down	Hori.	Hori.	Down Ex.
k.	MALAR	Pron.	Pron.	Pron.	Pron.	Pron.	Pron.	Pron.
l.	PROGNATH.	None	None	None	Med.	None	None	Med.
m.	CHIN	Med.	Med.	Med.	Med.	Med.	Med.	Med.

TABLE 2 (Continued)

ANTHROPOLOGICAL OBSERVATIONS OF 111 CHINESE

		8	9	10	11	12	13	14
a.								
b.	SKIN COLOR	15, 10	12, 9	14, 10	13, 12	18, 9	12, 9	9, 9
c.	HAIR:							
	Col.	Black	Black	Black	Black	Black	Black	Bl., D. Br.
	Quan.	Med.	Med.	Med.	Med.	Med.	Med.	Med.
	Form	Straight	Straight	Straight	Straight	Straight	Straight	Straight
d.	BEARD:							
	Col.	Black	...	...	...	...	...	...
	Quan.	Sm.	Sm.	Sm.	Sm.	Sm.	Sm.	Sm.
	Form	...	...	Straight	...	...	...	...
e.	EYE COL.:							
	Iris	L. Br.	L. Br.	L. Br.	L. Br.	L. Br.	L. Br.	L. Br.
	Sclerotic							
f.	EYEBROWS	Med.	Med.	Med.	Med.	Med.	Bushy	Med.
g.	BROW-RIDGES	Med.	Med.	Med.	Sm.	Sm.	Sm.	Perc.
h.	EYELIDS:							
	Opening	Round	Nar.	Round	Nar.	Nar.	Nar.	Nar.
	Dir.	Hor.	Obl.	Hor.	Obl.	Obl.	Obl.	Obl.
	Epican.	Pr.	Abs.	Pr.	Abs.	Pr.	Pr.	Pr.
i.	FOREHEAD:							
	Height	Med.	Med.	Med.	High	Med.	Med.	Med.
	Breadth	Broad	Broad	Med.	Med.	Broad	Med.	Broad
	Slope	Round	Round	Bulging	None	Round	Mod.	Mod. Ro.
j.	NOSE:							
	N. D.	Med.	Deep	Med.	Deep	Med.	Med.	Med.
	Sept.	Hori.	Hori.	Down	Hori.	Hori.	Hori.	...
k.	MALAR	Med.	Pron.	Sm.	Med.	Pron.	Med.	Pron.
l.	PROGNATH.	Sm.	None	None	None	None	None	None
m.	CHIN	Sm.	...	...	Med.	Med.	Med.	Med.

		22	23	24	25	26	27	28
a.								
b.	SKIN COLOR	12, 9	12, 9	12, 11	13, 9		12, 9	12, 10
c.	HAIR:							
	Col.	Black	Black	Black	Black		Black	Black
	Quan.	Med.	Med.	Med.	Med.		Sm.	Med.
	Form	Straight	Sm.Wavy	Straight	Straight		St.Sm.,Wavy	Straight
d.	BEARD:							
	Col.	...	...	...	...		...	...
	Quan.	Sm.	Sm.	Sm.	Sm.		Sm.	Sm.
	Form	...	...	...	...		...	...
e.	EYE COL.:							
	Iris	L. Br.	L. Br.	L. Br.	L. Br.		L. Br.	L. Br.
	Sclerotic	Yellowish	Yellowish	Yellowish	...		...	Yellowish
f.	EYEBROWS	Bushy	Bushy	Med.	Bushy		Med.	Bushy
g.	BROW-RIDGES	Sm.	Mod.	Sm.	Mod.		Mod.	Sm.
h.	EYELIDS:							
	Opening	Nar.	Nar.	Nar.	Nar.		...	Long
	Dir.	Obl.	Obl.	Sm. Obl.	Sm. Obl.		Hori.	Sm. Obl.
	Epican.	Pr.	Pr.	Abs.	Pr.		Abs.	Pr.
i.	FOREHEAD:							
	Height	Med.	Med.	Med.	Med.		Med.	Med.
	Breadth	Broad	Broad	Med.	...		Broad	Med.
	Slope	Mod. Ro.	None	Mod. Ro.	Mod. Ro.		Mod.	Mod. Ro.
j.	NOSE:							
	N. D.	Med.	Sm.	Med.	Mod.		Med.	Med.
	Sept.	Hori.	Hori.	Hori.	Hori.		Hori.	Up. Ex.
k.	MALAR	Pron.	Pron.	Pron.	Pron.		Exces.	Pron.
l.	PROGNATH.	None	None	None	None		Sm.	None
m.	CHIN	Med.	Med.	Med.	Med.		Med.	Med.

TABLE 2 (CONTINUED)

a.		29	30	31	32	33	34	35
b.	SKIN COLOR	15, 12	12, 10	13, 10	13, 10	13, 10	13, 10	12, 9
c.	HAIR:							
	Col.	Black	Black	Black	Black	Bl., Y.	Bl., Y.	Black
	Quan.	Med.	Sm.	Med.	Med.	Med.	Med.	Med.
	Form	Straight	Straight	Straight	Straight	Straight	Straight	Straight
d.	BEARD:							
	Col.	...	...	...	...	...	...	...
	Quan.	Sm.	Sm.	Sm.	Sm.	Sm.	Sm.	Sm.
	Form	...	...	...	...	...	...	...
e.	EYE COL.:							
	Iris	L. Br.	L. Br.	L. Br.	L. Br.	L. Br.	L. Br.	L. Br.
	Sclerotic	Yellowish	Yellowish	Yellowish	Yellowish	...	Yellowish	...
f.	EYEBROWS	Med.	Bushy	Med.	Med.	Med.		Med.
g.	BROW-RIDGES	Sm.	Mod.	Mod.	Mod.	Perc.	Mod.	Mod.
h.	EYELIDS:							
	Opening	Long	Long	Long	Long	Long	Long	Long
	Dir.	Sm. Obl.	Sm. Obl.	Sm. Obl.	Sm. Obl.	Sm. Obl.	Sm. Obl.	Sm. Obl.
	Epican.	Abs.	Pr.	Pr.	Pr.	Abs.	Pr.	Abs.
i.	FOREHEAD:							
	Height	Med.	Med.	Med.	Med.	Med.	Med.	Med.
	Breadth	Med.	Broad	Broad	Broad	Broad	Med.	Broad
	Slope	Mod. Ro.	Mod. Ro.	Mod.	Pron.	Mod. Ro.	Mod. Ro.	Mod.
j.	NOSE:							
	N. D.	Med.	Med.	Med.	Med.	Med.	Med.	Med.
	Sept.	Hori.	Hori.	Hori.	Hori.	Hori.	Hori.	Hori.
k.	MALAR	Med.	Pron.	Pron.	Pron.	Pron.	Exc.	Pron.
l.	PROGNATH.	None	Sm.	Sm.	Sm.	None	Pron.	Sm.
m.	CHIN	Med.	Med.	Med.	Med.	Med.	Sm.	Med.

a.		43	44	45	46	47	48	49
b.	SKIN COLOR	12, 9	10, 8	11, 8	12, 9	9	7	9
c.	HAIR:							
	Col.	Black	Black	Black, R.	Black	Black	Black	Black
	Quan.	Med.	Med.	Sm.	Med.	Sm.	Med.	Thick
	Form	Wavy	Straight	Straight	Straight	Straight	Straight	Straight
d.	BEARD:							
	Col.	Black	Black	Black, R.	...	...	...	...
	Quan.	Med.	Sm.	Bushy	Sm.	Sm.	Sm.	None
	Form	Wavy	Straight	Straight	...	...	...	...
e.	EYE COL.:							
	Iris	R. Br.	L. Br.	R. Br.	L. Br.	L. Br.	L. Br.	Br.
	Sclerotic	Yellowish	...	Yellowish	Yellowish	Yellowish	...	Yellowish
f.	EYEBROWS	Med.	Bushy	Med.	Med.	Med.	Med.	Med.
g.	BROW-RIDGES	Sm.	Sm.	Sm.	Pron.	Med.	Med.	Sm.
h.	EYELIDS:							
	Opening	Long	Long	Long	Long	Long	Long	Long
	Dir.	Obl.	Sm.	Hori.	Hori.	Hori.	Sm. Obl.	Sm. Obl.
	Epican.	Pr.	Pr.	Pr.	Pr.	Abs.	Pr.	Pr.
i.	FOREHEAD:							
	Height	Med.	High	High	Med.	Med.	Med.	Med.
	Breadth	Broad	Med.	Broad	Med.	Med.	Med.	Broad
	Slope	Mod.	Mod.	Mod.	Sm.	Sm.	None	Sm.
j.	NOSE:							
	N. D.	Med.	Med.	Deep	Deep	Med.	Med.	Med.
	Sept.	Hori.	...	Hori.	Up	...	...	...
k.	MALAR	Pron.	Mod.	Pron.	Pron.	Pron.	Pron.	Pron.
l.	PROGNATH.	None	None	None	Sm.	Sm.	None	None
m.	CHIN	Med.	Sm.	Sm.	Incon.	Med.	Med.	Med.

TABLE 2 (Continued)

a.		**36**	**37**	**38**	**39**	**40**	**41**	**42**
b.	Skin Color	13, 10	13, 10	14, 12	11, 9	10, 8	10, 8	11, 7
c.	Hair:							
	Col.	Bl., some Y.	Black	Black	Black	Black	Bl., Y.	Bl., Br.
	Quan.	Med.	Med.	Sm.	Med.	Med.	Med.	Med.
	Form	Sm. Wavy	Straight	Straight	Straight	Straight	Straight	Straight
d.	Beard:							
	Col.	...	...	...	Black	...	...	...
	Quan.	Sm.	Sm.	Sm.	Med.	Sm.	Sm.	Sm.
	Form	...	...	...	Straight	...	...	...
e.	Eye Col.:							
	Iris	L. Br.	L. Br.	L. Br.	L. Br.	L. Br.	L. Br.	L. Br.
	Sclerotic		Yellowish	Yellowish	Yellowish	Yellowish	Yellowish	Yellowish
f.	Eyebrows	Med.	Med.	Med.	Bushy	Med.	Med.	Med.
g.	Brow-ridges	Mod.	Mod.	Sm.	Sm.	Mod.	Mod.	Mod.
h.	Eyelids:							
	Opening	Long	Long	Long	Long	Long	Long	Long
	Dir.	Sm. Obl.	Sm. Obl.	Sm. Obl.	Sm. Obl.	Obl. (out)	Sm. Obl.	Sm. Obl.
	Epican.	Abs.	Abs.	Abs.	Abs.	Pr.	Pr.	Pr.
i.	Forehead:							
	Height	Med.	Med.	Med.	Med.	Med.	Med.	Med.
	Breadth	Broad	Broad	Med.	Broad	Med.	Med.	Broad
	Slope	Mod. Pron.	Mod. (r)	Mod.	None	Round	Mod. Ro.	Mod.
j.	Nose:							
	N. D.	Med.	Med.	Med.	Med.	Med.	Med.	Med.
	Sept.	Hori.	Hori.	Hori.	Hori.	Down (out)	Down (out)	Hori.
k.	Malar	Mod.	Pron.	Pron.	Pron.	Pron.	Mod.	Pron.
l.	Prognath.	None	None	Sm.	None	Sm.	None	None
m.	Chin	Med.	Med.	V. Slight	Med.	Med.	Med.	Med.

a.		**50**	**51**	**52**	**53**	**54**	**55**	**56**
b.	Skin Color	10	13	13	10	10	11	12, 10
c.	Hair:							
	Col.	Black	Black	Black	Black	Black	Black	Black
	Quan.	Thick	Thick	Thick	Thick	Med.	Med.	Med.
	Form	Straight	Straight	Straight	Straight	Straight	Straight	Straight
d.	Beard:							
	Col.	...	...	...	...	...	...	Black
	Quan.	None	None	Sm.	Sm.	Sm.	Sm.	Med.
	Form	...	...	...	...	...	...	Straight
e.	Eye Col.:							
	Iris	D. Br.	Br.	Br.	Br.	L. Br.	Br.	L. Br.
	Sclerotic	Yellowish	Yellowish	Yellowish	Yellowish	Yellowish	Yellowish	Yellowish
f.	Eyebrows	Subm.	Med.	Med.	Sm.	Med.	Subm.	Med.
g.	Brow-ridges	Sm.	Med.	Med.	Sm.	Med.	Sm.	Imp.
h.	Eyelids:							
	Opening	Long	Long	Long	Long	Long	Long	Long
	Dir.	Sm.	Sm. Obl.	Sm. Obl.	Sm. Obl.	Sm. Obl.	Sm. Obl.	Sm. Obl.
	Epican.	Pr.	Pr.	Pr.	Pr.	Pr.	Pr.	Pr.
i.	Forehead:							
	Height	Subm.	Med.	Med.	High	Med.	Med.	Med.
	Breadth	V. Broad	Broad	Broad	Med.	Med.	Med.	Broad
	Slope	None	Sm.	Sm.	Sm.	...	Sm.	None
j.	Nose:							
	N. D.	Sm.	Med.	Med.	Med.	Sm.	Deep	Med.
	Sept.	...	Down	Down	...	...	Up	Up
k.	Malar	Mod.	Subm.	Pron.	Pron.	Pron.	Pron.	Pron.
l.	Prognath.	None	None	None	None	None	Sm.	None
m.	Chin	Med.	Med.	Med.	Med.	Med.	Incon.	Med.

TABLE 2 (Continued)

a.		57	58	59	60	61	62	63
b.	Skin Color	10, 8	11, 9	10	14, 10	8, 9	10, 9	10, 9
c.	Hair:							
	Col.	Black	Bl., Y.	Black	Black	Black	Black	Black
	Quan.	Med.	Med.	Med.	Med.	Med.	Med.	Thick
	Form	Straight	St. Wavy	Straight	Straight	Straight	Straight	Straight
d.	Beard:							
	Col.	...	Bl., Br.	...	Black	...	...	Black
	Quan.	Sm.	Sm.	Med.	Med.	...	Sm.	Med.
	Form	...	Straight	Straight	Straight	...	...	Straight
e.	Eye Col.:							
	Iris	L. Br.	L. Br.	L. Br.	L. Br.	D. Br.	L. Br.	L. Br.
	Sclerotic	Yellowish		Yellowish		Yellowish	Yellowish	Yellowish
f.	Eyebrows	Med.	Bushy	Bushy	Med.	Med.	Med.	V. Bushy
g.	Brow-ridges	Mod.	Sm.	Mod.	Mod.	Mod.	Sm.	Mod.
h.	Eyelids:							
	Opening	Long	Long	Long	Long	Long	Long	Long
	Dir.	Hori.	Hori.	Sm. Obl.	Sm. Obl.	Hori.	Hori.	Hori.
	Epican.	Pr.	Pr.	Pr.	Pr.	...	Abs.	Abs.
i.	Forehead:							
	Height	Med.	Med.	V. High	Med.	Med.	Med.	Med.
	Breadth	Broad	Med.	V. Broad	Broad	Broad	Med.	Broad
	Slope	Mod.	Mod. (r)	Mod.	Mod.	Mod.	Mod.	Sm.
j.	Nose:							
	N. D.	Med.	Deep	Med.	Deep	Deep	Deep	Med.
	Sept.	Hori.	Down	...	Hori.	Hori.	Down	Hori.
k.	Malar	Mod.	Pron.	Pron.	Pron.	Pron.	Pron.	Pron.
l.	Prognath.	None	None	Sm.	Mod.	Sm.	None	Mod.
m.	Chin	Med.	Marked	Med.	Sm.	Med.	Med.	Med.

a.		71	72	73	74	75	76	77
b.	Skin Color	9, 8	12, 8	9, 7	10, 9	9, 7	10, 9	16, 9
c.	Hair:							
	Col.	Black	Black	Black	Black	Black	Black	Black
	Quan.	Med.	Med.	Med.	Med.	Med.	Med.	Med.
	Form	Straight	Straight	Straight	Straight	Straight	Straight	Straight
d.	Beard:							
	Col.	...	Black	...	Black	...	...	...
	Quan.	Sm.	Sm.	Sm.	Sm.	Sm.	Sm.	Sm.
	Form	...	Straight	...	Straight	...	...	...
e.	Eye Col.:							
	Iris	L. Br.	L. Br.	L. Br.	L. Br.	L. Br.	L. Br.	Br.
	Sclerotic	Yellowish	Yellowish	Yellowish	Yellowish	Yellowish	Yellowish	Yellowish
f.	Eyebrows	Med.	Bushy	Med.	Med.	Bushy	Med.	Med.
g.	Brow-ridges	Mod.	Mod.	Mod.	Mod.	...	Mod.	Sm.
h.	Eyelids:							
	Opening	Long	Long	Long	Long	...	...	Long
	Dir.	Sm. Obl.	Hori.	Sm. Obl.	Sm. Obl.	Hori.	Hori.	Hori.
	Epican.	Pr.	Pr.	Pr.	Pr.	Abs.	Abs.	Abs.
i.	Forehead:							
	Height	Med.	Med.	Med.	Med.	Med.	Med.	Med.
	Breadth	Broad	Broad	Broad	Med.	Broad	Broad	Broad
	Slope	Mod.	Mod.	Mod.	Mod.	Mod.	Mod.	Mod.
j.	Nose:							
	N. D.	Med.	Deep	Deep	Med.	Deep	Med.	Med.
	Sept.	Up	Up	Hori.	Down	Hori.	Hori.	Hori.
k.	Malar	Exces.	Pron.	Exces.	Med.	Pron.	Pron.	Exces.
l.	Prognath.	None	Sm.	None	Mod.	None	Mod.	Sm.
m.	Chin	Med.	Med.	Med.	Sm.	Med.	Sm.	Sm.

TABLE 2 (Continued)

a.		64	65	66	67	68	69	70
b.	SKIN COLOR	10, 9	10, 9	11, 9	12, 9	12, 9	13, 9	10, 9
c.	HAIR:							
	Col.	Black	Black	Black	Black	Black	Black	Black
	Quan.	Med.	Med.	Med.	Med.	Thick	Med.	Thick
	Form	Straight	Straight	Straight	Straight	Straight	Straight	Straight
d.	BEARD:							
	Col.	Black	...	...	Black	Black	...	Black
	Quan.	Sm.	Sm.	Sm.	Sm.	Med.	Sm.	Bushy
	Form	Straight	...	...	Straight	Straight	...	Straight
e.	EYE COL.:							
	Iris	L. Br.	L. Br.	L. Br.	L. Br.	L. Br.	L. Br.	L. Br.
	Sclerotic	Yellowish	Yellowish	Yellowish	Yellowish	Yellowish	Yellowish	Yellowish
f.	EYEBROWS	Bushy	Bushy	Med.	Med.	Bushy	Med.	Bushy
g.	BROW-RIDGES	Sm.	Mod.	Mod.	Mod.	Mod.	Mod.	Mod.
h.	EYELIDS:							
	Opening	Long	Long	Long	Long	Long	Long	Long
	Dir.	Hori.	Sm. Obl.	Sm. Obl.	Hori.	Hori.	Hori.	Hori.
	Epican.	...	Pr.	Pr.	Abs.	...	Abs.	Pr.
i.	FOREHEAD:							
	Height	Med.	Med.	Med.	Med.	Med.	Med.	Med.
	Breadth	Med.	Med.	Broad	Broad	Med.	Med.	Broad
	Slope	Mod.	Mod.	Mod.	Mod.	Mod.	Mod.	Mod.
j.	NOSE:							
	N. D.	Deep	Med.	Deep	Deep	Med.	Deep	Sm.
	Sept.	Up	Hori.	Hori.	Hori.	Hori.	Hori.	Hori.
k.	MALAR	Pron.	Pron.	Exces.	Pron.	Subm.	Pron.	Pron.
l.	PROGNATH.	Sm.	Sm.	Pron.	Med.	None	Sm.	None
m.	CHIN	Med.	Med.	Incon.	Med.	Med.	Med.	Pron.

a.		78	79	80	81	82	83	84
b.	SKIN COLOR	12, 9	12, 10	12, 9	14, 10	11, 9	21, 14	13, 9
c.	HAIR:							
	Col.	Black	Black	Black	Black	Black	Black	Black
	Quan.	Med.	Thick	Med.	Med.	Med.	Thick	Med.
	Form	Straight	Straight	Straight	Straight	Straight	Wavy	Straight
d.	BEARD:							
	Col.	Black	Black	...	...	...	...	Black
	Quan.	Med.	Sm.	Sm.	Sm.	Sm.	V. Sm.	Sm.
	Form	Straight	Straight	...	...	...	...	Straight
e.	EYE COL.:							
	Iris	L. Br.	L. Br.	L. Br.	L. Br.	L. Br.	L. Br.	L. Br.
	Sclerotic	Yellowish	Yellowish	Yellowish	Yellowish	Yellowish	Yellowish	Yellowish
f.	EYEBROWS	Med.	Med.	Med.	Med.	Med.	Bushy	Bushy
g.	BROW-RIDGES	Mod.	Mod.	Mod.	...	...	Mod.	Mod.
h.	EYELIDS:							
	Opening	...	Long	...	Long	...	...	...
	Dir.	Hori.	Hori.	Sm. Obl.	Hori.	Hori.	Sm. Obl.	Hori.
	Epican.	Pron.	Abs.	Pr.	Pr.	Pr.	Pr.	Abs.
i.	FOREHEAD:							
	Height	High	Med.	High	Med.	Med.	Med.	Med.
	Breadth	Broad	Broad	Broad	Med.	Broad	Broad	Broad
	Slope	Sm.	Mod.	Mod.	Mod.	Mod.	Mod.	Sm.
j.	NOSE:							
	N. D.	Med.	Deep	Med.	Med.	Med.	Med.	Med.
	Sept.	Hori.	Up	Hori.	Hori.	Hori.	...	Hori.
k.	MALAR	Pron.	Exces.	Pron.	Subm.	Pron.	Subm.	Pron.
l.	PROGNATH.	None	None	Sm.	None	None	None	None
m.	CHIN	Med.	Med.	Med.	Med.	Med.	Med.	Med.

TABLE 2 (Continued)

a.		85	86	87	88	89	90	91
b.	Skin Color	11, 9	10, 8	13, 7	9, 7	11, 7	10, 7	13, 10
c.	Hair:							
	Col.	Black	Black	Black	Black	Black	Black	Black
	Quan.	Med.	Thick	Med.	Med.	Med.	Med.	Med.
	Form	Straight	Straight	Wavy	Straight	Straight	Straight	Straight
d.	Beard:							
	Col.	Black	Black	Black	Black	Black	Black	...
	Quan.	Sm.	Sm.	Med.	Sm.	Sm.	Sm.	Sm.
	Form	...	...	Straight	...	...	...	...
e.	Eye Col.:							
	Iris	L. Br.	L. Br.	L. Br.	L. Br.	L. Br.	L. Br.	L. Br.
	Sclerotic	Yellowish	Yellowish	Yellowish	Yellowish	Yellowish	Yellowish	Yellowish
f.	Eyebrows	Bushy	Bushy	Bushy	Med.	Med.	Med.	Med.
g.	Brow-ridges	Pron.	Pron.	...	Mod.	Mod.	Mod.	Mod.
h.	Eyelids:							
	Opening	Long	...	...	...	...	Long	...
	Dir.	Hori.	Hori.	Hori.	Hori.	Hori.	Sm. Obl.	Sm. Obl.
	Epican.	Abs.	Abs.	Pr.	Pr.	Pr.	Abs.	Pron.
i.	Forehead:							
	Height	Med.	Med.	Med.	Med.	Med.	Med.	Med.
	Breadth	Broad	Broad	Broad	Broad	Broad	Broad	Broad
	Slope	Mod.	Sm.	Mod.	Mod.	Sm.	Sm.	Med.
j.	Nose:							
	N. D.	Med.	Med.	Med.	Med.	Deep	Deep	Deep
	Sept.	Up	Hori.	Up	Hori.	Down	Hori.	Hori.
k.	Malar	Exces.	Pron.	Pron.	Pron.	Pron.	Exces.	Pron.
l.	Prognath.	Sm.	Sm.	Mod.	Sm.	None	None	None
m.	Chin	Med.	Med.	Med.	Pron.	Pron.	Pron.	Pron.

a.		99	100	101	102	103	104	105
b.	Skin Color	12, 7	14, 9	13, 7	11, 7	...	9, 7	13, 10
c.	Hair:							
	Col.	Black	Black	Black	Black	...	Black	Black
	Quan.	Thick	Med.	Sm.	Med.	Med.	Med.	Thick
	Form	Straight	Straight	Straight	Straight	Straight	Straight	Straight
d.	Beard:							
	Col.	Black	...	Black	...	...	Black	...
	Quan.	Sm.	Sm.	Sm.	Sm.	V. Sm.	Sm.	Sm.
	Form	...	Straight	Straight	...	...	...	...
e.	Eye Col.:							
	Iris	L. Br.	L. Br.	L. Br.	L. Br.	L. Br.	L. Br.	L. Br.
	Sclerotic	Yellowish	Yellowish	Yellowish	Yellowish	Yellowish	Yellowish	Yellowish
f.	Eyebrows	Med.	Med.	Med.	Med.	Med.	Med.	Med.
g.	Brow-ridges	Mod.	Mod.	Mod.	Mod.	Sm.	...	Mod.
h.	Eyelids:							
	Opening	...	...	...	...	...	...	Obl.
	Dir.	Obl.	Sm. Obl.	Hori.	Sm. Obl.	Sm. Obl.	...	Sm. Obl.
	Epican.	Pr.	Pr.	Pr.	Pr.	Pr.	Pr.	Pr.
i.	Forehead:							
	Height	Med.	Med.	High	High	Med.	Med.	High
	Breadth	Broad	Broad	Broad	Broad	Broad	Broad	Broad
	Slope	Sm.	Sm.	Sm.	V. Sm.	Mod.	Sm.	Sm.
j.	Nose:							
	N. D.	Med.	Med.	Med.	Deep	Med.	Med.	Med.
	Sept.	Hori.	Down	Hori.	Hori.	Up	Up	Hori.
k.	Malar	Pron.	Pron.	Pron.	Pron.	Pron.	Pron.	Exces.
l.	Prognath.	Sm.	None	None	None	Mod.	None	Sm.
m.	Chin	Med.	Med.	Med.	Pron.	Med.	Med.	Sm.

TABLE 2 (Continued)

a.		92	93	94	95	96	97	98
b.	Skin Color	13, 9	10, 8	17, 9	13, 9	14, 11	14, 13	10, 8
c.	Hair:							
	Col.	Black	Black	Black	Black	Black	Black	Black
	Quan.	Thick	Thick	Med.	Thick	Med.	Thick	Med.
	Form	Straight	Straight	Straight	Straight	Straight	Straight	Straight
d.	Beard:							
	Col.	...	...	...	Black	Black	Black	Black
	Quan.	Sm.	Sm.	Sm.	Sm.	Sm.	Sm.	Med.
	Form	...	...	...	Straight	Straight	Straight	Straight
e.	Eye Col.:							
	Iris	L. Br.	L. Br.	L. Br.	L. Br.	L. Br.	L. Br.	L. Br.
	Sclerotic	Yellowish	Yellowish	Yellowish	Yellowish	Yellowish	Yellowish	Yellowish
f.	Eyebrows	Bushy	Med.	Med.	Bushy	Med.	Med.	Med.
g.	Brow-ridges	Mod.	Mod.	Mod.	...	...	Mod.	Sm.
h.	Eyelids:							
	Opening	...	...	...	...	...	...	...
	Dir.	Hori.	Hori.	Obl.	Hori.	Hori.	Sm. Obl.	...
	Epican.	Abs.	...	Pr.	Pr.	Pron.	Pr.	Pr.
i.	Forehead:							
	Height	Med.	Med.	Med.	Med.	Med.	High	Med.
	Breadth	Broad	Med.	Broad	Broad	Broad	Broad	Broad
	Slope	V. Sm.	Mod.	Mod.	Sm.	V. Sm.	Mod.	Mod.
j.	Nose:							
	N. D.	Mod.	Deep	Med.	Deep	Med.	Med.	Deep
	Sept.	Hori.	Hori.	Hori.	Hori.	Hori.	Down	Up
k.	Malar	Pron.	Pron.	Pron.	Pron.	Pron.	Pron.	Mod.
l.	Prognath.	None	Mod.	Sm.	Mod.	None	None	Mod.
m.	Chin	Pron.	Sm.	Med.	Med.	Pron.	Med.	Sm.

a.		106	107	108	109	110	111
b.	Skin Color	11, 7	9, 7	9, 9	11, 9	12, 9	—
c.	Hair:						
	Col.	Black	Black	Black	Black	Black	Black
	Quan.	Med.	Med.	Thick	Med.	Med.	Thick
	Form	Straight	Straight	Straight	Straight	Sm.Wavy	Straight
d.	Beard:						
	Col.	...	...	...	...	...	...
	Quan.	Sm.	...	...	Sm.	...	...
	Form	...	...	...	...	...	...
e.	Eye Col.:						
	Iris	L. Br.	L. Br.	L. Br.	L. Br.	L. Br.	Br.
	Sclerotic	Yellowish	Yellowish	Yellowish	Yellowish	Yellowish	Yellowish
f.	Eyebrows	Med.	Med.	Med.	Med.	Med.	Subm.
g.	Brow-ridges	Sm.	Mod.	Mod.	Mod.	Mod.	Mod.
h.	Eyelids:						
	Opening	Obl.	Obl.	Obl.	...	...	...
	Dir.	Sm. Obl.	...	Sm. Obl.	Hori.	Sm. Obl.	Sm. Obl.
	Epican.	Pr.	Pr.	Pr.	Pr.	Pr.	Pr.
i.	Forehead:						
	Height	Med.	High	High	Med.	Med.	V. High
	Breadth	Broad	Broad	Broad	Broad	Broad	V. Broad
	Slope	Sm.	Sm.	Sm.	Sm.	Sm.	None
j.	Nose:						
	N. D.	Med.	Med.	Med.	Med.	Deep	Med.
	Sept.	Hori.	Hori.	Hori.	Hori.	Hori.	Down
k.	Malar	Pron.	Pron.	Exces.	Pron.	Pron.	Mod.
l.	Prognath.	None	...	...	Sm.	Sm.	None
m.	Chin	Med.	Pron.	Pron.	Pron.	Med.	Pron.

TABLE 3

A SUMMARY OF THE METRICAL OBSERVATIONS, SHOWING THE EXTREMES, THE MEANS, AND THEIR PROBABLE ERRORS; STANDARD DEVIATIONS AND THEIR PROBABLE ERRORS; THE VARIABILITIES AND THEIR PROBABLE ERRORS (MALES ONLY)

Traits	No. of cases	Extremes	Means ± E. M.	σ ± E. σ	C. ± E. C.
Stature..........	108	1446–1833	1677 ±4.1	63.1 ±2.97	3.7 ±.177
H. H.	108	109–149	127 ± .51	7.8 ±3.36	6.1 ±.288
H. L.	109	169–203	187 ± .39	5.9 ± .27	3.2 ±.846
H. B.	109	139–170	153 ± .37	5.8 ± .26	3.8 ±.172
H. L. I.	108	58–81.71	67.94 ± .29	4.5 ± .21	....
L. B. I.	109	72.4–98.82	82.1 ± .27	4.2 ± .19	....
Hor. Cir.	59	501–582	550 ±1.46	16.6 ±1.03	3.0 ±.184
M. F. D.	109	94–127	108 ± .42	6.5 ± .29	6.0 ±.275
Biz. Diam.	109	127–157	141 ± .35	5.5 ± .25	3.9 ±.177
N. M. H.	109	98–142	122 ± .49	7.6 ± .35	6.2 ±.292
F. I.	109	73.9–100.7	86.4 ± .36	5.4 ± .25	....
N. H.	109	41–62	52.6 ± .27	4.2 ± .19	8.0 ±.368
N. B.	109	34–44	38.2 ± .15	2.4 ± .11	6.2 ±.28
N. I.	109	61.02–94.2	72.84 ± .44	6.8 ± .31	....

TABLE 4

A SUMMARY OF THE SALIENT POINTS CONCERNING THE DESCRIPTIVE TRAITS (MALES ONLY)

(1) *Skin Color*

Color Grade	Forehead		Forearm	
	No. of cases	Per cent	No. of cases	Per cent
7......................	1	.93	14	14.6
8......................	2	1.87	10	10.4
9......................	8	7.48	49	51.
10.....................	21	19.6	16	16.7
11.....................	13	12.13	2	2.08
12.....................	23	21.5	3	3.12
13.....................	20	18.5	1	1.04
14.....................	11	10.3	1	1.04
15.....................	3	2.79	..	..
16.....................	1	.93	..	..
17.....................	1	.93	..	..
18.....................	1	.93	..	..
19.....................	1	.93	..	..
20.....................	..	..	..	..
21.....................	1	.93	..	..

(2) *Hair Color:* generally black, except one dark-brown, one brown, five with slightly yellowish tinge, and one slightly red.

TABLE 4 (CONTINUED)

(3) *Quantity of Hair:* total cases, 105.

		Per cent
Scanty	5	4.76
Small	1	.95
Medium	79	75.24
Thick	20	19.05

(4) *Hair Form:* generally straight, except four slightly wavy, three wavy, and one curly.

(5) *Quantity of Beard:* total cases, 103.

		Per cent
Very scanty	5	4.85
Scanty	81	78.64
Small	4	3.88
Medium	11	10.68
Bushy	2	1.95

(6) *Eye Color:* all light-brown except one red-brown.

(7) *Sclerotic:* 92 cases with yellow patches (84.4 per cent).

(8) *Eyebrows:* total cases, 109.

Submedium	4	3.67
Medium	78	71.56
Bushy	26	23.85
Very bushy	1	.92

(9) *Brow-ridges:* total cases, 93.

Imperceptible	1	1.07
Perceptible	3	3.23
Slight	25	26.88
Moderate	53	56.99
Medium	8	8.60
Pronounced	3	3.23

(10) *Opening of Eyelids:* total cases, 77.

Narrow	21	27.3
Long	53	68.8
Medium	1	1.3
Round	2	2.6

(11) *Direction of Eye:* total cases, 106.

Slightly oblique	41	38.6
Oblique	29	27.4
Horizontal	36	34.0

(12) *Epicanthus:* total cases, 103.

Absent	25	24.3
Present	78	75.7

(13) *Height of Forehead:* total cases, 106.

Submedium	1	.94
Medium	90	84.91
High	13	12.27
Very high	2	1.88

TABLE 4 (Continued)

(14) *Breadth of Forehead:* total cases, 107.

		Per cent
Medium	35	32.7
Broad	69	64.5
Very broad	3	2.8

(15) *Slope of Forehead:* total cases, 107.

None	8	7.47
Very slight	3	2.80
Slight	26	24.30
Moderate	45	42.07
Round	22	20.56
Pronounced	2	1.87
Bulging	1	.93

(16) *Nasal Depression:* total cases, 108.

Slight	6	5.60
Medium	77	71.30
Deep	25	23.10

(17) *Nasal Septum:* total cases, 98.

Horizontal	69	70.4
Up (anterior)	14	14.3
Down	15	15.3

(18) *Malars:* total cases, 108.

Slight	1	.93
Moderate	9	8.33
Submedium	4	3.70
Medium	9	8.33
Pronounced	75	69.45
Excessive	10	9.26

(19) *Prognathism:* total cases, 109.

None	68	62.38
Slight	26	23.85
Moderate	12	11.01
Medium	1	.92
Pronounced	2	1.84

(20) *Chin:* total cases, 106.

Inconspicuous	2	1.89
Very slight	2	1.89
Slight	9	8.49
Submedium	1	.94
Medium	80	75.47
Pronounced	12	11.32

II. The Data Analytically Considered

To coördinate all the anthropological data regarding the Chinese and to consider them analytically, we need to be reminded again that China proper is a country of 1,532,000 square miles, and that her population as estimated in 1902 [1] is about 416,000,000. So, unless we have a sufficient number of data to prove that the Chinese are racially homogeneous (which we have not), we have no ground for considering them so. It has been customary for most anthropological writers on China to divide this country into two parts, the North and the South, and to compare the data from the respective regions, in order to draw conclusions. This, I think, is hardly doing justice to the problem. Nor has the line of division ever been clearly drawn. The usual practice is to call Shantung and Chihli, North China; Fukien and Kwangtung, South China. But Shantung, Chihli, Fukien, and Kwangtung are only four units of China's political divisions, and China has eighteen provinces. The respective sizes of these eighteen provinces demand our attention here (see Map I).

	Sq. miles		Sq. miles
Chekiang	36,680 [2]	Kwangsi	77,220
Chihli	115,830	Kwangtung	100,500
Fukien	46,332	Kweichow	67,182
Honan	67,954	Nganhui	54,826
Hunan	83,398	Shansi	81,852
Hupeh	71,428	Shantung	55,984
Kansu	125,483	Shensi	75,290
Kiangsi	69,498	Szechuan	218,533
Kiangsu	38,610	Yunnan	146,718

So, if we remember that the largest province of China (Szechuan) is larger than France, and that even the smallest province (Chekiang) has a size exceeding two thirds of the area of England, we must pause a while before we infer the anthropological status of one of these provinces from a casual study of another. If only because of the immense size of these areas, I am led to believe that it is safer to take the province as the unit for our analysis than to follow the usual practice of dividing China into two or three parts.

The physical traits chosen for the following analysis are three: stature, and the cephalic and nasal indices. The racial significance of the last two need not be discussed; they have been universally recognized. As to stature, there may be a question whether there is any advantage in coördinating the data. My reasons for choosing it are two: (1) it is the most widely studied; the distribution of its variation can be studied on a more solid basis than that of any other trait;

[1] Data taken from L. Richard's *Comprehensive Geography of the Chinese Empire* (M. Kennelly, S. J. T'usewei Press, Shanghai), p. 8.

[2] L. Richard, *op. cit.*, p. 8.

(2) it is by no means entirely devoid of racial significance, if only of a secondary sort; the distribution of its variation may at least serve as a basis for the study of other distributions.

On the whole, these three are chosen primarily because they are the most convenient. The omission of the descriptive characters is justified by the impossibility of comparing them.

(a) *Stature*

The following tabulated data are a compilation of all the studies that have been made on Chinese stature. It may be observed that only male adults (aged 18 years and over) are included.

TABLE 5

Author	No. of subjects	Native province of subject	Averages mm.	Extremes mm.
Hutcheson	232	Kwangtung	1608	....
Hagen	64	Kwangtung	1613	1504–1720
Girard	25	Kwangsi	1615	1528–1748
Hutcheson	267	Hunan	1615	....
Hagen	910	So. Kwangtung	1617	1410–1795
Legendre	100	Szechuan	1625	1469–1476
Hutcheson	258	Chekiang	1628	....
Hutcheson	9	Hupeh	1634	....
Whyte	742	?	1635	....
Shoemaker	380	Mixed	1652	....
Breton	15	Kwangtung	1658	....
Hutcheson	709	Kiangsu	1661	....
Hutcheson	5	Fukien	1663	....
Hutcheson	8	Kweichow	1666	....
Joyce and Stein	20	Kansu	1667	....
Shoemaker	?	?	1667	....
Weisbach	20	Shantung	1675	1510–1790
Koganei	942	Mixed	1676	1480–1860
Hutcheson	5	Shantung	1676	....
Li	109	Mixed	1678	1446–1833
Hutcheson	261	Chihli	1689	....
Total Subjects	5081	Averages ...	1651	1410–1860

I have been unable to construct a curve of distribution for the individual statures, because, with the exception of Hagen, Weisbach, Joyce, and myself, none of the authors has given any detailed measurements. In these four sets of data, the different provinces are very unequally represented. Any curve of distribution on this basis, therefore, will not be normal. The data as a whole do not contain an equal representation of the 18 provinces, so the average (1651) would have to be modified, if the factor of inequality could be eliminated. At all events, it can be calculated on a different scale. This I propose to do, after the averages of the provinces are ascertained. By eliminating those data which have not been definitely located, the following provincial averages are obtained:

TABLE 6

Province	No. of cases		Averages mm.
1. Chekiang	Hutcheson ......258 Li 17	275	1631
2. Chihli	Hutcheson......261 Li............ 7	268	1690
3. Fukien	Hutcheson...... 5 Li............ 10	15	1686
4. Honan	....	...	....
5. Hunan	Hutcheson......267 Li............ 9	276	1623
6. Hupeh	Hutcheson...... 9 Li............ 2	11	1638
7. Kansu	Joyce and Stein .. 20		1667
8. Kiangsi	Li...... 4		1714
9. Kiangsu	Hutcheson......709 Li............ 18	727	1661
10. Kwangsi	Girard .... 25 Li............ 1	26	1621
11. Kwangtung	Hutcheson......232 Hagen.......... 64 Hagen.........910 Breton.......... 15 Li............ 26	1247	1617
12. Kweichow	Hutcheson...... 8		1666
13. Nganhui	Hutcheson...... 29 Li............ 4	33	1653
14. Shansi	Li............ 2		1668
15. Shantung	Weisbach....... 20 Li............ 1 Hutcheson...... 5	26	1676
16. Shensi	Li............ 1		1739
17. Szechuan	Legendre........100 Li............ 2	102	1625
18. Yunnan	Li............ 2		1613

Of these 18 provinces, only Honan is unrepresented. No separate measurements of the province had been published, so far as I know, except by Koganei, who has among his 942 subjects 90 Honanese. But his data are presented in such a way that, although he has given the native places of his subjects, he has not given the provincial average either of stature or of any of the other measurements. I have found it possible to do this. By multiplying the number of persons in each province by the respective averages obtained here, subtracting the sum total so obtained from that of Koganei, and finally dividing the remainder by 90, I have obtained as the theoretical average for the Honanese the following figure, 1693 mm., a figure by no means absurd —in fact, just what is to be expected. When compared with the average for Chihli, its northern neighbor, it shows a difference of only three mm. So it is to be adopted for our present analysis.

The following summary is then arrived at:

1. Total number of cases considered, 5081.
2. Mean of the total, 1651 mm.
3. Provincial means.   (See Table 7.)
4. Extremes of provincial means, 1613 to 1730 mm.
5. Mean of provincial means, 1661 mm.

TABLE 7

Province	No. of cases	Means mm.	Province	No. of cases	Means mm.
1. Chekiang	275	1631	10. Kwangsi	26	1621
2. Chihli	268	1690	11. Kwangtung	1247	1818
3. Fukien	15	1686	12. Kweichow	8	1666
4. Honan	90	1693	13. Nganhui	33	1668
5. Hunan	276	1623	14. Shansi	2	1668
6. Hupeh	11	1638	15. Shantung	26	1680
7. Kansu	20	1667	16. Shensi	1	1730
8. Kiangsi	4	1712	17. Szechuan	102	1625
9. Kiangsu	727	1661	18. Yunnan	2	1613

However, the number of cases on which the different provincial averages are based varies enormously — from 1 to 1247. It does not take a statistician to see that equal weight should not be attached to the averages of Kwangtung and Shensi. If we exclude from consideration those provinces which have less than ten cases, we find the provincial average to be 1654.9 mm. If we go still a step further, and consider only those cases numbering over one hundred, the average is 1641 mm. Averaging these three, we get 1652. This last average may be called a weighted average, and be considered as a hypothetical average Chinese stature. It has the double advantage, not only of eliminating the local preponderance of one province, which is included in the first one (1651), but also of giving due weight to each case according to its degree of accuracy. Yet how close it is to the first average! And how close to the world average (1655)!

But this satisfactory result is not found in all the provinces. If we group the different provinces according to the customary classification, we find:

		Means	
Yunnan		1613?	
Kwangtung		1618	
Kwangsi		1621	
Hunan		1623	belong to the submedium class
Szechuan		1625	
Chekiang		1631	
Hupeh		1638	
Kiangsu		1661	
Kweichow		1666?	
Kansu		1667	belong to the medium class
Shansi		1668?	
Nganhui		1668	
Shantung		1680	
Fukien		1686	belong to the supermedium class
Chili		1690	
Honan		1693	
Kiangsi		1712?	belong to the tall class
Shensi		1739?	

Thus, so far as stature is concerned, the Chinese have at least three types. The variations are indeed very gradual; but, if we compare the established extremes, the difference is 7.2 cm. Nor is the grouping in any way haphazard (Map 2). The supermedium is found in the northeast, the medium in the centre and northwest, the submedium in the south, centre, and west. The meaning of this grouping, however, cannot be explained until we consider other factors.

(b) Cephalic Index

Haberer has made a good summary of all the studies on Chinese skulls previous to 1902. Since this, few have been published. For the sake of comparison, I have sifted out from Haberer's list the following craniological data.   It may be observed again that only male adult skulls are included.

Author	No. of cases	Author	No. of cases
Davis	32	Atgier	1
Spengel	11	Mochi	4
Ecker	1	Indian Museum	2
Broesike	10	Reicher	16
Schaafhausen	21	Haberer	28
Rüdinger	12	Virchow	1
Zaborowski	8		
Flower	17		174
ten Kate	10		

Of these 174 crania, the following percentages of indices are found:

Type	No. of cases	Per cent
Dolicho (up to 74.99)	27	15.50
Meso (75–79.99)	87	50.00
Brachy (80 and above)	60	34.49
	174	99.99

Koganei's series of 84 Chinese skulls, which is the only one of any importance that I have not included in the above table (because the individual measurements are not available), gives the following percentages:

TABLE 8

Type	Northern Chinese		Southern Chinese	
	No. of cases	Per cent	No. of cases	Per cent
Hyperdolicho	3	4.3	0	0
Dolicho	15	21.4	4	28.6
Meso	24	34.3	6	42.9
Brachy	21	30.0	4	28.6
Hyperbrachy	7	10.0	0	0
	70	100.0	14	100.1

It is clear then in both cases that the meso type is the dominant one. Koganei's division into North and South is, however, misleading. It would be clearer to record the first 70 as from Chihli, Shantung, and Shengking, and the last 14 as from Formosa, in accordance with actual facts. By incorporating Koganei's percentages into our own summary, we arrive at the following conclusion regarding the component factors of the Chinese male adult skull:

Type	No. of cases	Per cent
Dolicho	49	19.00
Meso	117	45.35
Brachy	92	35.65
	258	100.00

I have found it a somewhat profitless task to trace the distribution of these different types of skulls. Of the small number of which we can make use, few have been definitely located. Of these few, a large proportion seems to be open to question. Peking, Canton, Shanghai, for instance, are the dumping-grounds of a majority of these cases. But these are metropolitan cities, where men from all regions may die and lie buried, in spite of the Chinese love for home. To assume that the skulls are the indigenous products of these cities is, therefore, unwarranted. Again, to call skulls found in Sumatra, Southern Chinese, and those from Kouldja, Northern Chinese, may be fair assumptions. But these assumptions are to be proved. And the proofs I have been unable to secure. So, after a very diligent survey of the probable location of the types, I have found it necessary to give up in despair my scheme of locating them exactly. The only safe procedure left for me is to study these component types as a whole. Beyond this, no useful analysis can be made.

If we turn our attention from the dead to the living, we find these anthropometric measurements:

Type	No. of cases		Type	No. of cases
Weisbach	20		Hagen	64
Girard	25		Li	109
Birkner	6		Hagen	1
Koganei	942			
Stein and Joyce	20			1187

In these 1187 cases, the following types of cephalic indices are found:

Type	Per cent
Dolicho (up to 75.9)	14.41
Meso (76 to 80.9)	42.12
Brachy (81 and above)	43.47

Compared with the skulls, there is an increasing preponderance of the brachycephalic element and a corresponding diminution of the mesocephalic as well as of the dolichocephalic element. If the range of the different types is considered, it still holds true that the mesocephalic element dominates in the make-up of the living population of China. (Graph 1.) On the whole, however, the anthropometric results are more reliable, since they are based on a number of individual measurements almost five times as great as that of the skulls.

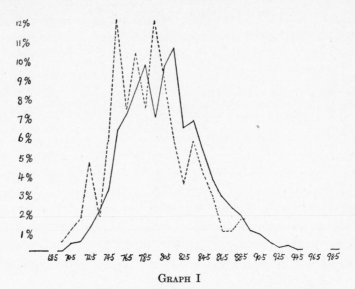

GRAPH I

———— Distribution of 1187 cephalic indices: data of Birkner, Girard, Hagen, Koganei, Li, Stein, and Weisbach.

------ Distribution of 173 cranial indices: data of Atgier, Broe-sike, Davis, Ecker, Flower, Haberer, ten Kate, Mochi, Schaaffhausen, Spengel, Reicher, Zaborowski, and the Indian Museum.

The distribution of the total results by provinces has not been as hopeless as the same attempt with skulls, although the results leave much to be desired. I have found it possible to establish the following averages:

TABLE 9

Provinces	No. of cases	Extremes	Means
1. Chekiang	16	73.96–86.20	81.855
2. Chihli	7	78.76–93.71	84.32
3. Fukien	11	77.39–88.51	82.53
4. Honan	....	....	....
5. Hunan	9	75.52–80.53	78.32
6. Hupeh	2	81.82–85.00	83.41
7. Kansu	20	72.00–81.00	76.54
8. Kiangsi	4	73.98–93.22	84.46
9. Kiangsu	19	78.61–98.82	85.14
10. Kwangsi	26	73.00–85.00	78.98
11. Kwangtung	92	....	....
12. Kweichow	....	....	....
13. Nganhui	4	75.51–83.96	80.86
14. Shansi	2	72.31–76.60	74.46
15. Shantung	26	67.62–89.32	78.21
16. Shensi	1	....	72.40
17. Szechuan	102	....	79.30
18. Yunnan	2	80.21–82.20	81.25

Working out the percentages of these three types of head form, we have:

TABLE 10

Provinces	No. of cases	Per cent dolicho	Per cent meso	Per cent brachy
1. Chekiang	16	6.25	39.50	54.25
2. Chihli	7	....	28.57	71.43
3. Fukien	11	....	45.45	54.54
4. Honan	..	....	....	....
5. Hunan	9	....	100.00	....
6. Hupeh	2	....	....	100.00
7. Kansu	20	30.00	65.00	5.00
8. Kiangsi	4	25.00	....	75.00
9. Kiangsu	19	....	15.79	84.21
10. Kwangsi	26	15.38	50.00	34.62
11. Kwangtung	92	4.46	36.95	58.59
12. Kweichow	..	....	....	....
13. Nganhui	4	....	50.00	50.00
14. Shansi	2	50.00	50.00	....
15. Shantung	26	19.23	61.54	19.23
16. Shensi	1	100.00	....	....
17. Szechuan	2	....	....	100.00
18. Yunnan	2	....	50.00	50.00

If we take the predominance of type (over 50 per cent) as a criterion, we may group the provinces in the following fashion:

1. The Brachycephalic Provinces

	Per cent		Per cent
Kiangsu	84.21	Fukien	54.54
Kiangsi	75.00 (?)	Chekiang	54.25
Hupeh	100.00 (?)	Szechuan	100.00 (?)
Chihli	71.43	Yunnan	50.00 (?)
Kwangtung	58.59	Nganhui	50.00

2. The Mesocephalic Provinces

	Per cent		Per cent
Hunan	100.00	Kwangsi	50.00
Kansu	66.00	Shensi	50.00 (?)
Shantung	61.54	Nganhui	50.00 (?)

The case of dolichocephaly, however, needs special consideration. Since it is a lesser element in the make-up of the Chinese population, its mere presence in any of the provinces is a significant fact; and we have found in

	Per cent		Per cent
Chekiang	6.25	Kwangtung	4.45
Kansu	30.00	Shansi	50.00 (?)
Kiangsi	25.00	Shantung	19.23
Kwangsi	15.38	Shensi	100.00 (?)

Barring the uncertain cases from consideration (that is, those provinces having less than five cases), we have reason to believe that the dolichocephalic cases are important in Kansu, Shantung, and Kwangsi, at least. Now these are, geographically, widely separated provinces; so the question arises whether the dolichocephalic elements in these three provinces are of the same type or different from one another. But before we can discuss this question, we have to consider another feature—that is, the nasal index.

(c) Nasal Index

Some of the craniological data are singularly deficient in the nasal index. The main reason for this is that many of the skulls measured have broken faces, and hence are not measurable in part. While the cranial indices for 174 cases are given, only 96 of these are complete for the nose. The same authors are, of course, responsible for these data. Classified, these 96 indices fall into the following groups:

	No. of cases	Per cent
Leptorrhinic	45	46.87
Mesorrhinic	34	35.41
Platyrrhinic	17	17.72
	—	
	96	

The cases of the living, numbering 235, present the following percentages:

	Per cent
Leptorrhinic	24.68
Mesorrhinic	59.57
Platyrrhinic	15.75

Thus, as in the cephalic index, the meso is the dominant type of Chinese nose. The decrease of the leptorrhinic type in the case of the living as compared to that of the dead is noticeable. I am not at all sure whether this is due to the paucity of craniological data or not. It is worthy of cursory notice here.

If we classify the heads of the living according to their provinces, with respect to types and means of the nasal index, we find the following:

TABLE 11

Provinces	No. of cases	Per cent lepto	Per cent meso	Per cent platy	Mean of nasal index
1. Chekiang	16	18.95	81.25	....	73.43
2. Chihli	7	42.85	57.15	....	70.02
3. Fukien	11	45.45	45.45	9.10	72.44
4. Honan	..	....	....	....	....
5. Hunan	9	33.33	66.66	....	71.35
6. Hupeh	2	50.00	50.00	....	....
7. Kansu	20	20.00	55.00	35.00	78.20
8. Kiangsi	4	....	100.00	....	....
9. Kiangsu	19	63.57	36.43	....	70.21
10. Kwangsi	26	7.69	50.00	42.31	82.05
11. Kwangtung	84	14.28	66.43	19.29	80.33
12. Kweichow	0	....	....	....	....
13. Nganhui	4	....	100.00	....	76.65
14. Shansi	2	100.00	....	....	64.65
15. Shantung	26	34.61	57.69	7.61	73.07
16. Shensi	1	....	100.00	....	75.00
17. Szechuan	2	....	50.00	50.00	72.98
18. Yunnan	2	....	50.00	50.00	69.45

Thus the platyrrhinic nose, like the dolichocephalic head, is a lesser element in the make-up of the Chinese physical traits. In general, the mesorrhinic is the dominant factor. The only exception is found in Kiangsu, where the leptorrhinic elements mount as high as 63.57 per cent.

(d) *Confirmatory Evidence*

So far our data are somewhat sparse; it would therefore be extremely risky to consider all the conclusions here arrived at as fully established. Many of them are based upon cases numbering less than ten; statistically speaking, the evidential weight is very slight. What we need is a greater number of data. Whether these conclusions are confirmed or not does not matter. What is important is that here we have *something* for somebody either to accept or to reject — in either case by virtue of his possession of *more* evidence than I can furnish.

I have myself found a set of incomplete data, in the *China Medical Journal*, which I consider valuable in this connection and which may serve as confirmatory evidence. They are published by Mr. S. H. Chuan of the Chinese Army College, and are incomplete because only the averages of the head length and the nasal breadth are given (except for the bi-parietal, which serves no useful purpose here). They, however, possess two virtues which are lacking in most other data: they are fairly large in number, and they are classified according to provinces, an extremely important fact.

The way in which I propose to utilize them is this. I have taken out at random one hundred cases of the anthropometrical measurements which I have already analyzed, and have worked out the correlation coefficient and the regressional equation between the head length and the cephalic index; the results are (X being the head length and Y the cephalic index):

$$r \text{ (cor. coef.)} = -.58$$
$$X = 250.93 - 79 Y$$
$$Y = 159.5 - .42 X$$

Now that we have all the values of X's given by Mr. Chuan, I think it reasonable to calculate the values of the corresponding Y's by the above equation (Y = 159.5 − .42 X).

In the same way, the correlation coefficient between the nasal breadth (X) and the nasal index (Y) works out:

$$r = .61$$
$$X = .19 Y + 21.62$$
$$Y = 1.98 X + 5.54$$

The total results so calculated, together with our own final results, may be summarized in the following tabulated form:

TABLE 12 $(Y = 159.5 - .42 X)$

Provinces	Chuan's data			Other results	
	No. of cases	Head length	Cephalic index (mean)	No. of cases	Cephalic index (mean)
1. Chekiang	17	187.0	80.96	16	81.85
2. Chihli	54	182.5	82.85	7	84.32
3. Fukien	7	183.0	81.64	11	82.53
4. Honan	14	188.0	79.54	..	....
5. Hunan	12	190.0	78.7	9	78.32
6. Hupeh	12	186.0	80.83	2	83.41
7. Kansu	20	....	....	20	76.54
8. Kiangsi	6	192.1	78.22	4	84.46
9. Kiangsu N.	6	192.0	78.49 ⎫	19	85.14
Kiangsu S.	14	182.5	82.85 ⎭		
10. Kwangsi	..	....	....	26	78.98
11. Kwangtung	50	198.0	76.34	92	81.50
12. Kweichow	6	193.0	77.44	..	....
13. Nganhui	17	192.2	78.77	4	80.86
14. Shansi	8	188.0	79.54	2	74.46
15. Shantung	11	189.0	79.12	26	78.21
16. Shensi	..	....	....	1	72.40 (?)
17. Szechuan	7	192.0	77.86	100	79.30
18. Yunnan	5	192.0	77.86	2	81.25
19. (?)	83	....	82.85	....	....
20. Manchus (Peking)	..	181.5	83.27	....	....

TABLE 13 $(Y = 167 X + 15.85;\ X\ being\ nasal\ breadth)$

Provinces	Chuan's data			Other results	
	No. of cases	Nasal breadth	Nasal index (mean)	No. of cases	Nasal index
1. Chekiang	17	36.4	76.65	16	73.43
2. Chihli	64	39.0	77.64	7	78.80
3. Fukien	7	36.0	75.92	11	72.44
4. Honan	14	33.3	71.46	..	....
5. Hunan	12	36.0	75.92	9	71.35
6. Hupeh	12	36.0	75.92	2	70.48
7. Kansu	..	....	....	20	78.20
8. Kiangsi	6	34.0	72.63	4	78.28
9. Kiangsu N.	6	38.2	79.65 ⎫	19	70.21
Kiangsu S.	14	38.0	79.31 ⎭		
10. Kwangsi	..	....	....	26	82.05
11. Kwangtung	50	40.0	82.65	92	86.33
12. Kweichow	6	36.0	75.97	2	....
13. Nganhui	17	33.5	71.79	4	76.65
14. Shansi	8	38.0	79.31	2	64.65
15. Shantung	11	33.6	71.96	26	73.07
16. Shensi	..	....	....	1	75.00
17. Szechuan	7	34.0	72.63	100	72.90
18. Yunnan	5	41.0	84.32	2	69.45

These two sets of data may be best described as supplementing rather than as confirming each other. They do, of course, in some cases confirm, — as a matter of fact to an amazing degree, — but still one is justified in calling it accidental only, rather than conclusive.

It is now possible for me to draw a final map of the nasal and cephalic indices, based on the last two tables. (Maps 3 and 4.)

III. The Data Synthetically Considered

So far our analysis has been an attempt to show in a discrete manner the range of variation of the different traits, and to trace the probable groupings of these traits according to provinces. The range of variation in the case of stature is from 1410 mm. to 1860 mm., the shortest Chinese being quite comparable to the Mawambi pygmy of Africa, though the tallest on record would be considered a giant even among the Saras. Our figures, however, exclude the cases of giantism and dwarfism. Regarding giantism, it is probably individually pathological, like the giantism found in other parts of the world, its description being found only in medical journals. Dwarfism, however, cannot be so dismissed. In all probability it forms an element in the make-up of the Cantonese population not to be ignored from an anthropological standpoint. Both B. Hagen and Duncan Whyte, whose data are the most extensive of this kind (1000 and 1621 cases, respectively), have put them on record. Hagen gives only one case of dwarfism (1225 mm.), but Whyte has two (46 and 48 inches respectively).

It may be noted that I have omitted Whyte's first series in my survey of Chinese stature. I did so for reasons which I have already indicated. Nominally the subjects are known as the Hoklos, according to Mr. Whyte's definition of this term. We must remember that the Hoklos are by no means a pure stock, just as the undefined Cantonese are not a pure one. What is more important is that Mr. Whyte himself has omitted these two extremely short subjects and four more on the ascending scale in his curve of distribution of the Hoklo statures which he studied. He excluded them from all his calculations in his treatise. It is not the recording of Hoklo dwarfs here which is important, for in all probability those recorded are not Hoklos. It is the presence of these elements in this series that we should consider. Since this is the only series which contains 1000 cases and more, and since it is the only series, too, which contains the dwarf elements, we may infer that there is about 1 per cent of dwarf elements in the make-up of the Cantonese population. If this is the case, the number of dwarfs in Kwangtung must reach a respectable size. I have no ground for believing that this condition does not extend to other neighboring provinces.

The range of group variation shows less extent than that of the individuals. Nevertheless, the presence of three types is very striking. Take the more established cases alone — Kwangtung (1618), Kiangsu (1661), and Chihli (1690), for instance: the differences are comparable to the differences between the average statures of the Spaniards (1620, according to Kolmogaroff), the Finns (1666, according to Wateff), and the Danes (1691, according to Makeprang and Hansen) in Europe. In general the provinces of the North show a greater average stature than those of the South, and there is a tendency for the average to diminish together with the latitude. But it would be a mistake to conclude that there is a sharply defined difference between the North and the South. Not that such a conclusion is entirely untrue. It is simply inaccurate. The term "South" and the term "North" are misnomers and have to be relegated to the anthropological waste-paper basket. Fukien, customarily taken as representative of the South, shows a greater average stature than Shantung, a Northern province. Kansu, an out-and-out Northern province, can be classified with Kweichow in the South. The problem is therefore much more complicated than the partitioner of China into the North and the South ever realized. Our object here is just an attempt to show the inadequateness of such a division.

The three types of Chinese stature are, strangely enough, correlated with three types of head form and three types of nasal form. In both the North and the South the meso type is more frequent. This is true for the craniological material as well as the anthropometrical material, although with some variations. The preponderance of the meso type needs special explanation. Haberer, whose study on the Chinese skulls still remains the best, speaks of them as "eine Mischforme mit dolichocephalem Vorderkopfe und brachycephalem Hinterhaupt." . . . "Er ist noch mesocephal," he comments further (p. 72). This would suggest that the present meso elements of the Chinese population are a by-product of interbreeding the two extreme types. If this were the case, the mesocephalic elements could hardly be considered a distinct group by themselves. There would be only two primary types left for further consideration. Of these two, the brachycephalic head and the leptorrhinic nose seem to have survived the onset of inbreeding better than their opposites, as they are the more numerous. But when we look at Maps 3 and 4 once more the distribution of these types gives us reason to think that, while the continuity of the distribution of the brachycephalic type is almost unbroken (except in the Province of Chihli), that of the dolichocephalic head form falls distinctly into two groups, the North and the South.

Here we may recall once more that, of the cephalic composition of the 258 skulls which we have examined, the dolicho elements attain 19 per cent; in the case of the living they constitute 14.41 per cent. Provincially they are important in Kansu, Shantung, and Kwangsi. Kwangsi is separated from Kansu by Szechuan and Kweichow, in both of which the meso elements are dominant. So it is possible to link these two provinces together by way of Szechuan and Kweichow. In the same way Shantung may be related to Kansu by way of Honan and Shensi, except that our conclusions regarding the cephalic index in Shensi and Honan are for the former based only on one case and for the other are entirely inferential. New evidences other than geographical contiguity have to be sought in order to establish their affinity on a firmer ground. Perhaps the first thing we may do is to see to what extent they agree in other characters besides the head form. Let us recall some of our former data once more. The mean nasal index, cephalic index, and average stature for these three provinces are as follows:

	Mean C. I.	Mean N. I.	Stature mm.
Shantung	78.21 ⎱ 79.12 ⎰	72.07 ⎱ 73.07 ⎰	1680
Kansu	76.54	78.20	1667
Kwangsi	78.98	82.05	1621

I do not propose to argue that stature is a permanent racial trait; but it cannot be mere chance that these three provinces belong to three distinct classes according to our categories. Then again look at the nasal indices. It may be true that these provinces all belong to the intermediate form, but they are such different kinds of mesos that one is almost akin to the leptorrhinic, while another is certainly not far from a platyrrhinic average. So it would appear that, aside from the head form, these three have nothing in common. They are widely different.

But it may be argued that averages are misleading in that they tend to disregard the peculiarities of individual subordinate elements in favor of those of the group, and that here we do not even have a measure of the dispersion to give us an approximate idea of individual variations. The question therefore should be examined in this light. The percentages of the different elements that enter into the composition of the mean cephalic index and the mean nasal index of these three provinces may be again compared here:

TABLE 14

Provinces	Cephalic Index			Nasal Index		
	Dolicho	Meso	Brachy	Lepto	Meso	Platy
Shantung ...	19.23	61.54	19.23	34.61	57.79	7.61
Kansu......	30.00	65.00	5.00	20.00	45.00	35.00
Kwangsi....	15.38	50.00	34.62	7.69	50.00	42.31

If we work on the hypothesis that the meso form is a cross between the dolicho and the brachy, or the lepto and the platy, we may reduce the above table to the following terms, for the sake of comparison:

TABLE 15

Provinces	Cephalic Index		Nasal Index	
	Dolicho	Brachy	Lepto	Platy
Shantung...............	50.00	50.00	63.50	36.50
Kansu..................	62.50	37.50	42.50	57.50
Kwangsi................	40.38	59.62	32.69	67.31

Mathematically speaking, according to the above table we are sure that in Shantung some leptorrhinic noses must match dolichocephalic heads, no matter in what way we may combine these two elements; equally, there must be some dolicho heads matching platyrrhinic noses in Kansu or Kwangsi. Here we have two types of dolichocephalic Chinese established. The curious point in this connection is that Kansu should be related more closely to Kwangsi than to Shantung. The explanation, however, must be sought from history.

Still it may be argued that these results are not conclusive. To this argument we may reply that hitherto we have studied only the types as such, and in our analysis it is their elements that are of the first importance. Now, in order to verify the conclusions arrived at, let us reverse the procedure and take in terms of a three-fold description the individual variations of the subjects as a group for a synthetic treatment. In other words, any subject measured, be it a living person or a skull, must have a head form belonging to one of these three classes:

Dolichocephalic .... D
Mesocephalic .... M
Brachycephalic .... B

And the proportion of head height to head length must belong to one of these three classes:

Chamecephalic C
Orthocephalic .... O
Hypsicephalic .... H

And finally, the nasal form must belong to one of these three classes:

Leptorrhinic.. L
Mesorrhinic.. M
Platyrrhinic.. P

Different groupings of these three traits will give rise to twenty-seven combinations, so theoretically we have twenty-seven individual types defined by these traits. But intermediate forms, as we have reason to believe (p. 43), are due to the extreme types. Eliminating these intermediate forms, we can reduce the combinations from twenty-seven to eight. Suppose we classify the Chinese according to the following eight categories: D. C. L., D. C. P., D. H. L., D. H. P., B. C. L., B. C. P., B. H. L., and B. H. P.

I have utilized the following craniological material for such analysis:

	Crania		Crania
Haberer.....................	37	Indian Museum	2
Mochi......................	5	Peabody Museum	3
Reicher	16	Anatomical Museum of	
ten Kate...................	10	München............	13
Quatrefages et Hamy	2		—
Zaborowski.................	8		114
Flower.....................	18		

Classifying them according to our categories and reducing them to percentages, we obtain the following results:

	Per cent		Per cent
D. C. L.	.88	B. C. L.	4.39
D. C. P.	7.02	B. C. P.	2.63
D. H. L.	20.17	B. H. L.	31.58
D. H. P.	5.70	B. H. P.	27.63

Counting head form and nasal form alone, this table clearly gives two types of dolichocephalic Chinese, and serves as strong confirmatory evidence of what has been postulated.

It is, however, more than confirmatory. It gives rise to new problems, and shows that the dominant brachycephalic type also tends to fall into two classes. But the distinction between these two types is certainly not shown in our head-form map. So far as our data are concerned, we have been unable to plot any such distinction, although we may be confident of its existence.

If the length-height proportion is taken into consideration, it is obvious that, absolute as the hypsi type is in its prevalence, the chamae factor also forms an element not to be altogether disregarded. But its significance is inexplicable at this stage.

Let us go back to the living once more and see whether the same conditions exist. The distinct brachycephalic provinces are Chihli, Kiangsu, and Fukien; other factors cannot be counted, as their status is quite uncertain. What, then, are their nasal indices? The following comparison may be made:

	Chihli		North Kiangsu (a)*	South Kiangsu (a)*	Kiangsu (b)*	Fukien	
	(a)*	(b)*				(a)*	(b)*
C. I.	82.85	84.32	78.49	82.85	85.14	81.64	82.53
N. I.	77.64	78.80	79.65	79.31	70.21	75.92	72.44

* (a) Chuan's data; (b) other data.

The two types of brachycephalic elements in Kiangsu are very apparent in this table. But here again our ground is not as solid as it might be, as one set of the Kiangsu data here is entirely inferential. Let us therefore go one step further and study the individual cases, in order to see whether we can find any pure type. I have made out the following list of what we may call the pure types according to the above categories. (See page 48.)

I. Author's Data

No. of Subject [1]	C. I.	N. I.	Type	Place
8	85	67.86	B. L.	Hupeh
9	87	64.4	B. L.	Kiangsu
20	82.4	64.8	B. L.	Chihli
28	81.25	90.24	B. P. }	Kwangtung
37	82.8	62.3	B. L. }	
39	86.2	61.8	B. L.	Chekiang
45	83.33	61.02	B. L.	Chihli
47	82.16	69.64	B. L.	Kiangsu
48	81.91	67.8	B. L. }	Fukien
51	88.51	64.91	B. L. }	
59	85.34	68.97	B. L.	Szechuan
67	81.96	69.94	B. L. }	Kiangsu
80	83.51	67.86	B. L. }	
81	75.52	62.50	D. L.	Hunan
83	90.56	66.67	B. L. }	Kiangsu
94	81.92	67.92	B. L. }	
100	84.07	69.64	B. L.	Fukien
102	90.06	64.15	B. L.	Kiangsu

[1] Cf. Table 1

II. Weisbach

	C. I.	N. I.	Type	Place
6	84.62	52.54	B. L. }	
7	84.07	89.47	B. P.	
9	71.94	68.63	D. L. }	Shantung
13	81.05	67.31	B. L.	
16	67.62	58.33	D. L.	
20	66.67	57.89	D. L. }	

III. Birkner

	C. I.	N. I.	Type	Place
3	74.0	89.52	D. P.	Shantung

IV. Hagen

	C. I.	N. I.	Type	Place
305	82.72	100.00	B. P. }	
311	84.83	97.5	B. P.	
315	93.35	68	B. L.	
318	87.36	62.75	B. L. }	Kwangtung
324	82.45	92.5	B. P.	
344	82.12	92.86	B. P.	
345	85.47	66	B. L.	
358	83.33	67.35	B. L. }	

V. Joyce

	C. I.	N. I.	Type	Place
352a	73	62	D. L. }	
343a	74	93	D. P. }	Kansu
355a	73	62	D. L. }	

VI. Summary

Type	No.	Type	No.
B. L.	18	D. L.	6
B. P.	3	D. P.	2

The summary shows clearly the existence of these four types. They are therefore realities. To take my own cases No. 28 and No. 102, Weisbach's No. 16, and Joyce's No. 343a: would it be possible for anyone to consider them as belonging to a homogeneous stock? Here they are:

TABLE 16

	28 (Li) Kwangtung	102 (Li) Kiangsu	16 (Weisbach) Shantung	343a (Joyce) Kansu
Stature..................	1472	1666	1740	1580
Head length	192	181	210	190
Head breadth.............	156	163	142	141
Cephalic index	81.25	90.06	67.62	74
Nose length	41	53	60	42
Nose breadth	37	34	35	39
Nasal index	90.24	64.15	58.33	93
Bizygomatic breadth.......	149	144	132	123
Nasion-menton height	111	136	127	107
Facial index.............	74.5	90.28	96	87

Here we may close our survey with a summary of the essentials:

(1) There are two types of dolichocephalic Chinese: the dolicho-leptorrhinic, more prevalent in Shantung, and the dolicho-platyrrhinic, more prevalent in Kansu and Kwangsi.

(2) The brachycephalic elements are numerically dominant, especially in the Yangtze Valley, with Kiangsu as the centre of its purest form. They are also of two types.

(3) The mesocephalic element is the most dominant, but is the cross of the two types.

(4) There is a trace of dwarf element in the South.

(5) A low-head type is also found.

BOOKS AND ARTICLES CONSULTED

1. Atgier, M. *Craniométrie Comparée de Cranes Mongoloïdes (Chine et Annam)*, Bulletins et Mémoires de la Société d'Anthropologie de Paris, Série 5, Vol. v (1904), pp. 391–395.

2. Birkner, F. (a) *Beiträge zur Rassenanatomie der Chinesen*, Archiv für Anthropologie, Vol. xxxii (N. F. iv, 1906), pp. 1–40; (b) *Haut und Haare bei sechs Chinesenköpfen*, in Archiv für Anthropologie, Vol. xxxiii (N. F. v, 1906), pp. 142–148.

3. Breton, M. (a) *Sur les Mensurations de 15 femmes et de 53 hommes tonquinois provenant de Hanoi et de Haiphong*, Bulletins de la Société d'Anthropologie de Paris, Série 2, Vol. i (1879), pp. 592–594; (b) *Mensurations de 32 Annamites de Saigon et de 15 Chinois cantonnais*, pp. 595–597.

4. Broca, Paul. *Etudes sur les variations craniométriques et de leur influence sur les moyennes*, ibid., pp. 756–820.

5. Chuan, S. H. *The Skull Measurements of Three Hundred Chinese*, in Supplement of The China Medical Journal, Vol. xxxiv, pp. 12–13.

6. Davis, J. B. *Thesaurus Craniorum*, Vol. i, 1867; Vol. ii, 1875.

7. Flower, W. H. *Osteological Catalogue of the Museum of the Royal College of Surgeons of London*, 1879.

8. Girard, Henry. *Notes sur les Chinois du Quang-si*, L'Anthropologie, Vol. ix (1898), pp. 144–170.

9. Haberer, K. A. *Schädel und Skeletteile aus Peking*. Jena, 1902.

10. Hagen, B. (a) *Über Körpergrosse und Wachstumsverhältnisse der Südchinesen;* Verslag en Med. K. Akad. Wettenschappen. Afd. Natuurk. 2″ reeks, Deel xx (1884) pp. 236–246; (b) *Typical Heads and Faces of Eastern Asiatic and Melanesian Peoples*. Stuttgart, 1907; (c) *Anthropologische Studien aus Insulinde*, 1889; Verh. K. Akad. Wettenschappen xxviii, pp. 1–149; (d) *Die Körpergrösse chinesischer Frauen*, Archiv für Anthropologie, Vol. xxvii (1902), pp. 265–266.

11. Hutcheson, A. C. *Report on the Height, Weight, and Chest-Measurements of Healthy Chinese*, Anatomical and Anthropological Supplement of The China Medical Journal, Vol. xxxiv (1920), pp. 13–16.

12. Iwanowski, Alexis. *Zur Anthropologie der Mongolen*, Archiv für Anthropologie, Vol. xxiv (1896–97), pp. 67–90.

13. Joyce, T. A. *Notes on the Physical Anthropology of Chinese Turkestan*, Journal of the Royal Anthropological Institute, Vol. xlii (1912), pp. 450–484.

14. Koganei, Y. (a) *Messungen an chinesischen Soldaten*. Mitt. a. d. Medizin. Fakultät Kais. Japanischen Universität, Tokyo, Vol. vi (1903–05); (b) *Kurze Mitteilung über Messungen an männlichen chinesen Schädeln*, Internationales Centralblatt für Anthropologie, Vol. vii (1901), p. 129.

15. Legendre, A. F. (a) *Etude anthropologique sur les Chinois du Setchouen*, Bulletins et Mémoires de la Société d'Anthropologie de Paris, Série 6, Vol. ii (1911), pp. 102–124; (b) *Les Lolos*, ibid., Série 5, Vol. i (1910), pp. 77–94.

16. Von Luschan, Felix. *Über Hautfarbentafeln*, Zeitschrift für Ethnologie, Vols. xlvii–xlviii (1915–16), pp. 402–405.

17. Meigs, J. A. *Catalogue of Human Crania in the Collections of the Academy of Natural Science*. Philadelphia, 1857.

18. Merrins, E. M. *Anthropometry of Chinese Students*, The Chinese Medical Journal, Vol. xxiv (1910), pp. 318–324.

19. Mochi, A. *Crani Cinesi e Giaponesi*, Archivo per l'Anthropologia e la Etnologia, Vol. xxxviii (1908), pp. 299–328.

20. Retzius, A. *Ethnologische Schriften*. Stockholm, 1864 S. 141 (Tab. II. fig. I).

21. Reicher, M. *Untersuchungen über die Schädelform der alpenländischen und mongolischen Brachycephalen*, Zeitschrift für Morphologie und Anthropologie, Vol. xv (1912–13), pp. 421–562; Vol. xvi (1914), pp. 1–64.

22. Quatrefages (A. de) et Hamy (E. T.). *Crania Ethnica: Les Cranes des Races Humaines*. Paris, 1882.

23. Schaaffhausen, H. *Die Anthropologischen Sammlungen Deutschlands*. Braunschweig, 1877–1908.

24. Talko-Hryncewicz, J. D. Zamyetki po antropologiyi syevernoi Kitaitsev. (*Notes sur l'anthropologie des Chinois du Nord*) Trudy Troitskosavsk-Kiakhta Otd. Priamur. Otd. Imp. Russ. Geog. Obshcestva. Vol. ii, pt. 3.

25. Ten Kate, H. F. C. *Zur Craniologie der mongoloiden, Beobachtungen und Messungen*. Berlin, 1882.

26. Ting, V. K. *Anatomical and Anthropological Association of China*, The China Medical Journal, Vol. xxxv, 1921.

27. Virchow, H. (a) *Alt chinesicher Schädel*, Zeitschrift für Ethnologie, Vol. xlv (1913), pp. 640–644; (b) *Das Sohlenpolster des Menschen nach Untersuchungen des Herrn Henckel*, Zeitschrift für Ethnologie, Vol. xlv (1913), p. 644.

28. Welcker, Hermann. *Kraniologische Mitteilungen*, Archiv für Anthropologie, Vol. i (1866), pp. 89–160.

29. Whyte, G. Duncan. (a) *Notes on the Height and Weight of the Hoklo People of the Kwangtung Province, South China*, Journal of Royal Anthropological Institute, Vol. xli (1911), pp. 278–300; (b) *The Height, Weight, and Chest-Measurements of Healthy Chinese*, The China Medical Journal, Vol. xxxii (1918), pp. 210–216, 322–328.

30. Zaborowski, M. *Sur cinq Cranes d'Hakkas et les origines chinoises*, Bulletin de la Société d'Anthropologie de Paris, Série 3 (1879), Vol. ii, pp. 557–578.

31. Zuckerkandl, E. *Reise der Österreichischen Fregatte Novara um die Erde in den Jahren 1857–1858.* Anthropologischer Theil. ii, Wien, 1867.

32. *Craniological Data from the Indian Museum.* Calcutta, 1909.

MAP 1. The 18 Provinces

52

 Supermedium

 Medium

 Submedium

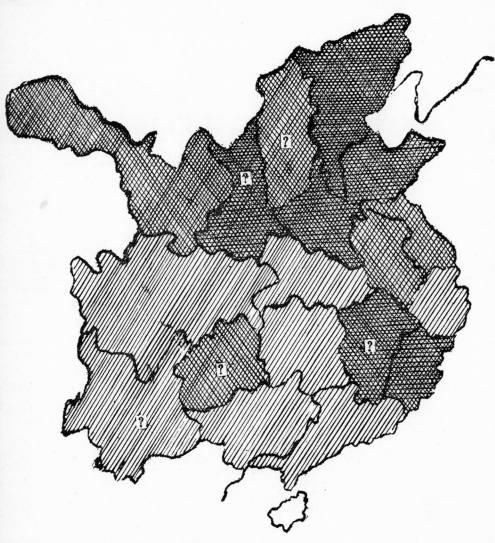

MAP 2. Average Stature

53

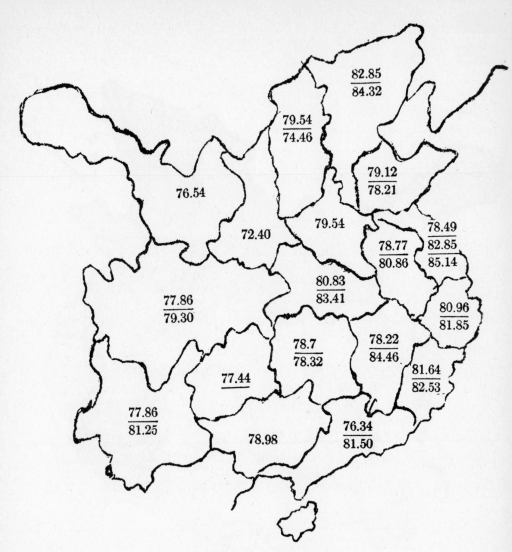

MAP 3. Average Cephalic Index
(*Results from Chuan's data underlined*)

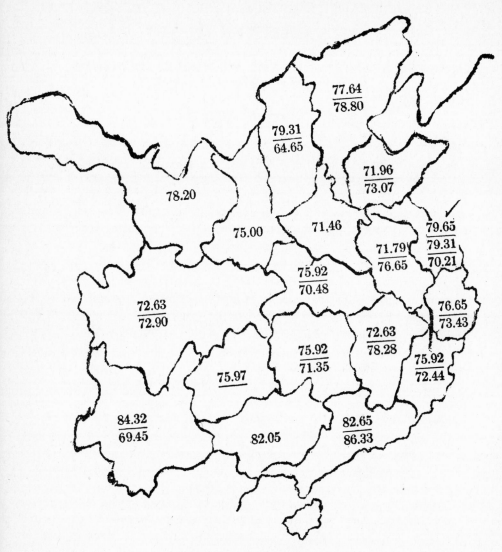

MAP 4. Average Nasal Index
(*Results from Chuan's data underlined*)

55

CHAPTER III

THE EVOLUTION OF THE WE–GROUP: ITS SIZE AS MEASURED BY THE CITY POINTS

Introductory

THE biological data, scattered as they are, have at least revealed the complexity of the physical make-up of the modern Chinese. In all the measurable traits we have considered, the ranges of their variations are almost as extensive as those of the Europeans. The anthropological problem of China is therefore comparable in magnitude to that of Europe, and the historical causes in operation must have been no less complicated. If the complexity is to be considered as a sequel to the past, it necessarily follows that the historical sources have to be tapped so that the present stream may be traced back to the ancient rivulets which have given rise to it. This is, however, no light task, because the scope of the problem covers such a large extent in both time and space. Archaeological inquiry seems at first to be the only right approach. In default of this type of data, the difficulty of making a second choice is extreme.

It is, however, not a hopeless task. The Chinese historians are diligent compilers. As a result of their activity for the past two thousand years and more, there has accumulated in China an amount of historical material, the richness of which is hardly surpassed by any other country even to-day. Within the time limit of our inquiry, it is possible to sift out of this material enough facts for an accurate statement concerning the essential changes of the Chinese during this period.

There are two aspects of this problem, the size of the We-group, and its components; both of these have undergone a process of evolution, not necessarily either concomitantly or altogether independently of each other. Each needs special consideration. The quantitative part may be taken up first. In the following chapter, I shall deal with the changes in its composition.

The source of material for both this and the following chapter is found in the Chinese Encyclopedia (Ch'in Ting Ku Chin T'u Shu Chi Ch'êng). It is fitting that I should say a few words here regarding this remarkable work. The compilation of this encyclopedia was undertaken and completed during the reign of Emperor K'anghsi, and, according to the researches of Mr. Lionel Giles, edited by Ch'ên Mêng-lei. Regarding the scope of this work, I can do no better than quote from Mr. Giles:

The total number of Chüan or books, which vary but little in size, is 10,000. . . . The table of contents alone . . . occupied no fewer than 40 Chüan. There are 9 columns to every page with 20 characters to each column. Allowing an average of 40 leaves, or 80 pages, to the Chüan, we get a total of 800,000 pages; 7,200,000 columns, and (assuming that each page is filled up) 144,000,000 characters. . . . [1]

The work as a whole, in the opinion of Mr. Giles, contains between three and four times as much matter as "the 11th Edition of the Encyclopædia Britannica."

I have found it possible to make use of two out of the thirty-two sections into which the Encyclopedia is divided. Section VI, which is extracted from the local history of different prefectures all over China, furnishes valuable data for the present chapter; Section XIV, which gives a list of nearly 4000 different surnames, single, double, and polysyllabic, will be the basic material of the following chapter.

Leaving Section XIV for later consideration, I have found in Section VI the dates at which, in the different districts, the walls of cities now occupied or abandoned were built. Working from these dates, I propose to reconstruct the routes along which the city points have moved, and infer on this basis the movement of the historical We-group during the successive periods.

The argument derives its validity from these ascertained facts:

(1) That, of all the Eastern Asiatic peoples, the earliest We-group Chinese are the most active wall-builders. The culmination of their activity is expressed in the famous Great Wall.

(2) That all the dates are recorded by the Chinese historians explicitly writing about the Chinese walls.

The obvious inference, then, is that, within China proper, wherever the city wall is found it indicates the presence of the We-group Chinese already in a settled condition. The expansion of the wall-building activity in historical times is therefore a safe barometer showing the expansion of the historical We-group.

It is not the purpose of this chapter to discuss the origin of the city walls, or the process of building, or the motive from which the build-

[1] *An Alphabetical Index to the Chinese Encyclopedia (Ch'in Ting Ku Chin T'u Shu Chi Ch'êng)*, pp. 8, 9. Compiled by L. Giles, M.A. Printed by order of the Trustees of the British Museum. Sold at the British Museum. London, 1911.

ing took place. These are important archaeological and historical themes, and have to be dealt with separately. The sole purpose here, as I have explained, is to examine the development of the wall-building activity as an unmistakable Chinese feature within the boundary of China proper.

General Considerations

The records of 4,478 city walls have been examined. These are, however, not all the city walls that have been built by the Chinese. There are walls which have been destroyed by flood; there are walls which have been buried by earthquakes. All these can be brought to light only by archaeological excavations. But on the whole, this number covers the majority of the cases. The following list shows their distribution by provinces up to 1644 A.D.:

Province	No. of Walls	Province	No. of Walls
Chekiang	144	Kwangsi	129
Chihli	547	Kwangtung	110
Fukien	69	Kweichow	48
Honan	544	Nganhui	229
Hunan	152	Shansi	399
Hupeh	226	Shantung	459
Kansu	240	Shensi	354
Kiangsi	194	Szechuan	219
Kiangsu	268	Yunnan	147

Provinces, however, vary in size. To show the relative density of the distribution of these city walls, a simpler spatial unit has to be selected. Below is shown the number of city walls per 1000 square miles found in each province:

Province		Province	
Chekiang	3.92	Kwangsi	1.69
Chihli	4.72	Kwangtung	1.10
Fukien	1.49	Kweichow	.71
Honan	8.01	Nganhui	4.17
Hunan	1.82	Shansi	4.87
Hupeh	3.16	Shantung	8.19
Kansu	1.91	Shensi	4.70
Kiangsi	2.79	Szechuan	1.02
Kiangsu	6.94	Yunnan	1.02

The relative density of the above distribution must be a result of many factors. First among these, perhaps, is the topographical condition, which differs in each province and must have served as a major factor in determining the wall-building activity of the community. This is mainly because, in the majority of cases, the city walls were built in order to defend the community from outside attack. The purpose is obvious in the case of the Great Wall along the northern frontier of China proper. Speaking generally, the majority of the 4478 city walls about which we have records were so designed. As such, the strategical importance of each place, determined partly by its land formation and partly by the political conditions of the time, is the most important factor. The mountainous districts, abundantly provided with naturally defensive positions, tend to lessen the necessity for artificial protection. In the plain, the necessity for wall building would increase. I offer this as the main reason to explain why Szechuan, a mountainous province, which is at least as old as Fukien, a less mountainous district, compares so poorly with it in the possession of the number of city walls.

The length of occupation is another determining factor, more important in some respects than topography. There could be no gainsaying that, a priori, the longer a district is occupied, the longer it is open to attack, and hence there are more occasions for the community to build walls, and more city walls accordingly are built. This is not theory, but a simple statement of plain facts. The following list shows the number of walls that were built in the eight periods previous to 1644 A.D. The division of time is mainly dynastic.

Periods	First built [1]	First mentioned [1]
A. (Previous to 722 B.C.)	163	. . .
B. (722–207 B.C.)	585	233
C. (206 B.C.–264 A.D.)	540	137
D. (265–617 A.D.)	419	77
E. (618–959 A.D.)	353	65
F. (960–1279 A.D.)	315	61
G. (1280–1367 A.D.)	96	33
H. (1368–1644 A.D.)	564	132
Total	3035	738
Doubtful	705	

[1] The records we have are of two kinds: one states definitely that such and such a city is built in this year; the other merely gives the earliest date at which the city wall is mentioned.

There are according to the above list 3035 city walls in China whose origins are definitely dated. Inasmuch as the periods into which the time is divided are of different lengths, the intensity of the wall-building activity therefore can be brought into the right perspective only when it is expressed in terms of x per year. Taking off the first period (A), which vanishes into an indefinite past, and excluding the mentioned and the doubtful cases, I have worked out the building intensity for the different periods as follows:

	No. of city walls built per year
B-period (516 years)	1.13
C-period (470 years)	1.15
D-period (353 years)	1.18
E-period (342 years)	1.03
F-period (320 years)	.98
G-period (88 years)	1.09
H-period (277 years)	2.04

The index of the intensity of the wall-building activity may be interpreted in several different ways. It may be considered as indicating the degree of contact with the You-group, or as showing the directions of growth of the We-group. I do not, however, mean to discuss this aspect here. What is worth noting is the steadiness and uniformity with which the wall-building activity is marked up to the last period. In the last period, the record of this activity almost doubles that of any of the preceding periods; this is undoubtedly due, partly at least, to the fact that in this period the records were better kept. If we can trace back all the referred cases to the different periods to which they belong, a different series of indices may be worked out. As it is, probably the more remote period is most inaccurately treated.

It cannot be true, however, that the city walls are all of the same type; for instance it cannot be true that if in the province of Shantung there is a living city wall to every 122 square miles, people can still practise farming. The truth is that the city walls are not all of the same type. In the main, two classes are plainly indicated: the living and the abandoned. (It may be added here, that when I say living and abandoned, I mean in the year 1644 A.D.) The following list shows the number of abandoned city walls and the percentage of the total number of cities found in each province:

Provinces	No. of living cities	No. of abandoned cities	Total	Per cent of abandoned cities
Chekiang	86	58	144	40.28
Chihli	135	412	547	75.32
Fukien	54	15	69	21.74
Honan	103	441	544	81.07
Hunan	73	79	152	51.97
Hupeh	60	166	226	73.45
Kansu	42	198	240	82.5
Kiangsi	95	99	194	51.03
Kiangsu	54	214	268	79.85
Kwangsi	96	33	129	25.58
Kwangtung	85	25	110	22.72
Kweichow	39	9	48	18.75
Nganhui	52	177	229	77.29
Shansi	108	291	399	72.94
Shantung	103	356	459	77.56
Shensi	71	283	354	79.95
Szechuan	119	100	219	45.66
Yunnan	65	82	147	55.78

The main cause of the abandonment of a city wall, aside from flood and war, which are not uncommon, is its age. In other words, the city has outlived its usefulness, or been ruined or destroyed and therefore abandoned. But whatever the cause of abandonment may be, it indicates the length of occupation. The city cannot be abandoned, unless it has been occupied. Therefore, other things being equal, the more abandoned cities there are in a province, the longer has been its age of occupation. The percentage of abandoned cities to the total is then a sure index of the length of occupation of each province. The following list shows the regrouping of the provinces according to the percentages of abandoned cities in a descending order:

Group I. Av. = 77.77 per cent

Kansu	82.50
Honan	81.07
Shensi	79.95
Kiangsu	79.85
Shantung	77.56
Nganhui	77.29
Chihli	75.32
Hupeh	73.45
Shansi	72.94

Group II. Av. = 48.94 per cent

Yunnan	55.78
Hunan	51.97
Kiangsi	51.03
Szechuan	45.66
Chekiang	40.28

Group III. Av. = 22.20 per cent

Kwangsi	25.58
Kwangtung	22.72
Fukien	21.74
Kweichow	18.75

The above grouping seems to be as natural as it can possibly be. Look at the enormous gap between Shansi and Yunnan, the last of

Group I and the first of Group II; look again at the enormous gap
between Chekiang and Kangsi, the last of Group II and the first
of Group III. (Graph 2.) Each group is therefore a compact whole
whose component parts show very little intra-group differences, and
therefore cannot be separated from each other. If this percentage is
taken as an index of age, it would show that Group I is more than
three times as old as Group III, and Group II is more than two thirds
younger than Group I.

Since this grouping is derived from the percentage of cities that are
abandoned, we may consider these three groups as the three archaeological zones of China proper. The richest zone represented by Group I
has undoubtedly been occupied by the Chinese the longest. If we
examine these provinces on Map 5 we shall find their location quite
in agreement with historical lessons. The zone includes all the provinces on the banks of the Hoang-ho and the historically noted provinces north of the Yangtze. In order to show the close affinity of the
provinces within this group, I have found out the extent of dispersion
of the provincial averages from the group average to be 3.21 per cent —
(mathematically speaking the standard deviation). In other words,
the average difference between the component average and the group
average for Zone I is just 3.21 per cent, a difference less than one fifth
of that between the last average of Group I and the first average of
Group II, which is 17.16 per cent.

The standard deviation of Group II is 5.35 per cent and that of
Group III, 2.53 per cent. Geographically, these two also form a united
whole. The only abnormality seems to be the province of Yunnan
which might be expected to be a member of Group III rather than
Group II. Perhaps the abnormality lies in our expectation, and is not
inherent in the facts. We shall see the explanation in its due place.

The distinction between these three zones is at any rate established.
It is obvious that if the city point is preceded by the We-group immigrants, there must have been two great movements of the historical
We-group in the periods under our consideration. The result of the
first movement is the occupation of the provinces of Group II — (Yunnan, Hunan, Kiangsi, Szechuan, and Chekiang), and that of the second
is the occupation of the provinces included in Group III. Whether
these movements were gradual or en masse, can be decided only by
a study of the intensity of the building activity in the different zones
during different periods. Table 17 shows the distribution of building
activities during each period in each of these three zones.

TABLE 17

| Periods | Group I (Total = 3266) | | | | Group II (Total = 856) | | | | Group III (Total = 356) | | | |
| | Sure Cases | | Doubtful Cases | | Sure Cases | | Doubtful Cases | | Sure Cases | | Doubtful Cases | |
	No.	Per cent	No.	Per cent	No.	Per cent	No.	Per cent	No.	Per cent	No.	Per cent
A	161	4.93	..	...	..	...	..	...	2	.56	..	...
B	526	16.10	232	7.1	48	5.61	1	.11	11	3.09	..	...
C	412	12.61	137	4.2	113	13.21	..	...	15	4.22	..	...
D	339	10.38	75	2.3	71	8.29	2	.23	9	2.53	2	...
E	206	6.3	56	1.71	115	13.41	7	.82	32	8.89	9	2.53
F	208	6.36	43	1.32	65	7.59	9	1.05	42	11.80	3	.84
G	64	1.96	28	.85	20	2.34	2	.23	12	3.37	16	4.49
H	174	5.32	87	2.66	244	28.50	29	3.39	146	41.01	..	...
?	518	15.86	...	...	130	15.20	..	...	57	16.00	..	...

The doubtful cases are undoubtedly greatly disturbing factors in this connection as they are unequally represented in the three zones. To compare the building activities of these three zones on an equal basis, it becomes necessary to reduce them in such a way that there is only one numerical value in each of these periods. By a mathematical formula to be explained in the appendix (p. 285), I have converted both of them to the different period as approximately as I can determine. Table 18 summarizes the results of this conversion.

TABLE 18

| Periods | Group I | | | | Group II | | | | Group III | | | |
| | a (Σ = 2090)[1] | | b (Σ = 3266)[2] | | a (Σ = 676) | | b (Σ = 856) | | a (Σ = 269) | | b (Σ = 356) | |
	No.	% Σ	No.	% Σ	No.	% Σ	No.	% Σ	No.	% Σ	No.	% Σ
A	161	7.7	391.34	11.98	..	...	17.98	2.10	2	.75	9.125	2.55
B	526	25.17	756.34	23.16	48	7.10	65.98	7.72	11	4.10	18.125	5.10
C	412	19.71	575.92	17.63	113	16.71	131.70	15.39	15	5.57	22.125	6.19
D	339	16.22	465.09	14.24	71	10.50	92.16	10.76	9	3.35	20.75	5.83
E	206	9.85	318.43	9.75	115	17.07	139.06	16.24	32	11.90	43.75	12.28
F	208	9.95	312.13	9.56	65	9.61	89.87	10.40	42	15.61	56.375	15.81
G	64	3.06	164.50	5.04	20	2.95	44.50	5.20	12	4.46	24.624	6.93
H	174	8.33	282.25	8.64	244	36.10	274.75	32.12	146	54.27	161.125	45.30

[1] Excluding the doubtful and the referred cases in the total number.
[2] Including the doubtful and the referred cases in the total number.

The graphs (Graph 3) based on this table show that there is really little difference between a and b, except in the H period of Group III. But even there it does not effect the order of the intensity of activity.

The culminating period for Group I is in B. In the case of both II and III, it is H. But II and III are not the same in spite of the identity in period of the climax. In Group II, the climax is reached gradually. In III it is a sudden jump; in fact, almost a freak. If the ogive curves (Graph 4) are examined, it will be seen that Group II attained fifty per cent of its total activity in the E period, while Group III did not reach that percentage until the F–G period.

The data may be again compared on a yearly basis. Table 19 shows: (1) the number of cities built per year in different periods and zones; (2) the period percentage of the different zones; (3) the zonal percentage of different periods. (The data of Table 18 are used, and the A period eliminated as it is impossible to reduce it to a yearly basis.)

TABLE 19

Periods	Total building activity of different periods	Group I			Group II			Group III		
		Building per year	Period percentages	Zonal percentages	Building per year	Period percentages	Zonal percentages	Building per year	Period percentages	Zonal percentages
B	1.133	1.019	18.63	89.94	.093	4.27	8.20	.021	2.18	1.86
C	1.148	.877	16.05	76.39	.240	11.01	20.99	.031	3.22	2.62
D	1.186	.960	17.56	80.87	.201	9.23	16.93	.025	2.59	2.20
E	1.031	.602	11.02	58.39	.336	15.39	32.59	.093	9.66	9.02
F	.984	.650	11.90	66.05	.203	9.32	20.63	.131	13.60	13.32
G	1.093	.730	13.35	66.79	.227	10.41	20.77	.136	14.12	12.44
H	2.034	.628	11.49	30.87	.880	40.36	43.26	.526	54.63	25.87

Total building activity of different zones } 5.466   2.180   .963

The period percentages as shown in Table 19 and in Graph 4a accordingly furnish another evidence to reënforce our argument that the building activity in Zone I is more steadily maintained and has a greater uniformity, and that its derivation from the average is but little; while in Zone II the dispersion is greater and in Zone III greater still. The degrees of dispersion of this activity in the different zones as measured by the standard deviation are as follows:

Group I.................................... 2.67
Group II.................................... 11.06
Group III.................................... 17.11

In trying to trace back the cause of the fluctuations of the building activity in the different zones, we are immediately confronted with a problem which I have so far not yet touched. I am inclined to call this the problem of the "point of saturation." Speaking generally, the number of cities that can be built in any region of definite size must be limited. When that limitation is reached, further building activity must be accompanied by abandonment. This need not mean that abandonment does not begin until this point is reached. But there cannot be further building without accompanying abandonment. It may be argued now that in any region, before the saturation point is reached, the building activity tends to fluctuate; after the saturation point is reached, the activity tends to normalize. So the dispersion of the activity is greater before the attainment of the point than after. The reasons are very plain. The building activity depends upon the builders. If a certain region is still capable of possessing more walls without a necessary concomitant abandonment, it shows also that there is still more room in that region for new settlers. As the movement of the settlers could not be determined on a per-year basis at a time when no organized immigration was conceivable, and as the causes of this movement are probably innumerable, hence functioning variably from year to year, it follows that the building activity of a region before its attainment of saturation, fluctuates with the movements of the settlers. The condition of affairs changes, however, when the point of saturation is reached. There is then no room for more walls. Thus further activity cannot be sustained, unless accompanied by abandonment. The causes of abandonment are probably of a variable character, but whatever the primary efficient cause may be, age always counts. It is usually the "aged city" which is abandoned; and as such, is a determining character. Since time persists with a dogged tenacity, so the rate of building activity has its limit of fluctuation. It cannot oscillate as in the non-saturated region. The proof of this whole theory lies in the facts themselves. In the three zones which we have considered, the oldest regions show the least fluctuation; the youngest, the greatest.

It now becomes imperative that we should devise a method to determine the saturation points of the respective regions. Since, by definition, the saturation point is that at which the greatest number of living city walls that are capable of being sustained in any region have been built, and beyond which further building activity must be accompanied by abandonment, the saturation point is to be determined by the greatest number of living cities in the most saturated region. Let us now apply this definition to Zone I which has the least probability of being unsaturated.

In the following list the number of living cities in the nine oldest provinces is given, with the area of each province, and the number of square miles in each province per city.

Province	No. of living cities	Size in square miles	Square miles per city
Kansu	42	125,483	2988
Honan	103	67,954	660
Shensi	71	75,290	1060
Kiangsu	54	38,610	715
Shantung	103	55,984	543
Nganhui	52	54,826	1054
Chihli	135	115,830	858
Hupeh	60	71,428	1190
Shansi	108	81,852	758

Thus it appears that if we express the saturation point in terms of the number of square miles per city, the figure shows a great provincial variation. This is exactly what might be expected, as topographical conditions vary with provinces. Since the topographic differences are generally very great, so are the different saturation points.

But it may be asked, how do we know that the saturation point in each province is constant in all the different periods? So far in the discussion it has been rather assumed that in the saturated province there is a relation between the rate of abandonment and the rate of building activity. But this is an implication that needs proof. Unless it is proved, there seems to be no solid ground for believing that there is a "fixed" saturation point in all the provinces all through the different periods. For climates may change, strategical importance vary, and conditions of natural resources shift from time to time — all these may disperse or concentrate the settlers in the respective regions. The rate of abandonment and that of building may therefore be different in accordance with the concentrating and the dispersing influences. They are two variables not necessarily concomitant with each other, although correlated to some degree. If a close correlation is to be maintained new evidences are certainly needed.

The question raised needs therefore some more detailed discussion. It seems to be necessary to show whether there is such a close correlation. But to do this, the dates of abandonment are necessary, which we unfortunately lack. It appears that at the present stage of our knowledge, it is impossible to prove the case either one way or the other. For my part, I rather believe there is no absolute saturation point, for the objections raised are certainly unanswerable. Nevertheless, this does not vitiate its existence. If it were true that the saturation point varies from period to period, it could still be postulated that, there is one point in each region which is the most saturated of all saturated points through different periods. It may be an unknown quantity, but it is as real as the notion of "marginal utility," and is the sign post of all migratory impulses. The task of proving its existence does not lie beyond the range of possibility as does the task of determining its general attribute. Therefore, I propose to proceed with this task. Table 20 shows the relative proportions of occupied and abandoned cities found in Zone I at 1644 A.D., the doubtful and the referred cases being excluded:

TABLE 20

Building periods	Occupied cities		Abandoned cities		Total
	No.	Per cent	No.	Per cent	
A.....................	10	6.2	151	93.8	161
B.....................	55	12.44	471	87.6	526
C.....................	53	12.90	359	87.1	412
D.....................	66	19.40	273	80.6	339
E.....................	73	35.50	133	64.5	206
F.....................	93	44.70	115	55.3	208
G.....................	52	81.25	12	19.75	64
H.....................	161	92.50	13	7.7	174
Total...........	563		1257		2090

Now, if we convert the total building activity of this zone to a per-century-per-100,000-square-mile basis, we obtain Table 21.

TABLE 21

INTENSITY OF BUILDING ACTIVITY IN ZONE I BETWEEN 722 B.C. AND 1644 A.D. EXPRESSED IN TERMS OF PER-CENTURY-PER-100,000 SQUARE MILES. 722 B.C., THE BEGINNING OF B-PERIOD IS TAKEN AS THE BASIS OF CALCULATION FOR TIME.

723 B.C. = 0
722 B.C. = 1

Mid-points of periods	No. of city walls built per-century-per-100,000 square miles	Mid-points of periods	No. of city walls built per-century-per-100,000 square miles
250...................	14.84	1500...................	8.75
550...................	13.04	1650...................	8.88
750...................	12.19	1850...................	9.46
950...................	13.21	2050...................	11.03
1150...................	13.97	2227...................	9.14
1350...................	11.67		

As plotted in Graph 5 the building activity in Zone I falls distinctly into two different periods. The 1400th year from 722 B.C. marks a very clear line of division. Previous to this period the building activity maintains an average of 13.61 with an average dispersion of 1.14: after that it falls to 9.68 with an average dispersion of 0.93. So in the second period, not only is the activity less intense, but the intensity also becomes more convergent: the explanation is not far to seek. I have already tried to show that the wall building activity in China as a whole, shows a very steady uniformity up to the H period (p. 103). In Table 18 we find the regional variations of these three Zones are well marked. If we may take these two tables as a help to the explanation of the phenomenon which we have found here, it would indicate that previous to the 1400th year counting from 722 B.C. (i.e. 678 A.D.), the Chinese population was most concentrated in Zone I. This explanation is attempted on the assumption that the degree of wall building activity is directly correlated with that of the concentration of the population. However it could not be taken as a ground for assumption that the population in Zone I becomes less concentrated after 678 A.D. That would be undoubtedly a false assumption and could not be attempted unless another false assumption is implied — that is, the population is a limited quantity. It may be true that there is a phenomenal increase of wall building activity in Zone II and III after 678 A,D.. indicative of a marked increase of population in these two zones; it may be true too that the chief source of human energy in the exploitation of these new regions is derived from Zone I; but it cannot be necessarily true that the population of Zone I, on this account, becomes less. On the other hand it does indicate that the wall building in Zone I has reached a point beyond which it cannot sustain itself with the same intensity; namely, it has reached the saturation point whose existence it is our purpose to prove.

The saturation point therefore does exist. If it exists in Zone I, there seems to be no reason for us to deny its existence in the other two regions. But it is possible that it had not yet been reached in 1644 A.D. This possibility is indicated by the wide fluctuations of the building activities in this region which we have noticed before. In the light of what we have come to know about these regions, the second and third zones are undoubtedly a great deal younger than the first; this again shows that they were probably far from being saturated in 1644 A.D. So for all these reasons, the other two regions are apparently incapable of being analyzed in the same way; and if so, it gives rise to the problem, "what are the relative ages of the different zones and regions?"

Here the age is measured by the length of occupation by the We-group and this in turn is measured by the history of the wall-building activities. Table 22 gives the different periodical rates of the cities built in Zone I that are abandoned by 1644 A.D. (the A period being excluded from calculation).

TABLE 22

	Interperiod durations [1]	Per cent
B–C	(493 years)	.5
C–D	(411.5 years)	6.5
D–E	(347.5 years)	16.1
E–F	(331 years)	9.2
F–G	(204 years)	35.55
G–H	(182.5 years)	12.25
$\frac{1}{2}$ H	(138.5 years)	7.5

[1] Interperiod duration, calculated from mid-point to mid-point: i.e., $\frac{1}{2}$ B + $\frac{1}{2}$ C equals 493 years, etc., the last one being $\frac{1}{2}$ H equals 138.5.

It is obvious that if we want to find out the abandonment rate of these city walls, we have only to reverse the time order and take 1644 A.D. as the starting-point; then count backward. The results then are as follows:

In the first 138.5 years, 7.5 %
In 321 years (7.5 + 12.25) 19.75 %
In 525 years (35.55 + 19.75) 55.37 %
In 856 years (55.3 % + 9.2 %) 64.5 % } of the total abandoned
In 1203.5 years (64.5 % + 16.1 %) 80.6 %
In 1615 years (80.6 % + 6.5 %) 87.1 %
In 2108 years (87.1 % + .5 %) 87.6 %

The above data, however, are rather local and applicable to Zone I only. In order to make this rate of abandonment universally representative, the following data on the basis of the abandoned cities as a whole are worked out:

TABLE 23

	Per cent of abandoned cities to total cities built
In the first 138.5 years	4.25
In 321 years	25.00
In 525 years	48.53
In 856 years	62.60
In 1203.5 years	78.76
In 1615 years	82.96
In 2108 years	88.89
In 2109 + X years	39.87

The two curves as plotted show some important differences. "The infant mortality" of the cities, so to speak, of the local curve is very much higher than that of the general curve. The old age mortality, on the other hand, is more pronounced in the general curve, while the local curve smooths into an indefinite remote period. But on the whole, the general curve, as it is based on a greater number of cases, must be nearer to the theoretical mean. Applying this curve to the analysis of the data, the following theoretical age of the different provinces may be deduced:

TABLE 24

THEORETICAL PROVINCIAL AGE[1] AT 1644 A.D.

Provinces	Theoretical age Years	Provinces	Theoretical age Years
1. Kansu	1580	10. Yunnan	690
2. Honan	1440	11. Hunan	600
3. Shensi	1320	12. Kiangsi	590
4. Kiangsu	1310	13. Szechuan	500
5. Shantung	1180	14. Chekiang	450
6. Nganhui	1170	15. Kwangsi	330
7. Chihli	1130	16. Kwangtung	300
8. Hupeh	1090	17. Fukien	290
9. Shansi	1080	18. Kweichow	260

[1] Calculation accurate to the tenth place only.

This seems to be the only satisfactory way to represent the relative lengths of occupation of the different provinces. Objections are not lacking, although the scheme as a whole is acceptable. It is hard to demonstrate the value of this scheme in a general way. To go over the salient features of the wall-building activity province by province seems to be the only choice at present as the next step of our inquiry. In doing this, not only the present estimation of the provincial age is to be reëxamined, but also the periodical changes of its wall-building intensity.

C. PROVINCIAL STUDIES

The following points are chosen for reasons that, although obvious, still need some elucidation. The general method of presentation would be to give the facts first, followed by a geographical distribution and then a discussion of their significance. So far as the facts go, the numerical survey of the wall-building activity must be taken as the most important category. It comprises the materials from which all the inferences are drawn. In the way of classifying these materials, no new criterion is introduced. The percentage table following the numerical tables is meant to give a bird's-eye view of the comparative status of the building activity in different provinces at different periods. It may be convenient to give the whole system of calculation here:

Let X = No. of walls built in any period in a province.

(a)
$$\frac{X}{\text{Total no. of walls built in the province } (1, 2, 3, 4, \text{ etc.})}$$
= per cent of the provincial total.

(b)
$$\frac{X}{\text{Total no. of walls built in the period } (A, B, C, D, E, \text{ etc.})}$$
= per cent of the periodical total.

(c)
$$\frac{\text{No. of walls built at the period that are abandoned at 1644 A.D.}}{X}$$
= per cent of the provincial period totals that are abandoned.

It will be seen that the abandonment curve that may be plotted for each province will be less generally satisfactory as compared with the curve as a whole, but it will give the provincial character in a greater relief; for this reason it is given together with the other two percentage curves.

The two indices aimed at, expressing the intensity of wall-building activity in each province, are calculated according to the following formula:

(d) Relative index =
$$\frac{X}{\text{no. of walls built per year in each province.}}$$
= periodical duration in term of years.

(e) Absolute index = no. of walls built per century per 10,000 square miles
$$= \frac{d \times 100}{\text{Provincial area in terms of 10,000 square miles.}}$$

The relative index therefore eliminates the durational inequality as the percentage system does not, so it puts the inter-period comparison on a more uniform basis. The absolute index makes the comparison on a still more objective basis, as it takes into account also the sizes of the provinces. But it must be noted that while these indices gain in one direction, they have lost all the local color characteristic and important in each period and province; so they should be studied together with the percentage system.

1. Kansu:

1. Area, 125,483 square miles.
2. Hypothetical age in 1644 A.D., 1580 years.
3. Building status in 1644 A.D.:
   (a) Total number of city walls found, 240.
   (b) Number of abandoned walls, 198.
   (c) Percentage of the total that are abandoned, 82.5 per cent.
4. History of the wall-building.

TABLE 25

(a) IN NUMBER

Building periods	Living		Abandoned		Total a [1]	Total b [1]
	Built	Referred	Built	Referred		
A..........	1	..	8	..	9	9
B..........	1	..	13	..	14	14
C..........	2	..	37	..	39	39
D..........	1	1	19	2	20	23
E..........	3	2	24	3	27	32
F..........	12	1	46	5	58	64
G..........	4	3	0	1	4	8
H..........	8	3	3	1	11	15
Doubtful			36			36
Total...	32	10	150	12	182	240
	42		198			

[1] Total a excludes the doubtful and the referred cases. Total b includes the doubtful and the referred cases.

(b) IN PERCENTAGES   (c) INDEX OF BUILDING INTENSITY

Building periods	Per cent of the provincial totals	Per cent of the period totals	Per cent of the "X" that are abandoned	Building periods	Relative index (No. of cities built per year)	Absolute index (No. of cities built per century per 10,000 square miles)
A.........	4.94	5.52	88.88	A.........	....	...
B.........	7.68	2.39	92.86	B........	.0271	.216
C.........	21.42	7.22	95.01	C........	.0830	.661
D.........	10.99	4.77	95.00	D........	.0566	.452
E.........	14.83	7.65	93.08	E........	.0789	.629
F.........	31.87	18.42	79.31	F........	.1813	1.444
G.........	2.20	4.17	....	G........	.0455	.362
H.........	6.04	1.95	27.27	H........	.0398	.317

2. Honan:

1. Area, 67,954 square miles.
2. Hypothetical age in 1644 A.D., 1440 years.
3. Building status in 1644 A.D.:
   (a) Total number of city walls found, 544.
   (b) Number of abandoned walls, 441.
   (c) Percentage of the total that are abandoned, 81.07 per cent.
4. History of the wall-building.

TABLE 26

(a) IN NUMBER

Building periods	Living		Abandoned		Total a	Total b
	Built	Referred	Built	Referred		
A..........	5	..	54	..	59	59
B..........	23	1	127	..	150	151
C..........	22	..	89	..	111	111
D..........	8	..	38	..	46	46
E..........	8	1	31	..	39	40
F..........	6	1	2	..	8	9
G..........	2	2	2	..	4	6
H..........	8	1	..	..	8	9
Doubtful	15		98			113
Total.......	82	6	343		425	544
	103		441			

(b) IN PERCENTAGES   (c) INDEX OF BUILDING INTENSITY

Building periods	Per cent of the provincial totals	Per cent of the period totals	Per cent of the "X" that are abandoned	Building periods	Relative index	Absolute index
A........	13.88	36.23	91.53	A.........	...	....
B........	35.38	25.62	84.67	B........	.291	4.278
C........	26.12	20.57	80.18	C........	.236	3.476
D........	10.82	10.95	82.61	D........	.130	1.917
E........	9.18	11.04	79.48	E........	.114	1.678
F........	1.88	2.55	25.00	F........	.025	.358
G........	.94	4.16	50.00	G........	.046	.669
H........	1.88	1.42	....	H........	.029	.425

3. Shensi:

1. Area, 75,290 square miles.
2. Hypothetical age in 1644 A.D., 1320 years.
3. Building status in 1644 A.D.:
    (a) Total number of city walls found, 354.
    (b) Number of abandoned walls, 283.
    (c) Percentage of the total that are abandoned, 79.95 per cent.
4. History of the wall-building.

TABLE 27

(a) IN NUMBER

Building periods	Living		Abandoned		Total a	Total b
	Built	Referred	Built	Referred		
A..........	..	..	21	..	21	21
B..........	2	..	75	4	77	81
C..........	2	1	39	17	41	59
D..........	13	2	39	5	52	59
E..........	9	3	16	7	25	35
F..........	9	1	10	..	19	20
G..........	10	3	3	2	13	18
H..........	15	1	2	..	17	18
Doubtful....			43			43
Totals......	60	11	205	35	265	354
	71		283			

(b) IN PERCENTAGES   (c) INDEX OF BUILDING INTENSITY

Building periods	Per cent of the provincial totals	Per cent of the period totals	Per cent of the "X" that are abandoned	Building periods	Relative index	Absolute index
A........	7.92	12.79	100.00	A........	...	....
B........	29.04	13.15	97.40	B........	.149	1.982
C........	15.48	7.59	95.12	C.......	.087	1.158
D........	19.63	12.40	74.98	D.......	.147	1.951
E........	9.43	7.08	64.00	E.......	.073	.971
F........	7.17	6.03	52.63	F.......	.059	.789
G........	4.91	13.55	23.08	G.......	.148	1.962
H........	6.42	3.02	11.76	H.......	.061	.815

4. Kiangsu:

1. Area, 38,610 square miles.
2. Hypothetical age in 1644 A.D., 1310 years.
3. Building status in 1644 A.D.:
   - (a) Total number of city walls found, 268.
   - (b) Number of abandoned walls, 214.
   - (c) Percentage of the total that are abandoned, 79.85 per cent.
4. History of the wall-building.

TABLE 28

(a) IN NUMBER

Building periods	Living		Abandoned		Total a	Total b
	Built	Referred	Built	Referred		
A..........	..	..	2	..	2	2
B..........	5	1	53	7	58	66
C..........	3	2	18	9	21	32
D..........	3	..	27	15	30	45
E..........	5	1	11	7	16	24
F..........	5	3	5	1	10	14
G..........	5	..	3	..	8	8
H..........	17	4	3	..	20	24
Doubtful ...	53					53
Totals......	43	11	122	39	165	268
	54		214			

(b) IN PERCENTAGE   (c) INDEX OF BUILDING INTENSITY

Building periods	Per cent of the provincial totals	Per cent of the period totals	Per cent of the "X" that are abandoned	Building periods	Relative index	Absolute index
A........	1.21	1.23	100.00	A........	....	....
B........	35.14	9.90	91.39	B........	.112	2.911
C........	12.73	3.89	85.71	C........	.045	1.157
D........	18.18	7.15	90.00	D........	.085	2.201
E........	9.70	4.53	68.75	E........	.047	1.212
F........	6.06	3.17	50.00	F........	.031	.809
G........	4.85	8.32	37.50	G........	.091	2.355
H........	12.12	3.55	15.00	H........	.072	1.870

5. Shantung:

1. Area, 55,984 square miles.
2. Hypothetical age in 1644 A.D., 1180 years.
3. Building status in 1644 A.D.:
    (a) Total number of city walls found, 459.
    (b) Number of abandoned walls, 356.
    (c) Percentage of the total that are abandoned, 77.56 per cent.
4. History of the wall-building.

TABLE 29

(a) In Number

Building periods	Living		Abandoned		Total a	Total b
	Built	Referred	Built	Referred		
A..........	..	..	6	...	6	6
B..........	..	6	39	116	39	161
C..........	2	1	26	64	28	93
D..........	5	2	26	9	31	42
E..........	3	1	6	5	9	15
F..........	17	..	8	1	25	26
G..........	21	3	..	..	21	24
H..........	19	23	..	3	19	45
Doubtful ...	47					47
Totals......	67	36	111	198	178	459
	103		356			

(b) In Percentage   (c) Index of Building Intensity

Building periods	Per cent of the provincial totals	Per cent of the period totals	Per cent of the "X" that are abandoned	Building periods	Relative index	Absolute index
A.........	3.37	3.69	100.00	A.........	....	....
B.........	21.90	6.66	100.00	B........	.076	1.352
C.........	15.73	5.19	92.90	C........	.060	1.065
D.........	17.42	7.40	83.90	D........	.088	1.575
E.........	5.06	2.57	66.70	E........	.026	.472
F.........	14.05	7.94	32.00	F........	.078	1.395
G.........	11.80	21.90	....	G........	.2385	4.275
H.........	10.67	3.38	....	H........	.069	1.228

6. Nganhui:

1. Area, 54,826 square miles.
2. Hypothetical age in 1644 A.D., 1170 years.
3. Building status in 1644 A.D.:
   (a) Total number of city walls found, 229.
   (b) Number of abandoned walls, 177.
   (c) Percentage of the total that are abandoned, 77.29 per cent.
4. History of the wall-building.

TABLE 30

(a) In Number

Building periods	Living		Abandoned		Total a	Total b
	Built	Referred	Built	Referred		
A..........	..	..	5	..	5	5
B..........	3	..	18	6	21	27
C..........	4	..	43	6	47	53
D..........	5	..	29	2	34	36
E..........	5	1	9	2	14	17
F..........	7	3	2	..	9	12
G..........	3	..	2	2	5	7
H..........	16	5	4	..	20	25
Doubtful....	47					47
Totals......	43	9	112	18	155	229
	52		177			

(b) In Percentages   (c) Index of Building Intensity

Building periods	Per cent of the provincial totals	Per cent of the period totals	Per cent of the "X" that are abandoned	Building periods	Relative index	Absolute index
A........	3.23	3.06	100.00	A........	...	....
B........	13.55	3.59	85.71	B.......	.041	.742
C........	30.30	8.72	91.50	C.......	.100	1.82
D........	21.92	8.12	85.40	D.......	.096	1.75
E........	9.04	3.97	64.30	E.......	.041	.75
F........	5.82	2.84	22.20	F.......	.028	.515
G........	3.23	5.20	40.00	G.......	.057	1.04
H........	12.90	3.55	25.00	H.......	.072	1.32

7. Chihli:

1. Area, 115, 830 square miles.
2. Hypothetical age in 1644 A.D., 1130 years.
3. Building status in 1644 A.D.:
   (a) Total number of city walls found, 547.
   (b) Number of abandoned walls, 412.
   (c) Percentage of the total that are abandoned, 75.32 per cent.
4. History of the wall-building.

TABLE 31

(a) In Number

Building periods	Living		Abandoned		Total a	Total b
	Built	Referred	Built	Referred		
A.........	2	..	33	..	35	35
B.........	10	..	47	40	57	97
C.........	7	..	64	26	71	97
D.........	4	2	23	17	27	46
E.........	15	..	16	9	31	40
F.........	18	1	21	20	39	60
G.........	4	4	1	5	5	14
H.........	33	32	..	2	33	67
Doubtful....	3		88			91
Totals......	93	39	205	119	298	547
	135		412			

(b) In Percentages   (c) Index of Building Intensity

Building periods	Per cent of the provincial totals	Per cent of the period totals	Per cent of the "X" that are abandoned	Building periods	Relative index	Absolute index
A........	11.73	21.48	94.4	A........	...	...
B........	19.12	9.75	82.5	B........	.111	.95
C........	23.82	13.15	90.1	C........	.151	1.30
D........	9.07	6.44	85.3	D........	.076	.66
E........	10.40	8.79	51.7	E........	.091	.78
F........	13.10	12.38	53.9	F........	.122	1.05
G........	1.68	5.20	20.0	G........	.057	.49
H........	11.08	5.86	...	H........	.119	1.03

8. Hupeh:

1. Area, 71,428 square miles.
2. Hypothetical age in 1644 A.D., 1090 years.
3. Building status in 1644 A.D.:
   (a) Total number of city walls found, 226.
   (b) Number of abandoned walls, 166.
   (c) Percentage of the total that are abandoned, 73.45 per cent.
4. History of the wall-building.

TABLE 32

(a) In Number

Building periods	Living		Abandoned		Total a	Total b
	Built	Referred	Built	Referred		
A..........	..	..	2	..	2	2
B..........	1	..	43	..	44	44
C..........	6	..	34	4	40	44
D..........	2	1	27	1	29	31
E..........	1	1	10	..	11	12
F..........	5	3	4	..	9	12
G..........	..	..	1	1	1	2
H..........	33	6	..	..	33	39
Doubtful....	1		39			40
Totals......	48	11	121	6	169	226
	60		166			

(b) In Percentages | | | | #### (c) Index of Building Intensity | |

Building periods	Per cent of the provincial totals	Per cent of the period totals	Per cent of the "X" that are abandoned	Building periods	Relative index	Absolute index
A........	1.18	1.22	100.00	A........	...	...
B........	26.10	7.53	97.70	B........	.085	1.19
C........	23.65	7.41	85.00	C........	.085	1.19
D........	17.15	6.92	93.2	D........	.082	1.15
E........	6.51	3.12	90.9	E........	.032	.45
F........	5.32	2.86	44.4	F........	.028	.39
G........	.58	1.04	100.00	G........	.011	.16
H........	19.51	5.85	....	H........	.119	1.67

9. Shansi:

1. Area, 81,853 square miles.
2. Hypothetical age in 1644 A.D., 1080 years.
3. Building status in 1644 A.D.:
   (a) Total number of city walls found, 399.
   (b) Number of abandoned, 291.
   (c) Percentage of the total that are abandoned, 72.94 per cent.
4. History of the wall-building.

TABLE 33

(a) In Number

Building periods	Living		Abandoned		Total *a*	Total *b*
	Built	Referred	Built	Referred		
A..........	2	..	20	..	22	22
B..........	10	..	56	51	66	117
C..........	5	..	9	7	14	21
D..........	25	1	45	15	70	86
E..........	24	..	10	13	34	47
F..........	14	1	17	2	31	34
G..........	3	1	..	1	3	5
H..........	12	6	1	..	13	19
Doubtful....	4		44			48
Totals......	95	9	158	89	253	399
	108		291			

(b) In Percentages   (c) Index of Building Intensity

Building periods	Per cent of the provincial totals	Per cent of the period totals	Per cent of the "X" that are abandoned	Building periods	Relative index	Absolute index
A........	8.72	13.5	90.9	A........	...	...
B........	26.10	11.28	84.9	B........	.128	1.57
C........	5.54	2.60	64.4	C........	.030	.37
D........	27.70	16.70	64.6	D........	.198	2.44
E........	13.41	9.64	29.4	E........	.0995	1.22
F........	12.25	9.85	54.8	F........	.098	1.20
G........	1.17	3.12	....	G........	.034	.42
H........	5.14	2.31	7.7	H........	.047	.58

10. Yunnan:

1. Area, 146,714 square miles.
2. Hypothetical age in 1644 A.D., 690 years.
3. Building status in 1644 A.D.:
   (a) Total number of city walls found, 147.
   (b) Number of abandoned walls, 82.
   (c) Percentage of the total that are abandoned, 55.78 per cent.
4. History of the wall-building.

TABLE 34

(a) In Number

Building periods	Living		Abandoned		Total a	Total b
	Built	Referred	Built	Referred		
A.........	..	..	..	..	..	..
B.........	..	..	1	..	1	1
C.........	3	..	4	..	7	7
D.........	1	..	4	..	5	5
E.........	5	..	20	..	25	25
F.........	1	..	5	..	6	6
G.........	1	..	2	..	3	3
H.........	50	3	7	..	57	60
Doubtful....	1		39			40
Totals......	61	3	43		104	147
	65		82			

(b) In Percentages   (c) Index of Building Intensity

Building periods	Per cent of the provincial totals	Per cent of the period totals	Per cent of the "X" that are abandoned	Building periods	Relative index	Absolute index
A........	...	...	....	A........	....	....
B........	.96	.17	100.00	B........	.0019	.013
C........	6.74	1.29	57.20	C........	.0149	.101
D........	4.81	1.18	80.00	D........	.0142	.097
E........	24.05	7.09	80.00	E........	.0732	.500
F........	5.76	1.91	83.30	F........	.0188	.130
G........	2.88	3.12	66.60	G........	.0341	.230
H........	54.80	10.12	12.30	H........	.2059	1.370

11. Hunan:

1. Area, 83,398 square miles.
2. Hypothetical age in 1644 A.D., 600 years.
3. Building status in 1644 A.D.:
    (a) Total number of city walls found, 152.
    (b) Number of abandoned walls, 79.
    (c) Percentage of the total that are abandoned, 51.97 per cent.
4. History of the wall-building.

TABLE 35

(a) In Number

Building periods	Living		Abandoned		Total a	Total b
	Built	Referred	Built	Referred		
A..........	..	..	..	..	..	..
B..........	3	..	12	..	15	15
C..........	10	..	20	..	30	30
D..........	2	..	8	..	10	10
E..........	3	..	11	1	14	15
F..........	10	..	7	..	17	17
G..........	4	..	1	..	5	5
H..........	36	4	2	..	38	42
Doubtful....	1		17			18
Totals......	68	4	61	1	129	152
	73		79			

(b) In Percentages   (c) Index of Building Intensity

Building periods	Per cent of the provincial totals	Per cent of the period totals	Per cent of the "X" that are abandoned	Building periods	Relative index	Absolute index
A.........	....	...	....	A........	...	...
B.........	11.62	2.56	80.00	B........	.029	.352
C.........	23.25	5.55	66.66	C........	.064	.765
D.........	7.75	2.39	80.00	D........	.028	.34
E.........	10.85	3.97	78.6	E........	.041	.49
F.........	13.17	5.4	41.2	F........	.053	.64
G.........	3.88	5.21	20.0	G........	.057	.68
H.........	29.44	6.75	5.27	H........	.137	1.65

12. Kiangsi:

1. Area, 69,498 square miles.
2. Hypothetical age in 1644 A.D., 590 years.
3. Building status in 1644 A.D.:
   (a) Total number of city walls found, 194.
   (b) Number of abandoned walls, 99.
   (c) Percentage of the total that are abandoned, 57.03 per cent.
4. History of the wall-building.

TABLE 36

(a) In Number

Building periods	Living		Abandoned		Total a	Total b
	Built	Referred	Built	Referred		
A..........		..	..	..	..	..
B..........	1	..	3	..	4	4
C..........	10	..	27	..	37	37
D..........	7	..	20	1	27	28
E..........	15	..	16	3	31	34
F..........	20	3	2	..	22	25
G..........	4	..	2	..	6	6
H..........	28	2	..	..	28	30
Doubtful....	5		25			30
Totals......	85	5	70	4	155	194
	95		99			

(b) In Percentages   (c) Index of Building Intensity

Building periods	Per cent of the provincial totals	Per cent of the period totals	Per cent of the "X" that are abandoned	Building periods	Relative index	Absolute index
A.........	....	...	....	A........	....	...
B.........	2.58	.68	75.00	B........	.0077	.11
C.........	23.83	6.86	73.00	C........	.0788	1.13
D.........	17.42	6.45	74.00	D........	.0765	1.11
E.........	20.00	8.79	51.60	E........	.0906	1.31
F.........	14.20	6.99	9.10	F........	.0688	.99
G.........	3.87	6.25	33.30	G........	.0682	.98
H.........	18.10	4.98	....	H........	.1010	1.46

13. Szechuan:

1. Area, 218,533 square miles.
2. Hypothetical age in 1644 A.D., 500 years.
3. Building status in 1644 A.D.:
    (a) Total number of city walls found, 219.
    (b) Number of abandoned walls, 100.
    (c) Percentage of the total that are abandoned, 45.66 per cent.
4. History of the wall-building.

TABLE 37

(a) In Number

Building periods	Living		Abandoned		Total a	Total b
	Built	Referred	Built	Referred		
A..........	..	..	..	..	..	..
B..........	1	..	8	..	9	9
C..........	4	..	25	..	29	29
D..........	1	..	13	1	14	15
E..........	4	..	17	..	21	21
F..........	8	1	7	1	15	17
G..........	..	..	2	..	2	2
H..........	86	14	..	..	86	100
Doubtful....			26			26
Totals......	104	15	72	2	176	219
	119		100			

(b) In Percentages   (c) Index of Building Intensity

Building periods	Per cent of the provincial totals	Per cent of the period totals	Per cent of the "X" that are abandoned	Building periods	Relative index	Absolute index
A.........	...	...	....	A........	...	...
B.........	5.12	1.53	88.89	B........	.017	.079
C.........	16.49	5.37	86.30	C........	.062	.28
D.........	7.96	3.34	93.00	D........	.040	.18
E.........	11.92	5.95	81.00	E........	.062	.28
F.........	8.54	4.77	46.60	F........	.047	.21
G.........	1.14	2.08	100.00	G........	.023	.10
H.........	48.82	15.22	....	H........	.311	1.42

14. Chekiang:

1. Area, 36,680 square miles.
2. Hypothetical age in 1644 A.D., 450 years.
3. Building status in 1644 A.D.:
   (a) Total number of city walls found, 144.
   (b) Number of abandoned walls, 58.
   (c) Percentage of the walls that are abandoned, 40.28 per cent.
4. History of the wall-building.

TABLE 38

(a) IN NUMBER

Building periods	Living		Abandoned		Total a	Total b
	Built	Referred	Built	Referred		
A...........	..	..	..	..	..	..
B..........	3	1	16	..	19	20
C..........	5	..	5	..	10	10
D..........	6	..	9	..	15	15
E..........	17	1	7	2	24	27
F..........	2	4	3	..	5	9
G..........	4	1	..	1	4	6
H..........	35	5	..	1	35	41
Doubtful....	2		14			16
Totals......	72	12	40	4	112	144
	86		58			

(b) IN PERCENTAGES   (c) INDEX OF BUILDING INTENSITY

Building periods	Per cent of the provincial totals	Per cent of the period totals	Per cent of the "X" that are abandoned	Building periods	Relative index	Absolute index
A.........	....	...	...	A........	...	...
B........	16.92	3.25	84.2	B........	.037	1.01
C........	8.94	1.85	50.0	C........	.021	.58
D........	13.42	3.58	60.0	D........	.043	1.15
E........	21.42	6.80	29.1	E........	.070	1.91
F........	4.47	1.58	60.0	F........	.016	.42
G........	3.57	4.16	....	G........	.045	1.24
H........	31.22	6.21	....	H........	.126	.34

15. Kwangsi:

1. Area, 77,220 square miles.
2. Hypothetical age in 1644 A.D., 330 years.
3. Building status in 1644 A.D.:
   (a) Total number of city walls found, 129.
   (b) Number of abandoned walls, 33.
   (c) Percentage of the total that are abandoned, 25.58 per cent.
4. History of the wall-building.

TABLE 39

(a) In Number

Building periods	Living		Abandoned		Total a	Total b
	Built	Referred	Built	Referred		
A...........	..	..	..	..	..	..
B...........	1	..	3	..	4	4
C...........	1	..	4	..	5	5
D...........	..	..	1	..	1	1
E...........	7	1	6	..	13	14
F...........	10	3	2	..	12	15
G...........	1	1	2	..	3	4
H...........	36	9	..	..	36	45
Doubtful....	26		15			41
Totals......	56	14	18		74	129
	96		33			

(b) In Percentages   (c) Index of Building Intensity

Building periods	Per cent of the provincial totals	Per cent of the period totals	Per cent of the "X" that are abandoned	Building periods	Relative index	Absolute index
A.........				A.......		...
B.........	5.42	.68	75.00	B.......	.0078	.10
C.........	6.77	.93	80.00	C.......	.0162	.21
D.........	1.35	.24	100.00	D.......	.0284	.37
E.........	17.58	3.68	46.20	E.......	.038	.49
F.........	16.21	3.82	16.70	F.......	.0375	.49
G.........	4.06	3.12	66.66	G.......	.0341	.44
H.........	48.62	6.39	....	H.......	.1300	1.69

16. Kwangtung:

1. Area, 100,000 square miles.
2. Hypothetical age in 1644 A.D., 300 years.
3. Building status in 1644 A.D.:
   (a) Total number of city walls found, 110.
   (b) Number of abandoned walls, 25.
   (c) Percentage of the total that are abandoned, 22.72 per cent.
4. History of the wall-building.

TABLE 40

(a) In Number

Building periods	Living		Abandoned		Total a	Total b
	Built	Referred	Built	Referred		
A..........	..	..	..	..	..	..
B..........	1	..	4	..	5	5
C..........	4	..	4	..	8	8
D..........	3	..	2	..	5	5
E..........	5	..	7	1	12	13
F..........	14	3	2	..	16	19
G..........	2	2	1	..	3	5
H..........	44	5	..	..	44	49
Doubtful....	2		4			6
Totals......	73	10	20	1	93	110
	85		25			

(b) In Percentages   (c) Index of Building Intensity

Building periods	Per cent of the provincial totals	Per cent of the period totals	Per cent of the "X" that are abandoned	Building periods	Relative index	Absolute index
A.........	...	...	....	A.........	....	....
B.........	5.38	.85	80.00	B........	.0097	.097
C.........	8.62	1.48	50.00	C........	.017	.17
D.........	5.38	1.19	40.00	D........	.0142	.142
E.........	12.90	3.4	58.40	E........	.0351	.351
F.........	17.21	5.07	12.50	F........	.0500	.500
G.........	3.22	3.12	33.3	G........	.0341	.341
H.........	47.30	7.9	....	H........	.1588	1.588

17. Fukien:

1. Area, 46,332 square miles.
2. Hypothetical age in 1644 A.D., 290 years.
3. Building status in 1644 A.D.:
   (a) Total number of city walls found, 69.
   (b) Number of abandoned walls, 15.
   (c) Percentage of the total that are abandoned, 21.74 per cent.
4. History of the wall-building.

TABLE 41

(a) In Number

Building periods	Living		Abandoned		Total *a*	Total *b*
	Built	Referred	Built	Referred		
A..........	..	..	2	..	2	2
B..........	..	..	2	..	2	2
C..........	2	..	..	..	2	2
D..........	3	..	..	..	3	3
E..........	3	..	3	..	6	6
F..........	11	2	3	1	14	17
G..........	3	..	1	..	4	4
H..........	28	1	1	..	29	30
Doubtful....	1		2			3
Totals......	50	3	12	1	62	69
	54		15			

(b) In Percentage   (c) Index of Building Intensity

Building periods	Per cent of the provincial totals	Per cent of the period totals	Per cent of the "X" that are abandoned	Building periods	Relative index	Absolute index
A........	3.23	1.23	100.00	A........	....	...
B........	3.23	.34	100.00	B........	.0039	.084
C........	3.23	.37	....	C........	.0043	.092
D........	4.84	.71	....	D........	.0085	.184
E........	9.68	1.70	50.00	E........	.0176	.378
F........	22.60	4.45	21.40	F........	.0438	.947
G........	6.46	4.17	25.00	G........	.0455	.982
H........	46.73	5.15	3.45	H........	.1046	2.26

18. Kweichow:

1. Area, 66,183 square miles.
2. Hypothetical age in 1644 A.D., 260 years.
3. Building status in 1644 A.D.:
   (a) Total number of city walls found, 48.
   (b) Number of abandoned walls, 9.
   (c) Percentage of the total that are abandoned, 18.75 per cent.
4. History of the wall-building.

TABLE 42

(a) In Number

Building periods	Living		Abandoned		Total a	Total b
	Built	Referred	Built	Referred		
A..........	..	..	..	..	..	..
B..........	..	..	..	..	..	..
C..........	..	..	..	..	..	..
D..........	..	..	..	..	..	..
E.........	..	..	1	..	1	1
F.........	..	..	..	..	..	..
G.........	1	..	1	..	2	2
H..........	36	1	1	..	37	38
Doubtful....	1		6			7
Totals......	37	1	3		40	48
	39		9			

(b) In Percentages   (c) Index of Building Intensity

Building periods	Per cent of the provincial totals	Per cent of the period totals	Per cent of the "X" that are abandoned	Building periods	Relative index	Absolute index
A.........	...	...	....	A.........	....	...
B.........	...	...	....	B.........	....	...
C.........	...	...	....	C.........	....	...
D.........	...	...	....	D.........	....	...
E.........	2.50	.28	....	E.........	.0029	.044
F.........	...	...	....	F.........	....	...
G.........	5.00	2.08	50.00	G.........	.0227	.342
H.........	92.50	6.57	2.71	H.........	.1336	.202

With the above fifty-four tables, and eighty graphs, we may say that we have finished the task of presentation and classification. There still remains, however, the task of coördination. In the general consideration, the problem of age and the problem of saturation point have already been touched upon; but both of them, as it has been pointed out, need detailed qualification. The provincial age constructed hypothetically on the abandonment curve especially needs more evidential confirmation. For this purpose, it is plain that the provincial abandonment curves can offer little help, as they differ only quantitatively from the general curve and on the whole are more remote from the hypothetical mean. But this cannot be taken as a ground for their complete exclusion from further consideration. They have their significance otherwise. Meantime, in order to testify to the value of the hypothetical age of the different provinces, a new angle of approach is needed. This is not particularly difficult at the present stage of our inquiry, if we remember that the essential part of our definition of age is "the length of occupation by the We-group measured by the wall-building activity." We have now the complete history of the wall-building activity of each province at our disposal. New light can be thrown on this problem, therefore, if the comparative building status of each province in the different periods is examined.

First of all let the meaning of the provincial age be examined more in detail. The wall-building activity as a yard-stick for the length of occupation implies that the occupation itself does not necessarily begin synchronously with the first building activity. It is a more than apparent truth that the occupation almost always precedes the wall-building activity; and when the building begins, a considerable length of time in many cases has already elapsed. To measure the length of occupation by beginning with the building activity is, as it appears, similar to the measurement of human age by beginning with the date of birth instead of that of conception. It is difficult to say whether this analogy can be stretched any further; whether, as may be possible, the length of occupation in the pre-building periods has its limit as does the pre-natal existence of all human beings. But this is not important in this connection. The point to be emphasized is that the age of the province, as we propose to call it, is only a relative index of the length of occupation; it is not even an approximate estimate of the actual length of occupation, as our data do not include the first appearance of the city-building activity in any of the provinces. But it does determine the *general* order according to which the different provinces are occupied by the We-group; and when we say one province is older than the other it means not much more than that the older province precedes the younger one in the order of occupation by the We-group. This leads us to the suggestion that the value of the hypothetical age that has been previously constructed may be tested by the general order in which the saturation points are attained by the different provinces. But one difficulty immediately appears: the suggestion is incapable of being carried out fully as the saturation point is an unknown quantity. Nevertheless, it furnishes a clue for the furtherance of our inquiry. Table 34 gives the accumulative percentages of the building activity of each province in the eight different periods.

The Ogive curves (Graph 87) plotted on the basis of Table 43 present clearly the temporal order according to which the provincial wall-building activity marches across its own mid-line. Now we may take this order as a test of the order of occupation. The fiftieth per cent is of course different from the saturation point, from the very fact that provinces which, as we have reason to believe are not saturated, also have their fifty per cent points no matter how limited is the number of walls that they possess. It is taken on the supposition that the earlier a province begins its wall-building activity, the earlier it will march across its mid-line; the curves clearly substantiate this point.

TABLE 43

ACCUMULATIVE PERCENTAGES OF THE BUILDING ACTIVITY OF DIFFERENT PROVINCES IN THE EIGHT SUCCESSIVE PERIODS

Provinces	Periods							
	A	B	C	D	E	F	G	H
1. Kansu....	4.94	12.62	34.04	45.03	59.86	91.73	93.93	100.00
2. Honan....	13.88	49.26	75.38	86.20	95.38	97.26	98.20	100.00
3. Shensi....	7.92	36.96	52.44	72.07	81.50	88.67	93.58	100.00
4. Kiangsu...	1.21	36.35	49.08	67.26	76.96	83.02	87.87	100.00
5. Shantung .	3.29	24.84	40.30	57.42	62.38	76.21	87.85	100.00
6. Nganhui ..	3.23	16.78	47.08	69.00	78.04	83.86	87.09	100.00
7. Chihli	11.73	30.85	54.62	63.74	74.14	87.24	88.92	100.00
8. Hupeh....	1.18	27.28	50.93	68.08	74.59	79.91	80.49	100.00
9. Shansi....	8.72	34.82	40.36	68.06	81.47	93.72	94.89	100.00
10. Yunnan...		.90	7.70	12.51	36.56	42.32	45.20	100.00
11. Hunan....		11.62	34.87	42.62	53.47	66.64	70.52	100.00
12. Kiangsi...		2.58	26.41	44.83	63.83	78.03	81.90	100.00
13. Szechuan..		5.12	21.61	29.57	41.49	50.03	51.17	100.00
14. Chekiang..		16.92	25.86	39.28	60.70	65.17	68.74	100.00
15. Kwangsi ..		5.34	12.19	13.54	31.12	47.33	51.39	100.00
16. Kwangtung		5.38	14.00	19.38	32.28	49.49	52.71	100.00
17. Fukien....	3.23	6.46	9.69	14.53	24.21	46.81	53.27	100.00
18. Kweichow.					2.50		7.50	100.00

At the outset, several outstanding features of this graph (87) need comment. The tripartite grouping here is again very striking. Thus one group marches across the border in the C period, one in the D–E periods and one in the F–G periods. This immediately suggests the tripartite divisions of the archaeological zones. But it is not so clearly marked; it has a head-province and a tail-province, both of which stand apparently quite apart from the rest of the groups. Let us compare the order of these two types of the tripartite divisions to ascertain their resemblances and differences:

TABLE 44

Provinces	Ranking[1] order a	Ranking[1] order b	Provinces	Ranking order a	Ranking order b
Kansu	1	10	Yunnan	10	17
Honan	2	1	Hunan	11	12
Shensi	3	3	Kiangsi	12	9
Kiangsu	4	5	Szechuan	13	13
Shantung	5	8	Chekiang	14	11
Nganhui	6	6	Kwangsi	15	16
Chihli	7	2	Kwangtung	16	14
Hupeh	8	4	Fukien	17	15
Shansi	9	7	Kweichow	18	18

[1] Order a according to the magnitude of abandonment; Order b according to the order of attaining half of the total activity.

So, on the whole, there is a close correlation between these two ranking orders. With two major exceptions, the members of the different archaeological zones are also the members of the corresponding fifty per cent divisions. So it may be concluded that the hypothetical age has a special value of its own, and as an indication of the length of occupation by the We-group, it is not far from the actual state of affairs. But the two exceptions need special consideration. Why should the hypothetically oldest province lag so much behind in marching across the fifty per cent border? Why should the province which heads the list of the second archaeological zone in its treasury of the abandoned walls drop to the second from the last position of the third fifty per cent division? These questions cannot be answered in any simple and direct way. To give them due consideration, it is necessary that we should survey the changes of building status as a whole. We may now proceed to do this.

The graphs showing the periodical contribution to the total number of walls in each province may be examined first (Graphs 7–24). A remarkable feature of Kansu among this group is visible at the first sight. Of the first nine provinces (Graphs 7–15) which belong to the archaeological Zone I, the "apex" of Kansu appears the latest. The apex of the other eight provinces is found in B or C or D, but that of Kansu province did not appear until the F-period. In that period, it may be noted, Kansu's building activity towers way above all the other provinces (Graph 7). But if the intensity is reduced to terms of the absolute spatial and temporal unit, the climax of Kansu building activity is quite colorless compared with the other provinces (Graph 69). The situation as a whole shows that the building activity of Kansu has never been very intense, and its most intense period appears very late in comparison with the other provinces of the zone to which it belongs.

Why then such a great percentage of abandoned walls? The answer is found in Table 5 and Table 10. Both of these indicate that what is noticeable with Kansu is, not the abundance of the abandoned walls, but the scarcity of the living. Its number of living cities is virtually the lowest, with the exception of Kweichow, which is in every respect the youngest province in China. This has made the percentage of the abandoned city walls excessively large, and in turn makes the province old according to our system of calculation. All these facts may be accounted for by the extraordinary geographical and geological situation that is found in this province. It is not as fertile as the other provinces that attract great population; yet it is strategically almost the most important province in Chinese history, and a gateway for most of the barbarian invasions. These two factors are sufficient to account for both the scarcity of the living and the abundance of the deserted walls in this province. Nevertheless Kansu is very old and its age is proved by the fact that it has a fair share of the building activity of all the periods (Graphs 25–32).

With Yunnan we have a different set of data with which to deal. Graph 78 shows that the absolute index of this province has always been low, and Graph 42 shows that its abandonment rate has been uniformly high. If the abnormality of Kansu is explained by geography, the abnormality of Yunnan may be explained by history. This province, according to history, was opened earlier than any other of the southwest provinces, but was colonized very late. It was due to the enterprise of a few adventurers that this province was opened in the late Han dynasty (our C period), and the first opening has necessitated the building of a number of cities which were, however, not kept up as the colonization has been a very spasmodic one until of late. It is this factor that throws the proportion of the abandoned to the living out of balance.

With these two exceptions explained, the age-scale in the light of our analysis seems at least satisfying for the present purpose. Any further elaboration on this topic would exaggerate its importance. There are, however, new questions which demand our immediate attention: they are —

(1) The general boundary line of the sphere of the wall-building activity in different periods.

(2) The line of the most intensive activity.

The first question may be answered by Graphs 25–32. If we take five per cent of the total period activity as a criterion of the full activity, we find the activity extends itself in the following order: (Compare the age-scale).

TABLE 45

A period: Kansu, Honan, Shensi, Chihli, Shansi.
B. + Kiangsu, Shantung, Hupeh.
C. + Nganhui, Kiangsi, Hunan, Szechuan.
D. + 0.
E. + Yunnan, Chekiang.
F. + Kwangtung.
G. + 0.
H. + Kwangsi, Fukien, Kweichow.

It is clear then that previous to 722 B.C. the wall-building activity is confined to only five provinces; in B period it extends to eight, in C period to twelve, and so forth. It is not until the H period that all eighteen provinces come under its sphere of influence. There is, of course, no sharp line of division. There are fringes and margins, nuances and shades of the wall-building activity which either precede or follow those centers of full activity within the sphere. But it is these centers of full activity that we have to study now, especially to ascertain the approximate route which the line of change follows.

Table 46 shows a coördinate summary of all the absolute indices of the building activity in different periods and different provinces. Table 47 reduces all the absolute indices to their respective ranks. Table 48 shows the first five most intensive provinces in each period. Table 49 shows the two most intensive periods of each province.

TABLE 46

ABSOLUTE INDICES OF THE BUILDING ACTIVITY OF DIFFERENT PROVINCES
IN DIFFERENT PERIODS

Provinces	Periods						
	B	C	D	E	F	G	H
1. Kansu.........	.216	.661	.452	.629	1.444	.362	.317
2. Honan.........	4.278	3.476	1.917	1.678	.358	.669	.425
3. Shensi.........	1.982	1.158	1.951	.971	.789	1.962	.815
4. Kiangsu........	2.911	1.157	2.201	1.212	.809	2.355	1.870
5. Shantung......	1.352	1.065	1.575	.472	1.395	4.275	1.228
6. Nganhui.......	.742	1.82	1.75	.75	.515	1.04	1.32
7. Chihli.........	.95	1.30	.66	.78	1.05	.49	1.03
8. Hupeh........	1.19	1.19	1.15	.45	.39	.16	1.67
9. Shansi........	1.57	.37	2.44	1.22	1.20	.42	.58
10. Yunnan.......	.013	.101	.097	.500	.130	.230	1.37
11. Hunan........	.352	.765	.34	.49	.64	.68	1.65
12. Kiangsi.......	.11	1.13	1.11	1.31	.99	.98	1.46
13. Szechuan......	.079	.28	.18	.28	.21	.10	1.42
14. Chekiang......	1.01	.58	1.15	1.91	.42	1.24	.34
15. Kwangsi.......	.10	.21	.37	.49	.49	.44	1.69
16. Kwangtung	.097	.17	.142	.351	.500	.341	1.588
17. Fukien........	.084	.092	.184	.378	.947	.982	2.26
18. Kweichow.....				.044		.342	.202

TABLE 47

RANKING ORDER OF THE ABSOLUTE INDICES OF THE BUILDING ACTIVITY OF
DIFFERENT PROVINCES IN DIFFERENT PERIODS

Provinces	Periods						
	B	C	D	E	F	G	H
1. Kansu.............	102	66	80	69	25	90	98
2. Honan.............	1	3	12	18	91	65	83
3. Shensi.............	9	40	11	54	59	10	57
4. Kiangsu	4	41	8	36	58	6	14
5. Shantung...........	29	46	22	79	27	2	34
6. Nganhui...........	63	15	16	62	72	48	30
7. Chihli.............	55	32	67	60	47	77	49
8. Hupeh.............	38	39	42	81	86	109	19
9. Shansi.............	23	89	5	35	37	85	70
10. Yunnan............	122	113	116	74	111	101	28
11. Hunan.............	92	61	97	76	68	64	20
12. Kiangsi............	112	44	45	31	51	53	24
13. Szechuan...........	120	100	107	99	103	114	26
14. Chekiang...........	50	71	43	13	84	33	96
15. Kwangsi...........	115	104	88	78	75	82	17
16. Kwangtung	117	108	110	93	73	95	21
17. Fukien.............	119	118	106	87	56	52	7
18. Kweichow..........				121		94	105

TABLE 48

THE FIVE PROVINCES OF EACH PERIOD WHICH SHOW THE GREATEST
ABSOLUTE INDICES OF BUILDING ACTIVITY

Periods	Ranks				
	1	2	3	4	5
B........	Honan	Kiangsu	Shensi	Shansi	Shantung
C........	Honan	Nganhui	Chihli	Hupeh	Shensi
D........	Shansi	Kiangsu	Shensi	Honan	Nganhui
E........	Chekiang	Honan	Kiangsi	Shansi	Kiangsu
F........	Kansu	Shantung	Shansi	Chihli	Kiangsi
G........	Shantung	Kiangsu	Shensi	Chekiang	Nganhui
H........	Fukien	Kiangsu	Kwangsi	Hupeh	Hunan

TABLE 49

THE TWO PERIODS FOR EACH PROVINCE WHICH SHOW THE GREATEST
ABSOLUTE INDICES OF BUILDING ACTIVITY

Kansu..............	F. and C.	Yunnan.............	H. and E.
Honan..............	B. and C.	Hunan..............	H. and C.
Shensi..............	B. and G.	Kiangsi.............	H. and E.
Kiangsu.............	B. and G.	Szechuan............	H. and E.
Shantung............	G. and D.	Chekiang...........	E. and G.
Nganhui.............	C. and D.	Kwangsi............	H. and F.
Chihli..............	C. and F.	Kwangtung.........	H. and F.
Hupeh..............	H. and B.	Fukien.............	H. and G.
Shansi..............	D. and B.	Kweichow..........	G. and H.

Cross-references to the four tables above show several salient features
that need further comment here. First of all, the vast range and the
great variation in the intensity of the wall-building activity tend to lead
us to believe that it is the function of a slow but steady movement of the
population, rather than a sudden rush. This, however, need not be
the case. Table 48 shows that the most intensive areas are confined
to several provinces and excluded from others up to 1644 A.D., although
the centers shift from period to period. The excluded provinces are
generally among the youngest and what I have tried to call the "unsaturated regions." Their abandonment curves as well as the building
curves, which are full of dashes and spurs, show that they have never
attained the balance and equilibrium of the older provinces. But it
should be recalled that although these excluded provinces are unsaturated they are within the sphere of the building activity, at least
during and before 1644 A.D. The most scientifically determinable date
for the beginning of their inclusion within the sphere is perhaps

the apex-period. For in the pre-apex-period the activity may be of any nature; while the apex-period makes a definite point of the beginning of serious activity. Table 50 is based on Table 48 and Table 49. It defines the sphere of the building activity by including: (1) the most intensive areas of the periods, (2) the apex-provinces in the period. The general principle is that any province which once lies within the sphere always remains in it. Thus no province appears twice in either (1) or (2); but provinces which have appeared in (2) may reappear in (1) in any succeeding period although the reverse does not occur. This procedure is justified by the fact that the degree of intensity indicated in (1) is related to the building activity of the period as a whole, while that in (2) is not.

TABLE 50

B. (1) Honan, Kiangsu, Shensi, Shansi, Shantung.
   (2) Hupeh.
C. (1) Nganhui, Chihli, Hupeh.
   (2) Kansu, Hunan.
D. (1) 0.
   (2) 0.
E. (1) Chekiang, Kiangsi.
   (2) Yunnan, Szechuan.
F. (1) Kansu.
   (2) Kwangsi, Kwangtung.
G. (1) 0.
   (2) Fukien, Kweichow.
H. (1) Fukien, Hunan, Kwangsi.
   (2) 0.

A comparison of this table with Table 45 will show that they agree with each other quite clearly. As they are based on different types of data, their agreement proves that the method devised here to solve the problem of the expansion of the sphere of building activity is fundamentally reliable. But there is an important difference regarding the province of Szechuan which in the last table (50) did not figure even secondarily until the E period; while in the attainment of the membership of the sphere, it ranks as early as C period. It will be recalled that the special geographical features of Szechuan have been considered in the early part of the chapter. Now, Table 45 takes the local feature of each province into consideration, while the last one does not. It appears, therefore, that in order to do justice to Szechuan, its membership card should be dated C period rather than E period. Since these two have respective merits peculiar to each, to make a final map of the expansion of the building activity these two tables

may be combined. The principle is to take the province into the sphere
at the earliest period according to these two tables. Table 51 shows
the result of this combination and furnishes the data on which the accompanying maps following this chapter are based. Marginal area
refers to those provinces which have appeared in the period either in
Table 45 or (2) of Table 50. Only those provinces which have appeared in (1) of Table 50 are taken into the sphere of full activity. The
province that shows the greatest absolute index in any period is taken
as the center of the period.

TABLE 51

THE EXTENSION OF THE SPHERE OF BUILDING ACTIVITY UP TO 1644 A.D.

| Periods | Sphere | |
	Central region	Marginal region
A period		Kansu, Honan, Shensi, Chihli, Shansi.
B period	Honan, Kiangsu, Shensi, Shansi, Shantung.	Kansu, Chihli, Hupeh.
C period	B. + Nganhui, Chihli, Hupeh.	Kansu, Kiangsi, Hunan, Szechuan.
D period	C. + 0	Kansu, Kiangsi, Hunan, Szechuan.
E period	D. + Chekiang, Kiangsi.	Kansu, Hunan, Szechuan, Yunnan.
F period	E. + Kansu.	Hunan, Szechuan, Kwangtung, Kwangsi, Yunnan.
G period	F. + 0	Hunan, Szechuan, Kwangtung, Kwangsi, Yunnan, Fukien, Kweichow.
H period	G. + Fukien, Kwangsi, Hunan.	Szechuan, Kwangtung, Yunnan, Kweichow.

The maps below (6–13) showing the expansion of the wall-building
activity in the eight successive periods may be taken as an index to
the evolution of the We-group. The index so worked out indicates
clearly that the area occupied by the modern Chinese is the result of a
slow and gradual expansion. Its constant increase marks unmistak-
ably the vitality of the We-group. The We-group, however, has suffered internal changes to which the next chapter will be devoted.

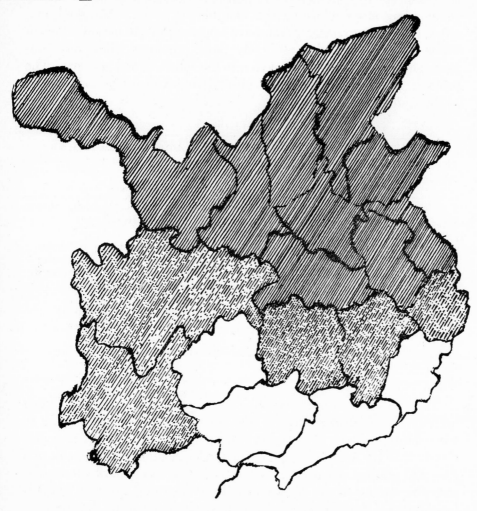

The first zone ▨
The second zone —·—·—
The third zone ☐

MAP 5. The three archaeological zones

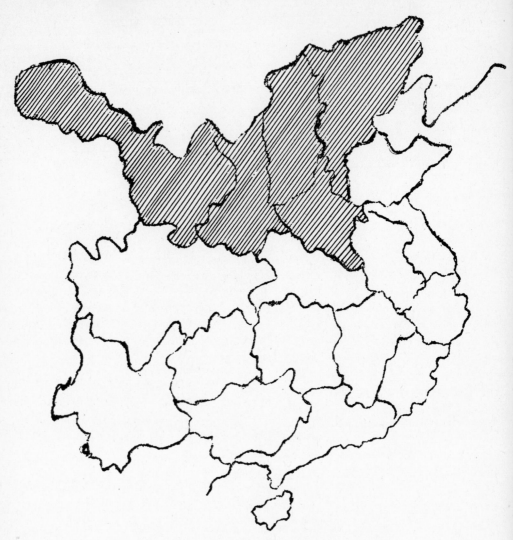

Marginal region

Central region

The centre

MAP 6. The Sphere of Building Activity of A-period

100

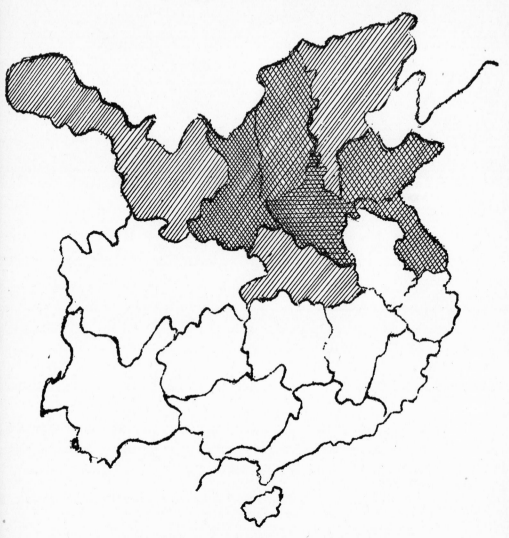

MAP 7. The Sphere of Building Activity of B-period

101

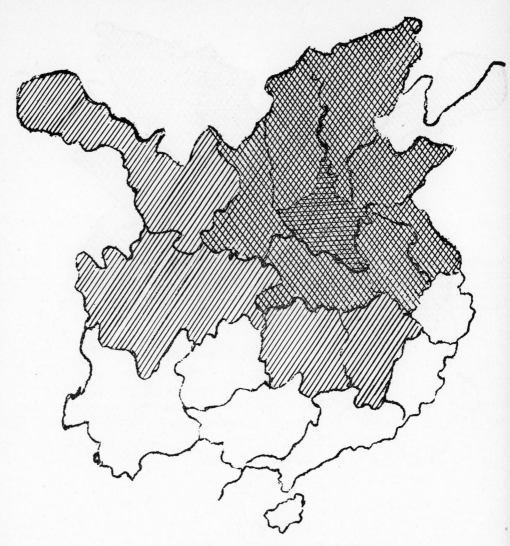

Map 8. The Sphere of Building Activity of C-period

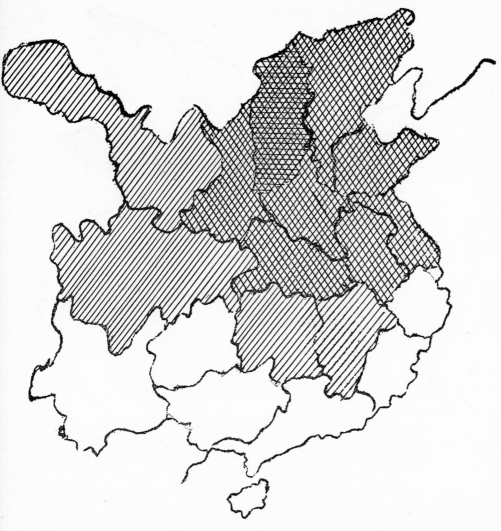

MAP 9. The Sphere of Building Activity of D-period

103

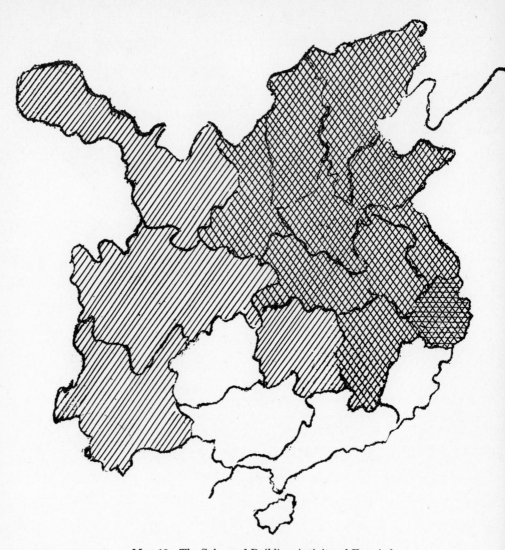

MAP 10. The Sphere of Building Activity of E-period

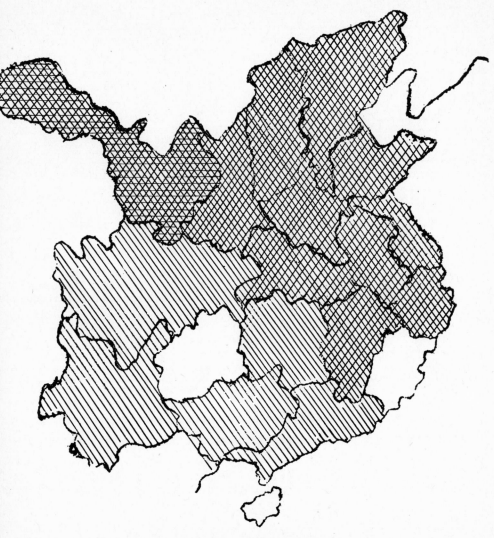

MAP 11. The Sphere of Building Activity of F-period

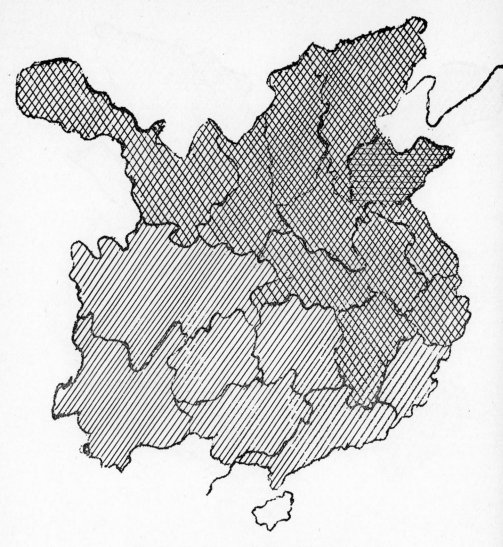

Map 12. The Sphere of Building Activity of G-period

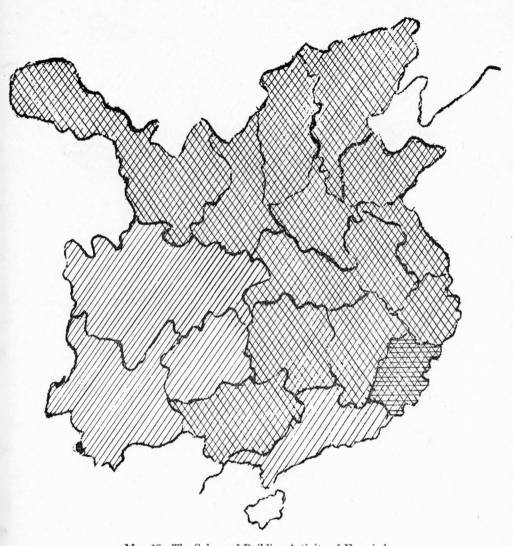

MAP 13. The Sphere of Building Activity of H-period

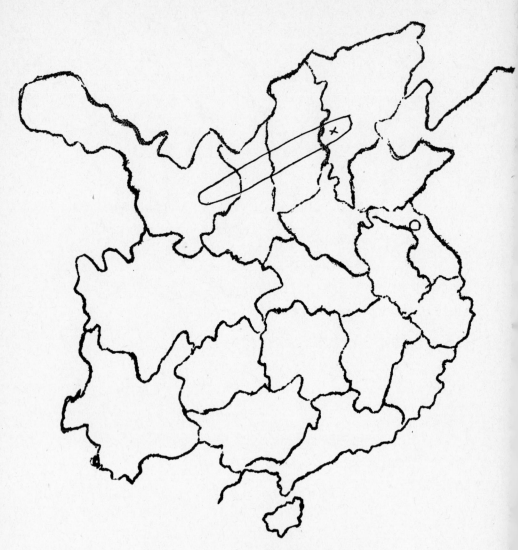

MAP 14.   Centres of the Changes in the D-period

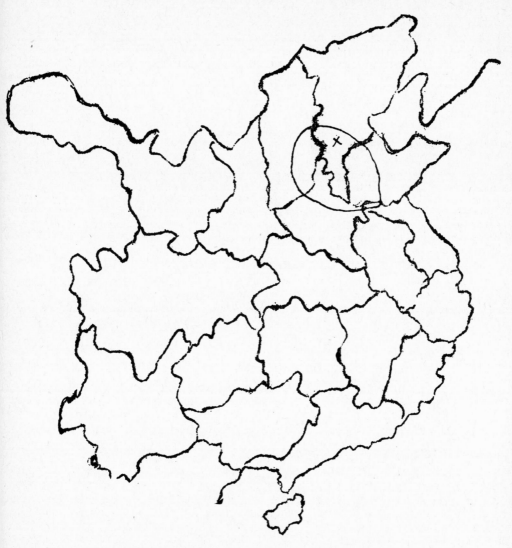

MAP 15. Centres of the Changes in the E-period

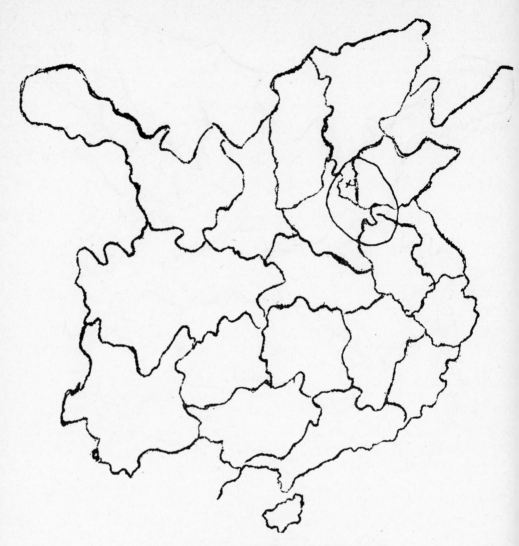

Map 16. Centres of the Changes in the F-period

110

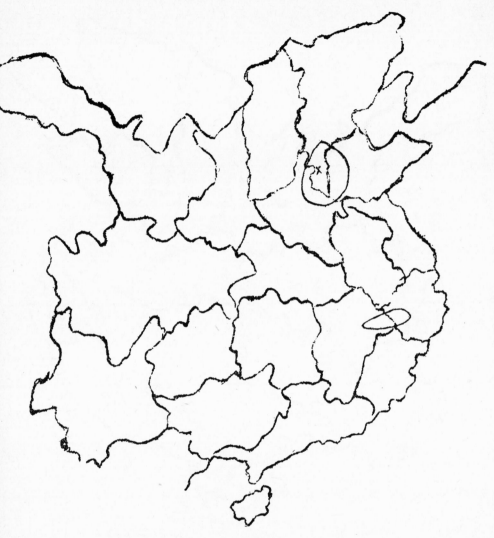

MAP 17. Centres of the Changes in the G-period

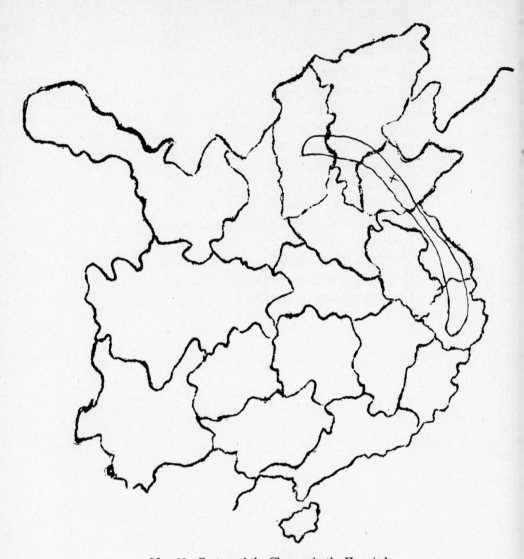

MAP 18. Centres of the Changes in the H-period

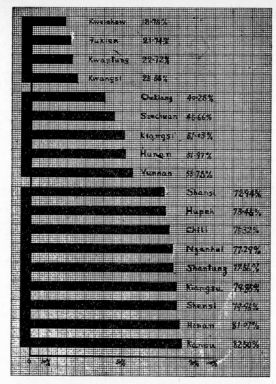

GRAPH 2. Percentages of the total number of cities
that were abandoned in each province at 1644 A.D.

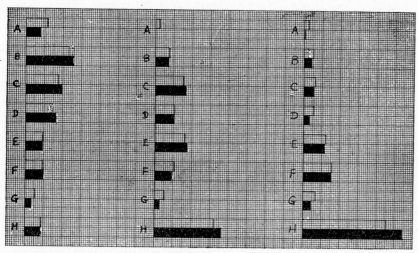

GRAPH 3. The two sets of data showing the building activity in the eight different
periods of the three different zones compared.

■■■■ = a-data
☐ = b-data

113

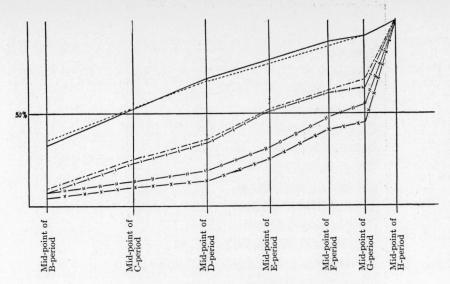

Mid-point of B-period   Mid-point of C-period   Mid-point of D-period   Mid-point of E-period   Mid-point of F-period   Mid-point of G-period   Mid-point of H-period

GRAPH 4. Ogive curves showing the accumulative rates of building in the eight successive periods of the three different zones.

Table 18.—		Group I	Group II	Group III
	a-data:	———	—ı—ı—	—x—x—
	b-data:	··········	—·—·—	—ıı—ıı—

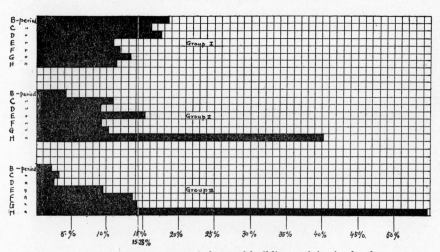

GRAPH 4a. Periodical percentages of the total building activity in the three zones.

114

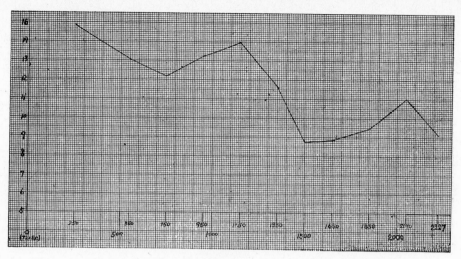

GRAPH 5. Change of intensities of building activity of different periods in zone I.
(Table 12)

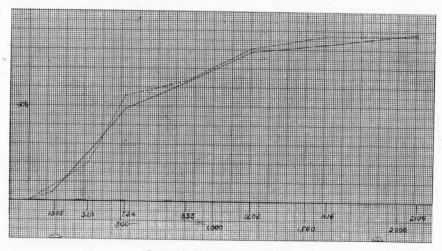

GRAPH 6. Abandonment curves

——— of the whole area   - - - - - of zone I

115

7 Kansu   8 Honan   9 Shensi   10 Kiangsu   11 Shantung

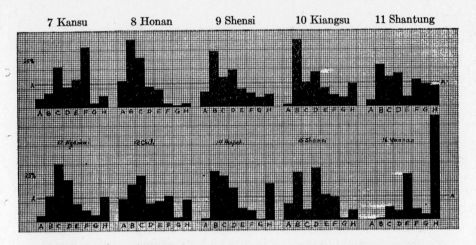

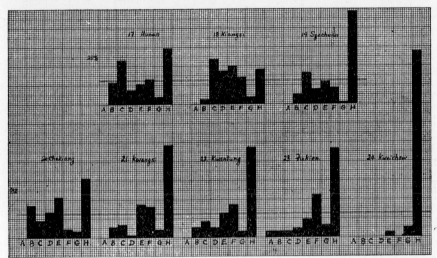

GRAPHS 7–24. Provincial building activity as distributed in the eight periods.
(Table 25b–42b, first column.) AA = average line = 125%

116

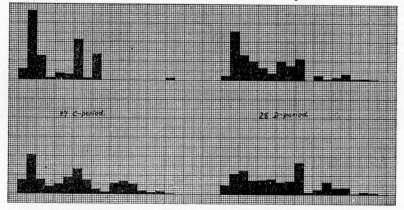

25 A-period   26 B-period

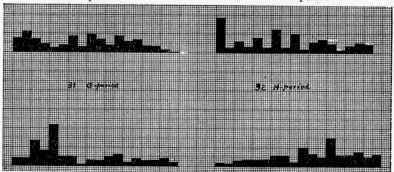

29 C-period   30 D-period

GRAPH 25–32. Periodical building activity as distributed in the eighteen provinces. (Table 25b–42b, second column.)

117

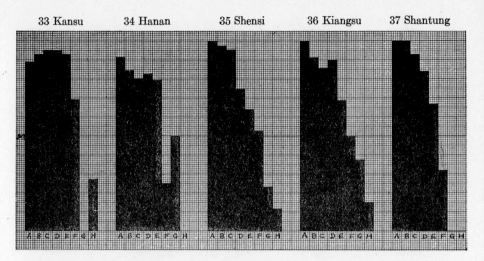

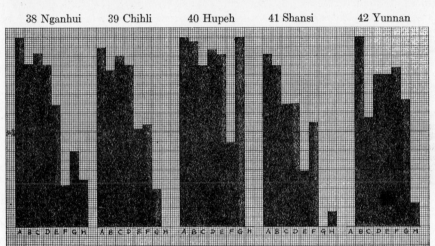

GRAPHS 33–42. Percentage of the "X" that are abandoned.
(Table 25b–42b, third column.)

118

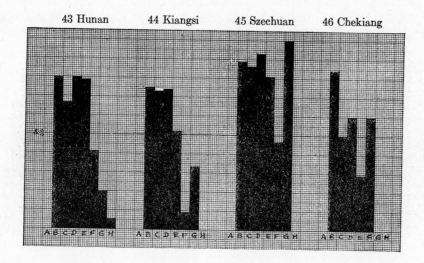

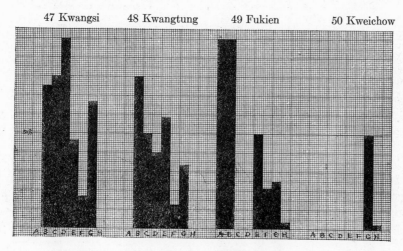

GRAPHS 43–50.   Percentage of the "X" that are abandoned.
(Table 25b–42b, third column.)

119

51 Kansu 52 Honan 53 Shensi 54 Kiangsu 55 Shantung 56 Nganhui

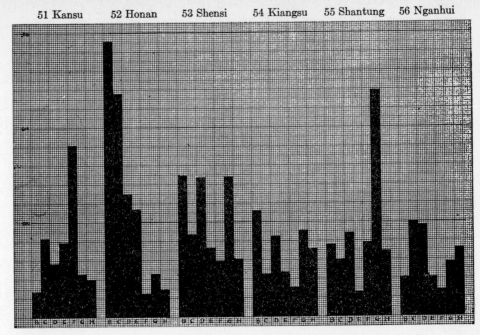

57 Chihli 58 Hupeh 59 Shansi 60 Yunnan 61 Hunan 62 Kiangsi

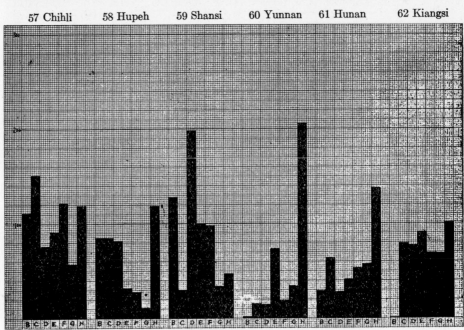

GRAPHS 51–62. Relative Indices. (Table 25c–42c.)

120

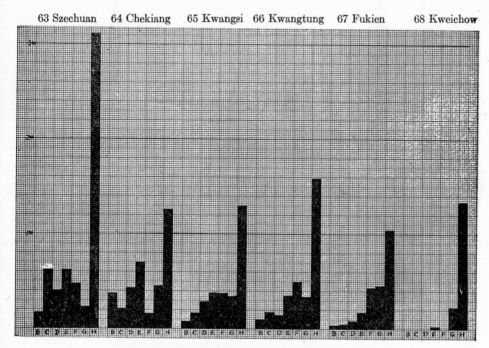

63 Szechuan   64 Chekiang   65 Kwangsi   66 Kwangtung   67 Fukien   68 Kweichow

GRAPHS 63–68.   Relative Indices.   (Table 25c–42c.)

121

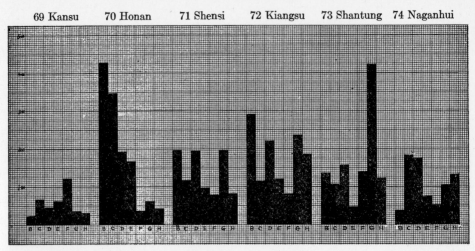

69 Kansu   70 Honan   71 Shensi   72 Kiangsu   73 Shantung   74 Naganhui

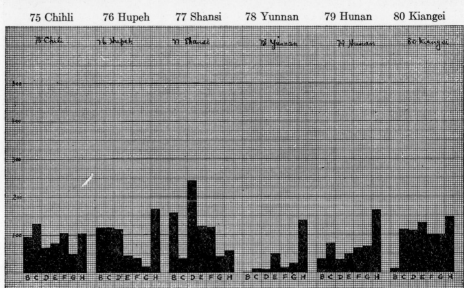

75 Chihli   76 Hupeh   77 Shansi   78 Yunnan   79 Hunan   80 Kiangei

GRAPHS 69–80. Absolute Indices. (Table 25c–42c.)

122

81 Szechuan   82 Chekiany   83 Kwangsi   84 Kuxesitung   85 Fukien   86 Yuveichow

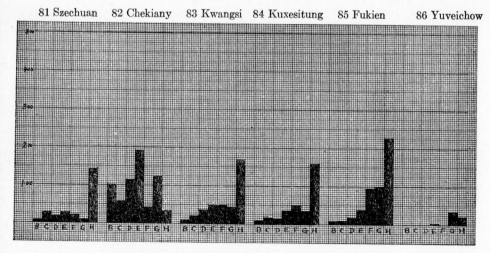

GRAPHS 81–86.   Absolute Indices.   (Table 25c–42c.)

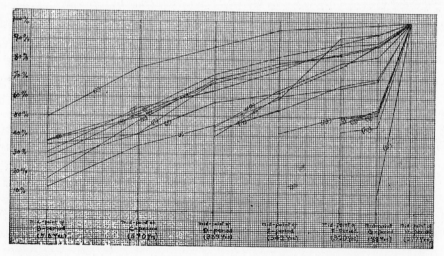

GRAPH 87.   Progressive rate of building activity in the eighteen provinces.   (Table 43.)

CHAPTER IV

THE EVOLUTION OF THE WE–GROUP: AN ESTIMATE OF THE CHANGE OF ITS CONSTITUENTS BASED ON A STUDY OF THE ORIGIN OF SURNAMES

THE traditional accounts of the origin of surnames go back to mythological ages. The earliest account tells us that, in ancient China, people married regardless of close blood-relationship. In the reign of Fuhsi (one of the mythological kings) endogamous marriages were for the first time forbidden and the observance of marriage rites enforced. The surname system was also established, and "the fundamental part of human relationship was adjusted to a correct basis," as the Chinese historian usually phrases it. The chief function of the surname in the opinion of most Chinese historians is to regulate the marriage system. In present-day China, any proposition of marriage between a man and a woman of the same surname stands ill in public opinion and is actually forbidden by civil law. For, according to a universal Chinese proverb, prevailing already in the days of Confucius, "marriage among the same surnames is never prolific"; and the national psychology of China does not like unprolific marriages.

Functionally, therefore, the surname is exclusively concerned with the regulation of sex-relations. But as a symbol, it is attached to other factors of equal social significance. It serves to denote the relationship of all the people in China on the male side. It is from the symbolic side that all the propositions in this chapter are to be deduced. The simple axiom which is to serve as the pivot of the whole series of arguments is this: like surnames of the same origin denote blood-relationship.

The modifying phrase, "of the same origin," as will be seen, is very important; for the close corollary of this axiom is that like surnames do not necessarily denote any blood-relationship, if they are of different origins.

The importance of this study may be seen in another way. It has already been said that the Chinese do not have a definite name for themselves. Yet in spite of this lack of conscious unity, there does exist a vague consciousness of kind among the people, which is proved by the fact that they all call themselves "Descendants of the Yellow

Emperor." As a matter of fact, "Descendants of the Yellow Emperor" is a phrase which the Chinese literati of the present day still employ as the most appropriate appellation for the "racial" group to which they belong.

Evidently the derivation of this phrase is more worthy of scientific inquiry than the derivation of the term "Chinese," which has already cost an enormous amount of labor without a proportionate return.

What, then, is the derivation of this phrase? Disregarding the mythological period, it is said, according to both Ssū-ma Chíen and the Confucian Classic, that Huangti had twenty-five sons, fourteen of whom were given distinct surnames by the gracious will of the Father-Emperor. It has been vaguely supposed that all surnames are derived in one way or another from these fourteen. Chinese genealogists, who are usually tireless workers, have made it a point, as far as possible, to trace the myriad of surnames to this origin. One of the shortest and best ways to prove that one is a genuine well-bred Chinaman is to show that one's surname has an authentic derivation. Judging by the tenacity with which the Chinese have practised ancestor worship, it must not be considered an absurd way of identification.

Neither need it be supposed that when one is once able to trace his surname back to one of the fourteen primary surnames, he is necessarily a genuine descendant of the Yellow Emperor; for woman, who counts fifty per cent biologically in the make-up of any Chinese, is genealogically altogether excluded from the calculation; and there is no assurance that the descendants of the Yellow Emperor have entirely refrained from marrying into the other tribes, which may be considered barbarians, and with which the Chinese would hesitate to identify themselves. Again, the surname system, although first created by the Yellow Emperor's clan, is not exclusive and peculiar to the descendants of that clan; the descendants of other tribes coexistent with that of the Yellow Emperor within the boundary of China proper also have surnames, either in their own way, or after that of the Yellow Emperor. But on the surface, the distinction is by no means always clear. Since it is socially a privilege to possess the surname of the Yellow Emperor's descendants, the incentive to give up certain surnames and adopt others is very strong. Many of the surnames that have survived, nominally traceable to the fourteen primary surnames, are probably not what they were, for the disturbing elements that have entered into the system have long been existent. The forces that impaired the purity of the system are, moreover, quite complicated. To disentangle some of these factors and trace back their origin will be one of the chief tasks of this chapter.

The term "Descendants of the Yellow Emperor" is, then, ethnologically as significant as that of "We-group." The two are not exactly the same thing, but they can be treated as closely identified with each other. For reasons that will be clear further on, these two terms can sometimes be used interchangeably. It is quite justifiable for us to go one step further and define the We-group as the descendants of the Yellow Emperor. But at present we shall not use them as synonymous, as they suggest two different types of relationship.

The Sources of Material

Ancestor worship, according to some philosophers of the West, is the main source of all the social evils that are found in China. This may all be true. But there is another aspect of ancestor worship which need not be so vehemently condemned. It has made the Chinese the most thoroughgoing genealogists of the world, for which fact the anthropologists, at least, have reason to be grateful. Genealogy in China is a regular science, if it may be so called. This has made possible the existence of a rich mass of genealogical material. The development of this branch of inquiry has other sources of stimulation, besides the deep-rooted psychology of ancestor worship. The barbarian invasions of the third and fourth centuries had made the cultivated Chinese of those days extremely apprehensive of the danger of the infusion of foreign blood; so they made a determined effort to keep the family record as clean as possible. Thus within the compass of two hundred years no less than forty-one systematic treatises on genealogy appeared in book form, the longest consisting of 690 chapters, according to the bibliographical account of the official history of the Sui dynasty. These are only the ones which survived up to the time when the history was written. There were undoubtedly many more which were written but destroyed, and still more which were written but unknown. The flourishing state of this branch of inquiry has continued with many vicissitudes up to the present time. It has been a custom in China for many generations for everybody, from the middle class up, to keep a full genealogical record, zealously guarded, in the ancestral hall. After the invention of the printing press it was usually printed, whenever the family could afford it. Otherwise, it was kept in manuscript form. The literature has grown so voluminous that even the making of a simple bibliographical list would be an impossible task. But the Encyclopedia gives an excellent summary of the best available knowledge, from which all our information is to be derived. It consists of abstracts and a compilation. The abstracts, in general, are concerned with the facts of the origin of the different surnames; the compilation is a vast national biography of all the prominent Chinese up to 1644 A.D. classified according to their surnames.

THE NUMBER OF SURNAMES AND ITS GROWTH

The total number of surnames given in the Encyclopedia is 3736 (my own counting), including all those recorded up to 1644 A.D. But the revised edition of Wên Hsien Túng Káo, published in the Ming dynasty,[1] gives a total of 4657; while Chêng Chíao, the most eminent Sung encyclopedist, gives a list of 2117 (my own counting).[2] These numbers are perhaps inaccurate. I have no way of finding out to what extent they represent the actual number. The task of verification is not important in this connection, as it really does not matter what the actual number is, so long as we know that it is unusually large. The number, however, becomes very vague as we go back beyond the Sung period. It cannot be estimated even approximately, until we go back to the mythological period of Huangti, who created fourteen surnames for his children. From 14 to 3736 or 4657, the increase is remarkable. The time consumed in the process was approximately 3900 years (2282 B.C. to 1644 A.D.). The nature of the growth may be considered under several headings.

(a) *Self-Segregation.* When surnames were first created, they were more like official titles of a later day than permanent appellations. They were established explicitly to reward the virtuous, that they might be socially recognized. The permanency of the surname is a result of social ossification and comparatively absent in the early phase of its development. In the early period, the important thing was that the virtuous ones should have a surname, but it was not necessary that the same surname should be retained through generation after generation. They might change, if they would; and the change was especially common when the clan grew too large — as did the royal house of the Chou dynasty.

The changes, however, were by no means haphazard. They fall into 28 definite groups which the Sung encyclopedist was able to classify.

---

[1] First edition published in 1319, revised by Wang Chi, and published later: see Giles.

[2] Encyclopedia, section xiv, book 14, p. 11.

The substitution of the name of the place where one was born for the original surname is one of the commonest changes. Chêng Chíao found 125 in the Sung period which had originated in this way. Other changes are made by taking the name of the province, or the district, or the title, or one's rank in the family, as the substitute. On the whole, self-segregation is the commonest course of the increase in the number of surnames, according to Chêng Chíao's statistics. More than 60 per cent of the total number of surnames are due to this cause.

(b) *Foreign Surnames*. The barbarians who settled in China retained their tribal names, which form more than 15 per cent of Chêng Chíao's collection. These names are generally polysyllabic, while the pure We-group surnames are, as a rule, monosyllabic.

(c) *Arbitrary Changes*. From Chinese history we learn that it was a common practice on the part of the Emperors to bestow the royal surnames on faithful ministers and brave warriors as rewards, on gentlemen and ladies of the court as favors, and on chieftains of barbarian tribes as a sign of good-will. In the Han dynasty, for instance, many of the Hsiung-nu tribes were given the surname "Liu," the surname of the imperial clan. On the other hand, if the displeasure of his or her majesty were incurred, some surname with a bad meaning would be imposed on the imprudent subject as a substitute for his original name. A notable example of this is found in the Táng dynasty, when the Empress Dowager, who usurped the throne, having discovered that some royal prince was plotting to dethrone her, punished him by depriving him of his royal surname (Li); and imposing on him as a substitute, "Hui," a venomous snake noted for its treachery and poison. The contribution of this type to the total number is, however, very small; but as a disturbing element it has been subtle and important.

(d) *Adaptation*. After long settlement the foreign elements began to feel that they were socially ostracized, because they retained their old tribal polysyllabic names. A desire for assimilation became intense; as a consequence, a monosyllabication of these polysyllabic names took place. The ninety-nine tribal names of the Tungus tribes which ruled Northern China (386 A.D. to 558 A.D.) were entirely monosyllabicated. The history of Wei has given a complete list of these 99 tribal names and their Chinese equivalents.[1] They took the most common Chinese surnames as their equivalent. The result of the step taken by this barbarian tribe is the addition of an important element of con-

---

[1] *History of Wei:* section 113.

fusion, which almost deprived of genealogical significance the whole system of surnames. We have noticed that it was in this time that genealogical study began to flourish. The purpose was, of course, to keep out the foreign blood as much as possible. But the effort, though more or less steadily maintained for some time, was not as successful as had been expected. Equally important disturbing elements came in later on; and they took the same step as the Wei tribes. It is plain, therefore, that the indigenous surnames which survived up to 1644 A.D. are polygenetic. This is especially true with the commoner surnames.

But although the confusion is great, its sources are localizable. The problem here is not allied to the difficulty of securing material. The material, on the contrary, is very abundant. The problem is: From what angle are these materials to be studied? It is possible to make a study of the origins of the surnames, and to classify them on a basis that has ethnical significance. If this is to be undertaken, several conditions have to be fulfilled:

(1) The origin given for the surname must not be fictitious; it should be definite.

(2) Whatever is given should be verifiable by other material.

(3) The origins given must be classifiable on an ethnical basis.

The fulfillment of the last condition is plainly dependent upon that of the first two. But neither the first nor the second condition can be satisfied in any simple and direct way, considering the nature of our material given in the Encyclopedia. To illustrate this point I have translated the first five samples of the original material regarding the origin of the surnames given in the Encyclopedia.

1. *Tung:* The surname Tung originated with Tung Pu-tzu, one of the seven friends of Emperor Shun (2255–2206 B.C.). It spread out from the district of Píng-yüan (Shansi). (Section XIV, book 21, P. 1.)

2. *T'ung:* The descendants of Lao-T'ung, one of the sons of Chuan-ti (one of the Emperors in the mythological age) took the personal name of their grandfather as their surname. This name is now (Sung dynasty) found in the district of Chien-ch'ang. It originally spread from the district of Po-hai (Chihli). [Footnote by Chêng Ch'iao: Taking the personal name of the grandfather as the surname of the family was practised only in the Chou dynasty; it is doubtful whether this system was found in the time of the Five Emperors (Chuan-ti being one of the Five Emperors)]. (*Ibid.*, p. 8.)

3. *Mêng:* According to Fêng-su-túng, the masters of Tung-meng took their surname from the mountain Mêng-shan. In the Ch'in dy-

nasty (246–207 B.C.), a general by the name of Mêng Ao was recorded. The son of Mêng Ao was Mêng Wu; the son of Mêng Wu was Mêng Kua. All of them served the Ch'in dynasty. This surname spread from the district Ngan-ting, where Mêng Ch'uan of the Sung dynasty (960–1280 A.D.) was born; he passed the civil service examination in the first year of Hsiang-fu (1008 A.D.). In the same dynasty, Mêng Chi of T'ai Chou and Mêng Chu of Feng Chou were known. [Footnote by Chêng Ch'iao: The mountain Mêng is 80 li northwest of the Fei district; there is also Tung-Mêng, which lies 75 li northwest of the Fei district, and east to the Mêng mountain. The descendants of the family whose original duty was to take care of the sacrifice to the mountain Mêng took their surname from the name of the mountain.] (*Ibid.*, p. 11.)

4. *Kung:* Kung originated from the surname Chi (the surname of the royal house of the Chou dynasty: 1122–247 B.C.). According to the commentator of Ch'un Ch'iu, Tso Chiu-ming, the descendants of the two sons Kung-yen and Kung-wei of Duke Chao (541–510 B.C.), the feudal lord of the Lu-principality (occupying a part of modern Shantung province), who was directly related to the royal house, took this name as their surname: In the Later Han dynasty (25–220 A.D.) there was Kung Chien, who held the title Chu-chüeh-tu-wei. [Footnote by Chêng Ch'iao: Kung-yen and Kung-wei were originally known as Kungtzu-yen and Kungtzu-wei (meaning, Prince Yen and Prince Wei). The suffix of the title, "tzu," was taken off, and "Kung" alone was used as an abbreviated form of the original. Chao Kung lost his principality; so the descendants of his two sons took the surname after their title. (*Ibid.*, Book 22, p. 1.)

5. *Wêng:* (a) In the Han dynasty, there was Wêng Po. In the T'ang dynasty, Wêng I was born in Loyang. Wêng Yi of the period of the Five Dynasties (907 A.D. to 960 A.D.) was born in Pu-tien (Chêng Ch'iao).

(b) The Wêng family of the Yen-Kuan district began with the son of Emperor Chao of the Chou dynasty born of his concubine. He was given the mountain Wêng, later on his descendants took their surname from the mountain. It also spread from Ch'ien-T'ang (Chekiang).

These serve as samples of the material that we have to deal with; the descriptions of the origin of the rest of the 3736 surnames are about the same, but naturally with more or less detail, in accordance with the type of the surname that is dealt with.

A careful analysis of these five samples shows that the three requisite conditions for an ethnical classification of the origins of the surnames cannot be easily fulfilled. If we take the "Descendants of the Yellow Emperor" as our starting point, only three out of the five are directly related to the Yellow Emperor. (2, 4, 5: see note 1.) The origins of the other two are certainly definite, but they are not classifiable. It is possible that one of the Seven Friends of Emperor Shun (Tung I) was directly related to the Yellow Emperor; but equally possible that he was not. The same thing may be said of the Mêng origin. So these two are not classifiable. Regarding verification, the problem is still more difficult. There are practically no means of verifying the accuracy of the different ancient authors, in the absence of first-hand antiquarian material. The case under consideration is, therefore, of uncertain value.

So far only the cited samples are discussed. It has been noted that there are no surnames of fictitious origin in the first five examples. But it is not to be inferred that the whole series is as definite as these five. There are many surnames of fictitious origin. For example, the barbarian tribes of the North which invaded China all claimed their descent from the Yellow Emperor so as to establish a close relationship with the subjects whom they ruled. This is, of course, absurd and extremely disturbing. There are many surnames of this type; consequently they cannot all be classified.

The material as a whole is therefore not adaptable to the scheme of approach that we have advocated. The procedure necessarily has to be reversed, and a way of approach adapted to the material at our disposal must be found. The nature of the data may be studied a little further.

In the above five examples we are given:

(1) The approximate origin of the surname.

(2) The approximate date of its first appearance.

(3) The centre of its spread.

This, however, is not all. In the above translation I have omitted all the biographical sketches of individuals bearing the surnames whose origin is described. The number of sketches varies considerably with different surnames, depending upon the spread of the surname and the prominence of those who bore it. There are thirty-seven attached to the Tung; forty-four to the T'ung; forty-eight to the Mêng; fifty to the Kung; and forty-three to the Wêng. Others have none; still others have thousands. In these sketches, generally speaking, both the date and the birthplace of the subject are given. Unknown cases are many; but known cases are more. All told, there are more than 50,000 of these biographical sketches of the men of prominence in China, from the earliest historical record up to 1644 A.D. So in addition to the above, the data consist of:

(4) The number of prominent men that bear a certain surname, and are recorded in history.

(5) The dates and the places of their births.

It is therefore possible to find out from these data: (1) the spread of the surname up to 1644 A.D., by a comparative study of the locations of the prominent men in different periods. Assuming that the centres of the different surnames are indicated by the birthplaces of those prominent men that bear the surname, it follows that the result of this study will serve as a basis for mapping out the centres of all the great surnames. (2) And so, since we know the approximate origin of a number of these surnames, we shall be able to locate the descendants of all the groups that have been found in China proper as well as the Descendants of the Yellow Emperor, the nucleus of the We-group. The ethnical strata of different parts of China may find a clear expression in this way.

On this basis, I had proceeded with the analysis of the data for a long while before I realized that the problem of location is of greater magnitude than I had realized. It is, in fact, a problem by itself. The reasons are that the geographical names of China, like those of Europe, have suffered many changes, due to political divisions and redivisions in different dynasties; and the birthplaces of the different prominent men are given the names used in the period in which they were born. To reduce all these records to a unified geographical terminology, it is necessary that all these names should be identified with the modern names. So far as I know, the Chinese historical geographers have not yet completed this task. The most recent historical atlas [1] published by the Peking National University, for instance, gives only the relative positions of the places; it is difficult to identify them on the maps with absolute assurance, because no longitude and latitude are given. It is, however, not an impossible task, but it is a very laborious one; and the lack of an alphabetical index of Chinese names makes it almost ten times more laborious than if an index were provided. To attempt it as a whole would be beyond the scope and province of the present work, so I have decided to make another turn of this inquiry and narrow it down to a partial study.

[1] Su Chia-yün, 1922.

Ten surnames that have given rise to the largest number of men of prominence are chosen for analysis according to the plan that has been discussed. If the spread of these ten surnames can be taken as an indication of the spread of the groups that are responsible for their origins, the results that are to be obtained from this analysis will give a safe index to the ethnical strata in different parts of China.

The Ten Test Surnames

Arranged alphabetically, the ten surnames chosen are: Chang, Ch'ên, Chu, Hu, Kuo, Li, Liu, Wang, Wu, Yang. The order of description will be (a) the origin, (b) migration, and enumeration of men of prominence found in each period in different parts of China.

I. Chang

(a) *Origin*

Account 1:

"The surname Chang originated from the surname Chi and began with the fifth son of Shao-hao, one of the sons of the Yellow Emperor. This son of Shao-hao was the first bow-maker in China; therefore, he was given the surname Chang, which is made up of two radicals — Kung or bow, and Ch'ang or long." (From the *Genealogy of the State Councilors of the T'ang dynasty, the History of T'ang*, quoted by the Encyclopedia, book 233, page 1.)

Account 2:

"The family Chang served the State of Chin (1106–376 B.C.) for generations. When Chin was divided into three (376 B.C.), this family continued to serve the State of Han (one of the three post-Chin states — 403–230 B.C.). The family was a branch of the royal house of Chin. . . . The surname originated with the member named Chieh-chang, whose descendants took his personal name as their surname. . . ." (*Ibid.*, page 2.)

". . . Yü-wên Chou conferred on the Ch'a-lo tribe (a Hsien Pei tribe) the surname Chang. . . ." (A preface to the *Genealogical Record of the Chang Family*, by Sung Lien, quoted, book 252, page 2.)

Conclusion: The first two accounts agree on the fact that the earliest Chang originated from the surname Chi and is traceable to the Yellow Emperor. For the house of Chin is a branch of the royal house Chou, whose surname is Chi, and a branch of the Descendants of the Yellow

Emperor. The third account shows that the Changs after 557 A.D. include a Tunguse element in addition to the Descendants of the Yellow Emperor. Explicitly, therefore, we have two ethnical types of Chang since 557 A.D.

(b) *Migrations and Centres*

Account 1:

"Chang Yuan was born in Yenshih, Honan; the family moved from Honei (Shensi or Shansi) to Honan in the Han dynasty." (The monument inscription of Chang Yüan in Chang's ancestral Hall — *Collected Essays of Ts'ai Chung Lang*, quoted, book 233, page 1.)

Account 2:

". . . After the disastrous event of Yüng-Chia (317 A.D.) the Chang family began to move southward across the Yangtze Valley. . . ." (*Collected Essays of Chang Yen-Kung*, quoted, *ibid*.)

Account 3:

". . . The Changs of Ch'a-lo origin flourish mainly between Yen and Tai. . . . They are not found south of the Yangtze. . . ." (Sung Lien, *Ibid*.)

Account 4:

". . . Chang Wei migrated southward with Yüan-ti and settled in Chiang-tso (left bank of the Yangtze). After six generations, one member moved northward to Loyang again. . . . Changs of Hotung (Shansi) were on the direct line beginning with Chang Hua, whose son moved to Hotung from Fan-yang. Changs of Shih-hsing (Shantung) were also a branch of Chang Hua's descendants; this branch migrated southward with Chin Yüan-ti (317 A.D.). One was an officer at Chü-chiang (Kwangtung) and settled in that province. . . . Changs of Fen-yi (Shensi) began with Chang Hao. . . . One, his grandson, served Shu, during the period of "The Three Kingdoms" (221–265 A.D.); later on the members moved from Chien-wei (Szechuan) to Hsia-pang (Shensi). . . . Changs of Wu-chün (Kiangsu) descended from the fourth son of Chang Hua. . . . Changs of Lo-ch'ang (S. Chihli) descended from Chang Liang. . . . Changs of Ho-chien (Chihli) descended from Chang Er. . . . Changs of Chung-shan (Nganhui) descended from Chang Ts'ang. . . . There are Changs of Chi (Honan) and Changs of Chêng Chou (Honan)." (*Genealogy of the State Councilors of the T'ang dynasty, the History of T'ang*, quoted, book 233.)

Account 5:

"Changs of Chü-chiang (cf. Account 4) at the time of Chang Chiu Ling (once State Councilor to T'ang Hsüan Tsung, 713 A.D.) first entered Szechuan." (*History and Topography of Szechuan*, quoted, book 233.)

Conclusion: The original Changs were first found in the provinces of Honan, Shensi, and Shansi, etc. Their first southward push began in 317 A.D. The Changs of Ch'alo origin had not yet crossed the Yangtze at the beginning of the Ming Dynasty — Sung Lien's time. So the Changs north of the Yangtze, and particularly in Chihli, were derived from both Hsien-pei and the Yellow Emperor; south of the Yangtze, the Changs were less heterogeneous, according to the records.

TABLE 52

PERIODICAL AND PROVINCIAL DISTRIBUTION OF THE RECORDED CHANGS

Provinces	Periods					
	C	D	E	F	G	H
I Chekiang	1	1	6	8	6	35
II Chihli	1	78	53	37	22	54
III Fukien	..	..	2	10	2	20
IV Honan	8	5	29	30	9	26
V Hunan	..	..	1	4	..	3
VI Hupeh	..	5	5	9	..	15
VII Kansu	..	14	1	1	1	0
VIII Kiangsi	..	..	3	12	6	18
IX Kiangsu	..	29	18	14	1	35
X Kwangsi	..	..	..	..	1	2
XI Kwangtung	..	..	5	1	1	15
XII Kweichow	..	..	..	..	..	4
XIII Nganhui	..	..	9	13	..	28
XIV Shansi	1	11	25	12	4	57
XV Shantung	1	6	18	22	10	36
XVI Shensi	6	9	17	10	1	31
XVII Szechuan	..	2	13	8	1	11
XVIII Yunnan	..	..	1	0	1	1
Unknown	56	77	99	85	7	2

II. Ch'en

(a) *Origin*

Account 1:

". . . The surname Ch'ên was derived from the surname Wei, which was taken by the descendants of Emperor Shun in the Chou dynasty. . . ." (*Genealogy of the State Councilors of the T'ang dynasty, the History of T'ang*, quoted, book 117, page 1.)

Account 2:

". . . There are four different groups of Ch'êns: (1) the descendants of Emperor Shun; (2) the Pai family, which has substituted Ch'ên for Pai since the Sui dynasty; (3) Ch'ên of Wan-nien, the descendants of Liu Chiao, who took this surname during the Han dynasty; (4) Ch'ên of Kuanling, which was monosyllabicated from Hou-mo-ch'ên, a Tungus tribe. . . ." (*Ibid.*, page 2.)

Conclusion: The surname Ch'ên is a compound of four elementary forms. The main stem is from Emperor Shun, traceable back to the Yellow Emperor. The main foreign element is the Tungus, introduced in 494 A.D.

(b) *Migration*

Account 1:

". . . Ch'ên Shih of T'ai-chiu (Honan) was noted in the latter part of the Later Han dynasty. When the royal house of Chin moved southward, one of his descendants followed and made his home at Wu-hsing (Kiangsu)." (*Collected Essays of Ch'ên Lung-chuan*, quoted, book 117, page 2.)

Account 2:

". . . From the period of the Five Dynasties (907–960 A.D.) to the disastrous year of Ching K'ang (1127 A.D.) when continuous war was devastating the Central Plain (Honan and the surrounding provinces), the men of "Caps and Gowns" of this region, in order to escape from the barbarian domination (Khitan), mostly migrated southward and made their homes in Wu (Kiangsu), Yüeh (Chekiang), Min (Fukien), and Kwang (Kwangtung). There they instructed their descendants with the books with which they had escaped from the north. . . . Now the families in the southwest, most cultivated in poetry and history are found in Min (Fukien); and among these, the Ch'êns stand out most prominently. All the four branches of Ch'êns in Min came originally from Ku-shih (Honan). Authentic records show that they are the direct descendants of Shun." (A preface, by Wang Shih-chêg, to the *Genealogical Record of the Family Ch'ên*, quoted, book 130, page 4.)

Account 3:

South of the Yangtze, the line of Ch'ên began with Ch'ên Kuei. Later on it spread out to twenty-one large branches and fifty-four small branches; one branch, found originally in Yin-t'ien (Honan), migrated to Mu (Nganhui), then to Huai-yu (Nganhui), to Pu (Fukien), and Chüan (Fukien), then backward to Ch'ao (Nganhui): this migration took more than one thousand years. (A preface, by Chang Chün, to the *Genealogical Record of the Family Ch'ên*, quoted, book 130, page 13.)

Conclusion: Account 1 shows that the first southward migration of the Ch'êns took place at the same time as the Changs. Another southward push of the same surname took place almost 800 years later (907–1129 A.D.). The second account also shows that there was a general southward push of population giving place to the invading Khitans.

TABLE 53

PERIODICAL AND PROVINCIAL DISTRIBUTION OF THE RECORDED CH'ÊN

Provinces	Periods				
	D	E	F	G	H
I Chekiang	..	15	100	7	136
II Chihli	4	6	9	7	12
III Fukien	1	15	100	7	136
IV Honan	4	5	11	6	18
V Hunan	..	2	4	..	9
VI Hupeh	1	2	1	..	31
VII Kansu	2	2	..	..	..
VIII Kiangsi	..	4	19	2	26
IX Kiangsu	74	16	10	4	55
X Kwangsi	..	..	..	..	..
XI Kwangtung	..	5	7	4	35
XII Kweichow	..	..	..	..	6
XIII Nganhui	3	4	4	2	27
XIV Shansi	2	..	2	2	16
XV Shantung	1	1	1	1	26
XVI Shensi	..	..	..	..	10
XVII Szechuan	1	1	13	..	4
XVIII Yunnan	..	..	..	..	4
Unknown	20	10	..	..	..

III. Chu

(a) *Origin*

Account 1:

"Chu Hui . . . is a native of Wan, Nan-yang (Honan); he comes from a family renowned for generations. . . . [Footnote: the ancestor of this family sprang from Wei-tzŭ, the founder of the royal house of Sung (1111–286 B.C.); the descendants of the house went to Tang, and changed their surname from Sung to Chu. Afterwards, they migrated to Wan.]" (*Biography of Chu Hui, Hou Han Shu,* quoted, book 66, page 1.)

Account 2:

The surname Chu was derived from T'sao. Among the descendants of Chuan-yü, there was one known as Lu Chung, who had six sons. The fifth was named Ngan. When Wu-wang of Chou (1134–1116 B.C.) succeeded the Shang dynasty, the descendants of Ngan were given the feudal title Chu (677–249? B.C.) and made a dependent principality under the control of the State of Lu (1122–249 B.C.). After it was incorporated into the State of Ch'u, which took place in 469 B.C., the members of the royal house of Chu took Chu as their surname . . . and settled in Hsiang district (Honan). . . . In the Later Han dynasty, when political persecution was at its height, the Chus moved southward to Tan-yang, thus beginning the Chus of Tan-yang. (*Genealogy of the State Councilors of the T'ang dynasty, the History of T'ang,* quoted, book 66, page 1.)

Account 3:

"Chu (one radical) was originally Chu (two radicals) which was derived from T'sao. . . . The most noted of their descendants are found in: (1) Pei-kuo (Honan); (2) Tan-yang (Kiangsu); (3) Yung-ch'eng (Honan); (4) Wu-chün (Kiangsu); (5) Ch'ien-t'ang (Chekiang); (6) I-yang (?); (7) T'ai-k'ang (Cheng-chou, Honan); (8) Tan-yang (?); (9) Honan. All these nine branches were well known both in the dynasty of Han and of T'ang. Another derivation of Chu was the mono-syllabication of K'o-chu-hun; and a third was that of Ko-chu-hun. Both were Tungus tribes. The Chus of the two latter origins are found mainly in Honan (now Shantung and Honan).

Conclusion: Here again there are two main origins. The exotic element was, like the previous two, introduced between the fifth and the sixth centuries A.D. The main stem, although having two versions, is traceable back to the Yellow Emperor.

(b) *Migration*

Account 1:

". . . The monumental inscription of Chu in Ch'iung-lung Shan (Su-chou), which is unfortunately incomplete, has the following remnants: 'For 429 years, sixteen generations have stayed in Hsia-pê (Kiangsu). . . . From the third year of P'ing-shih [1] to the year of Jen-hsü of Hui-ch'ang (842 A.D.), 842 years have elapsed.' This monument was erected by the Chus of the T'ang dynasty, who set down the date at which their ancestors crossed the Yangtze." (*History of Su-chou*, quoted, book 66, page 2.)

Account 2:

"My grandfather told me that our family formerly resided in the district Hsi (Nganhui), which according to tradition branched off from the central stem in Wu-chün (Su-chou). . . . During the T'ien-yu era of T'ang (904–907 A.D.), when Wu-yüan (Hui-chou, Nganhui) was first conquered, T'ao Ya, the governor of Hsi-chou, commissioned our ancestor to guard it with three thousand soldiers. He was buried in Lien-t'ung after death, and the children all settled down there. Their descendants afterwards scattered to different districts. One branch, however, is still found in Lien-t'ung, which claims direct descent from the commissioner, although it cannot be confirmed. My grandfather is the eighth generation from the commissioner, who came to Cheng-ho (Chien-ning, Fukien) in the Hsüan-ho era (1119–1126 A.D.). Now, I have already had grandchildren, so our family has already been settled in Min for five generations. . . ." (A postscript to the *Genealogy of the Family Chu of Ch'a-yüan*, by Chu Hsi, quoted, book 76, page 1.)

Conclusion: The earliest Chus of the main stem were found both in Shantung and Honan. In the middle of the Han dynasty and about the beginning of the Christian Era, they crossed the Yangtze valley and settled in Su-chou, from which they spread to Nganhui and Fukien. The records also show that the Chus south of the Yangtze belong to the main stem. The Chus of Tungus derivation are found mainly in Honan.

---

[1] The third year of P'ing-shih cannot be identified; the year Jen-hsü of Hui-ch'ang corresponds to 842 A.D., the second year of the reign of T'ang Wu-tsung. So counted backward from 842 A.D., the third year of P'ing-shih is correspondent with the first year of the Christian era, which is the first year of Yüan-shih of Han P'ing-ti.

TABLE 54

PERIODICAL AND PROVINCIAL DISTRIBUTION OF THE CHUS

Provinces	Periods				
	D	E	F	G	H [1]
I Chekiang	7	2	8	3	14
II Chihli	2	7	..	1	4
III Fukien	..	..	9	..	7
IV Honan	..	3	9	..	9
V Hunan	..	..	2	..	8
VI Hupeh	3	1	2	1	17
VII Kansu	..	..	..	..	..
VIII Kiangsi	..	1	6	1	14
IX Kiangsu	12	2	9	3	23
X Kwangsi	..	..	1	..	..
XI Kwangtung	..	..	..	..	8
XII Kweichow	..	..	..	..	6
XIII Nganhui	..	6	..	..	5
XIV Shansi	5	1	1	..	9
XV Shantung	..	2	1	2	10
XVI Shensi	..	1	2	..	4
XVII Szechuan	..	4	4	..	..
XVIII Yunnan	..	..	..	..	6
Unknown	..	22	9	..	5

[1] Royal house excluded.

IV. Hu

(a) *Origin*

Account 1:

"Hu Kuang, a native of Hua-yung, Nan-chün (Hupeh), derived his surname from Wei, the surname of Emperor Shun." (*Collected Essays of Ts'ai Chung-lang*, quoted, book 83, page 1.)

Account 2:

"State of Hu, a principality of the fourth order in the Ch'un-ch'iu period is to be identified with modern Yin-chou (Honan). It was incorporated into the State of Ch'u in the fifteenth year of Ting-kung of Lu (485 B.C.). The descendants of the royal house took the state name as their surname. Another account records that Hu-kung Man was made a noble at Ch'ên; his descendants also had this surname. The Hu of Lo-ling district (Shantung) afterwards took the surname Li. . . . The Hu of Honan was originally Hê-ku, a Tungus tribe." (*Chêng Ch'iao*, quoted, *ibid.*)

Account 3:

"... Hu Sho's ancestors shared the surname with the royal house of Ch'u (whose surname was Hsiung). They were made noble at Hu, and their descendants converted the state name into their surname. . . ." (*Collected Essays of Ts'ai Chung-lang,* quoted, *ibid.*)

Conclusion: The Hus have three origins: (1) from Emperor Shun; (2) from Hsiung, which belonged to the You-group in the B period; and (3) from the Tungus tribe in the fifth century A.D.

(b) *Centres and Migrations*

Account 1:

"Hus are found in Ngan-ting (Shansi and Kansu), and Loyang (Honan)." (*Shang-yu-lu,* quoted, book 83, page 12.)

Account 2:

"Hu Ta-hai is a native of Wu-tu (Nganhui). . . . Most members of this family died for the royal house of Ming (H period); . . . two survived and settled in Shantung." (Preface to the *Genealogy of Hu Ta-hai,* by Chang Fung-i, quoted, book 86, page 14.)

Account 3:

"... Hus of T'ao Yüan (Kiangsu) migrated from Ssŭ-ming. . . ." (Preface to the *Genealogy of the Family Hu,* by Shih Chien, quoted, book 86, page 15.)

Conclusion: These accounts do not show exactly the line of migration of any of these Hus, whatever their origins. It is certain, however, that the earlier Hus were found in several centres: Shensi, Kansu, Hupeh, Honan, and perhaps more. But the date of origin of any of these centres cannot be ascertained. In the Ming dynasty they appeared definitely south of the Yangtze valley. When they crossed the river cannot be determined. It is probable that the Hus were found south of the Yangtze very early, since one of the origins is allied to the royal house of the State of Ch'u, whose territory reached the Yangtze Valley. But this cannot be verified. Account 2 is interesting in that it shows a northward movement.

TABLE 55

PERIODICAL AND PROVINCIAL DISTRIBUTION OF HUS

Provinces	Periods					
	C	D	E	F	G	H
I Chekiang	..	..	1	14	5	23
II Chihli	1	..	..	1	2	4
III Fukien	..	..	1	7	1	9
IV Honan	3	2	..	2	1	3
V Hunan	4	..	1	3	..	18
VI Hupeh	..	..	..	..	1	24
VII Kansu	..	..	..	..	..	1
VIII Kiangsi	1	11	..	11	2	21
IX Kiangsu	..	2	..	13	..	5
X Kwangsi	..	..	..	..	..	..
XI Kwangtung	..	..	..	2	..	3
XII Kweichow	..	..	..	..	..	4
XIII Nganhui	..	4	..	10	2	13
XIV Shansi	2	1	1	..	1	7
XV Shantung	..	..	..	7	4	11
XVI Shensi	..	17	..	1	..	5
XVII Szechuan	1	..	1	1	..	2
XVIII Yunnan	..	..	..	..	..	4
Unknown	2	3	5	20	..	6

V. KUO

(a, b) *Origin, Centres and Migrations*

Account 1:

"Kuo originated from Chi, the surname of the royal house of the
Chou dynasty; it was originally 'Wo,' but later gutturalized to 'Kuo.'"
In the Later Han dynasty, there was Kuo Chuan, whose family for
generations made its home at Yang-chü (Shansi). The Kuo of Hua-yin
(Shensi) branched off from T'ai-yüan. The Kuo of Chung-shan
(Nganhui) made their home at Kucheng. The Kuo of Ch'ang-lo (Shan-
tung?) are also a branch of the T'ai-yüan stem." (*Genealogy of the State
Councilors of the T'ang dynasty, the History of T'ang*, quoted, book 528,
page 1.)

Conclusion: This is the first time that we come across a surname
that is relatively free from confusion with other origins. It is a unique
example of genealogical purity. But this, it must be observed, is true

only as far as the record [1] goes. There is no other account of the migration of this surname; so we have to proceed directly to the distribution of the Kuos in different provinces and periods.

TABLE 56

PERIODICAL AND PROVINCIAL DISTRIBUTION OF KUOS

Provinces	Periods						
	B	C	D	E	F	G	H
I Chekiang	..	..	..	..	6	..	9
II Chihli	2	3	2	7	7	12	38
III Fukien	..	..	..	..	3	5	14
IV Honan	..	11	1	3	16	2	34
V Hunan	..	..	..	1	1	..	11
VI Hupeh	..	..	3	2	1	1	35
VII Kansu	..	2	2	2	1	..	2
VIII Kiangsi	..	..	..	2	19	9	49
IX Kiangsu	..	..	2	..	5	2	4
X Kwangsi	..	..	..	..	..	..	..
XI Kwangtung	..	2	..	..	2	1	8
XII Kweichow	..	..	..	..	..	..	..
XIII Nganhui	..	..	..	2	2	1	4
XIV Shansi	..	5	16	4	9	3	22
XV Shantung	2	..	..	1	4	1	31
XVI Shensi	..	2	3	13	2	6	24
XVII Szechuan	..	..	..	2	5	..	9
XVIII Yunnan	..	..	..	..	..	..	3
Unknown	..	30	8	9	16	2	14

VI. LI

(a) *Origin*

Account 1:

"Li was derived from 'Ying'; the family descended from Chuan-yü and had many noted jurists in the early period. In the latter part of the Chou dynasty, Li Er, the founder of Taoism, was born. . . . The royal house of T'ang (618–960 A.D.) was directly descended from this famous teacher. . . ." (*Genealogy of the Royal House of T'ang, History of T'ang*, quoted, book 381, page 1.)

[1] There are several reasons why we have to make this statement with reserve. In the biographical sketches, I have found two instances of Kuos of foreign origin: Kuo Yung being a Mongol, and Kuo Tsung-i being a Shato.

Account 2:

"Li of Liu-ch'eng (Chihli) descended from a Khitan chieftain and later migrated to Wan-nien (Shensi). . . . Li of Wu-wei (Kansu) was originally Ngan derived from the surname Chi and directly related to the Yellow Emperor. In the early period, this family settled in the West, Nganhsi (Parthia). During the Later Han dynasty, one of the branches came back to China and made its home in Loyang (Honan). Between the Chin and the Wei dynasty, they migrated westward to Nganting (Shensi). From Nganting they moved to Liao-tso; and from Liao-tso they came to settle at Wu-wei. The noted member of this family in the time of the Northern Wei (386–583 A.D.) was known as Nan-t'o-san-p'o-lo. In the T'ang dynasty this family was given the royal surname Li.[1]

"There is another Li of Korean derivation.

"Li of Chi-t'ien descended from the Chi-ah-tieh tribe at the northern bend of the Huang-ho (Inner Mongolia).

"Li of Tai-po (Chihli and Shansi) was originally Chu-hsieh, a tribal name of Sha-to-li. They changed to Li in the T'ang dynasty with the consent of the Emperor." (*Genealogy of the State Councilors of T'ang, the History of T'ang*, quoted, book 381, page 5.)

Account 3:

"There are seventeen groups of Lis: the main stem was descended from the eminent jurist Kao-yao in the time of the Emperor Yao (2557–2256 B.C.); then the families Hsü, Ping, Ngan, Tu, Hu, Hung, Kuo, Ma, Chang, Tung, and Lo all have substituted Li for their original surnames. The tribes Hsien-yü, A-pu, A-tieh, Shê-li and Chu-hsieh have, by the gracious favor of his majesty, the Emperor of the T'ang dynasty, taken 'Li' as their surname. . . ." (*Chêng-Ch'iao*, quoted, book 381, page 5.)

Conclusion: The royal house of T'ang is chiefly responsible for introducing the exotic elements into this family. The tribes that have been given the name Li are mainly of Turkish origin, while the other twelve cases of conversion are originally of quite a mixed character; but in the main they are more related to the descendants of the Yellow Emperor than other tribes, dependent, of course, also on the time of conversion.

---

[1] This is plainly a false case; they are apparently of exotic origin, and claimed their descendance from the Yellow Emperor so their family might be made socially respectable.

(b) *Centres and Migrations*

"Li" is now found in almost every nook and corner of China proper. To trace its spread and migration is therefore a very fascinating task. But we can do only part of the work in the present connection as the materials provided are not sufficient to serve as a basis for constructing a complete genealogical table from the earliest period to the present time. But even this partial table could prove very valuable in illuminating the nature of the migration of the historical We-group at large in certain periods. In the T'ang dynasty, we have had occasion to point out, genealogical study was very careful. One of the first things for the genealogist to do is naturally to trace the line of the royal house as far back as possible. On page 146 the complete table is constructed according to the record given in the official History of T'ang on the Genealogy of the royal house. (Quoted, book 381, pages 1–3.)

The eminent and astute Sung encyclopedist, Chêng Ch'iao, observed that previous to the time of Li Shan the records are not reliable, but after him full credibility must be given to the record. So we must take the record in the same spirit. The important points to be noted here are these: (1) the earliest record about the main stem of Li shows it is found in Honan; (2) two main branches began about the third century B.C.; (3) the Chihli branch later on spread to Manchuria, Honan, Shensi, and Hupeh, and probably some other provinces which cannot be identified; (4) the Kansu branch later spread out to Chihli, Honan, Shansi, Shantung, and some others; (5) the migrations previous to 618 A.D. are limited in the south by the Yangtze River; (6) in the T'ang dynasty (960 A.D.) there were 37 branches of Li which spread all over China proper.

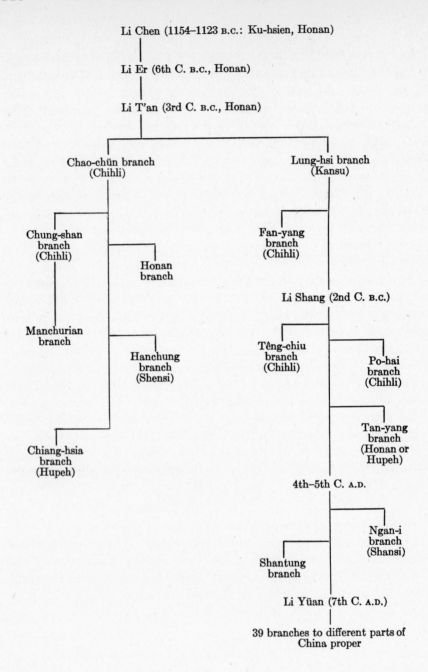

TABLE 57

PERIODICAL AND PROVINCIAL DISTRIBUTION OF LIS
(ROYAL HOUSE EXCLUDED)

Provinces	Periods					
	C	D	E	F	G	H
I Chekiang	..	..	..	10	3	5
II Chihli	4	77	62	36	8	25
III Fukien	..	..	1	22	..	8
IV Honan	13	7	19	36	..	36
V Hunan	..	1	11	4	..	1
VI Hupeh	3	4	1	6	..	12
VII Kansu	9	29	23	2	3	1
VIII Kiangsi	..	..	..	23	..	19
IX Kiangsu	1	..	4	16	4	19
X Kwangsi	..	..	..	4	..	1
XI Kwangtung	..	..	..	10	3	9
XII Kweichow	..	..	..	..	..	1
XIII Nganhui	1	1	4	13	3	18
XIV Shansi	2	7	1	39	6	4
XV Shantung	2	..	7	17	6	4
XVI Shensi	2	8	22	7	4	22
XVII Szechuan	9	24	15	16	1	3
XVIII Yunnan	..	..	..	..	1	1
Unknown	23	19	..	47	4	17

VII. LIU

(a) *Origin*

Account 1:

". . . The descendants of Shih Hui, who remained in Chin (Shensi), took the surname Liu. . . ." (*The Thirteenth Year of Wen Kung, Tso Chuan, Ch'un Ch'iu*, quoted, book 327, page 1.)

Account 2:

". . . The Lius of Tung-chün (Honan) and Tiau-yin were all of Hsiung-nu origin. Emperor Han Kao-tsu (206–195 B.C.) married one of his nieces to a Hsiung-nu chieftain. The Hsiung-nu rule of descent for the surname being matrilineal, their children took the surname Liu. . . ." (*Chêng Ch'iao*, quoted, book 327, page 2.)

Account 3:

There are five different groups of Lius: (1) the descendants of Yao; (2) the descendants of Wang Chi (father of Chou Wen-wang); (3) the conversion of Lou; (4) the conversion of Hsiang; (5) the conversion of Hiungnu.

Conclusion: The main stem is again traceable back to Huang-ti, the Yellow Emperor. The Hiungnu blood was introduced into the family in the Han dynasty.

(b) *Migration and Centres*

Account 1:

"There are twenty-five centres of Lius; the P'ên-ch'eng branch (Hsü-chou, Kiangsu) belongs to the noblest line." (*Wan-wei-yu-pien*, quoted, book 343, page 17.)

Account 2:

". . . Chou Shih, in his tribute to Nao-tsu, said that the line of the royal house of Han sprang directly from Emperor Yao. . . . In the Chou dynasty this line prospered mainly in the State Ch'in. . . . The grandfather of Kao-Tsu first moved to Fêng (N. Kiangsu). . . ." (*The Biography of Kao-tsu, Ch'ien Han Shu*, quoted, book 327, page 1.)

Account 3:

". . . When the State of Ch'in subjugated the State of Wei, the Lius moved to Ta-liang (Honan); the grandfather of Han Kao-tsu moved again to P'ei (N. Kiangsu)." (Foot-note of *Ch'un-ch'iu*, quoted in Account 1, a.)

Account 4:

"The descendants of the royal house of Han spread out to the following centres: (1) the Lius of Pên-ch'eng (Kiangsu); (2) the Lius of Wei-shih (Honan); (3) the Lius of Lin-huai (Kiangsu); (4) the Lius of Nan-yang (Honan); (5) the Lius of Kuang-ping; (6) the Lius of Tan-yang; (7) the Lius of Ts'ao-chou (Shantung)." (*Genealogy of the State Councilors of T'ang dynasty, History of T'ang*, quoted, book 327, page 2.)

Conclusion: The earliest Lius were found in Shensi and Kansu. In the third century B.C., they migrated southwestward to Honan and Kiangsu. Then a dynasty (Han) was created by one of the members in Kiangsu, whose descendants migrated to various parts of the Chinese domain. From the seventh to the ninth century, there were seven large centres; before the sixteenth century, the number grew to twenty-five.

TABLE 58

PERIODICAL AND PROVINCIAL DISTRIBUTIONS OF THE LIUS

Provinces		Periods				
		D	E	F	G	H
I	Chekiang	1	1	19	..	15
II	Chihli	41	25	36	7	28
III	Fukien	..	1	41	2	16
IV	Honan	19	22	18	6	26
V	Hunan	..	1	3	3	7
VI	Hupeh	1	1	2	..	11
VII	Kansu	1	..	..	1	0
VIII	Kiangsi	1	1	21	9	82
IX	Kiangsu	125	20	10	..	18
X	Kwangsi	..	..	..	..	0
XI	Kwangtung	..	..	1	..	5
XII	Kweichow	..	..	..	..	9
XIII	Nganhui	..	1	5	4	11
XIV	Shansi	5	2	9	1	13
XV	Shantung	16	8	7	7	38
XVI	Shensi	3	5	8	2	14
XVII	Szechuan	..	..	6	2	11
XVIII	Yunnan	..	..	..	..	1
Unknown		15	80	24	5	25

VIII. Wang

(a) *Origin*

Account 1:

"The Empress Hsiao-Yüan was the aunt of Wang Mang (the noted usurper between the two Han dynasties, 22 A.D.–25 A.D.) who claimed his direct descendancy from Huangti, the Yellow Emperor, and the Emperor Shun. . . ." (*Biography of Empress Hsiao-Yüan, Ch'ien Han Shu*, quoted, book 253, page 1.)

Account 2:

"Chou Ling-Wang's (571 B.C.–542 B.C.) son, Chin, was the founder of the Wangs of T'ai-yüan (Shensi). Several generations from Chin, Wang Chien was noted as the general in Ch'in. During the disaster of the Yüng-Chia era (307–313 A.D.) a branch remained in T'ai-yüan, and did not follow the general trend of migration going south. . . ." (*Tomb Inscription of Honorary Wang . . . of Shenchou*, by Ch'en Tzŭ-ang, quoted, book 253, page 1.)

Account 3:

"The origin of Wang was by no means monogenetic. There was the Wang that was derived from Chi of the Chou dynasty; there was the Wang that was derived from Wei; there was the Wang that was derived from Tzu; and there was the Wang that was of foreign origin. . . . There were again four different sources of the foreign Wangs: (1) derived from K'o-p'in (one of the 99 Toba tribes) found in Honan (now Honan and Shantung); (2) derived from Kan-er, found in Fêng-i (Shensi); (3) from Korea, found in Yün-Chou (Chihli); (4) from A-pu-Ssǔ (Nü-Chên), found in Ngantung (Chihli). . . ." (*Chêng Ch'iao*, quoted, book 253, page 3.)

Account 4:

". . . Wang's ancestry belongs to the Nüchên tribe. . . . His home was now in Po-Yang (Shantung). . . ." (*Tomb inscription of Wang. . . . Collected Essays of Huang Hsüeh-shih*, quoted, book 253, page 3.)

Conclusion: Wang is absolutely the commonest surname in China, and this according to Chêng Ch'iao is mainly due to its heterogeneous origin. Taking the foreign origin alone, there are at least three distinct types: the Koreans, the Tungus, and the Nüchên.

(b) *Centres and Migrations*

Account 1:

"Having incurred the displeasure of his father, Emperor Chou Ling-Wang (cf. a, 2), Chin, once the heir-apparent, was disinherited and degraded to the rank of commoner. People thence called his family 'Wang-Chia' (king's relative), and ever since they have taken 'Wang' as their surname. This line had been prominent in the state of Wei (Shansi and Honan) for some time (403 B.C.–225 B.C.). To escape the consequence of civil war in the latter part of Ch'in (210 B.C.–204 B.C.), one branch migrated to Lang-ya (Shantung). This branch has been very eminent up to the present dynasty (T'ang). Another branch at the same time migrated to T'ai-yüan (Shansi): this line branched off further during the time between Han and T'ang (266–216 A.D.) into the (1) Wangs of Wan-nien (Shensi); (2) Wangs of Chung Shan who were found in Wu-wei and Ku-tsang (Kansu), then in Lo-ling (Shantung); (3) Wangs of Hua-yin (Shensi). The Wangs of Chin-chao (Shensi) were descendants of one of the younger sons of Wen-wang; this line was originally located in Shantung; it moved to Shensi by a decree of Han

Hsüan-ti (73–49 B.C.). The Wangs of Wen-hsien (Honan) branched off from the main stem in T'ai-yüan in the Chin dynasty (205–420 A.D.)." (*Genealogy of the State Councilors of the T'ang dynasty, History of T'ang*, quoted, book 253, page 2.)

Account 2:

"In the fifth year of the Chia Yu era (1060 A.D.) Wang Yüng-hsien, a man of literary fame in Hsiang-tung (Honan), showed me the genealogical record and asked me to write a preface for him. He remarked that his family was directly descended from the Lang-ya stem, a branch of which prospered in Chên-ting for some time; then it spread all over the region south of the Yangtze. . . . " (A preface to the *Genealogical Record of the Wangs of Yü-ch'i in Heng-yang (Hunan)*, by Ou-yang Hsiu, quoted, book 280, page 1.)

Account 3:

". . . The Wangs of Chin Hua (Chekiang) all branched off from the main stem in Feng-ling (Kansu). . . ." (*Monumentary Inscription about the Virtuous Family, Wang of P'u-yang, Shench'i*, by Sung Lien, quoted, book 280.)

Account 4:

"The ancestral line of Wang is traceable back to the Chin heir-apparent, the son of Chou Ling-Wang. In the Chin dynasty (265–420 A.D.) there were 21 eminent branches. The records were revised in the T'ang dynasty, and three preëminent branches were mentioned. The Wangs of Min (Fukien) were founded by Wang Shen-tzu, who declared himself the king of Min in 909 A.D., and started the line of Wang in this province at that time. Among his descendants, one branch was known in Hsing-hua (Fukien). Sixteen generations from the first settler in Hsing-hua, one of the members migrated to Hai-yang (Ch'ao-chou, Kwangtung) in the Chin-yen era (1276–1278 A.D.) as a consequence of civil war." (Preface to the *Genealogical Record of the Wangs of Cheng-hai, Nan Wan*, by Lo Heng-hsin, quoted, book 200.)

Conclusion: The Wangs were originally found in Honan and Shansi, first branched off in the third century B.C., crossed the Yangtze about the fourth century A.D., came to Fukien in the tenth century, and migrated to Kwangtung in the thirteenth century.

TABLE 59

PERIODICAL AND PROVINCIAL DISTRIBUTION OF THE WANGS

Provinces	Periods				
	D	E	F	G	H
I Chekiang.........	2	3	38	3	45
II Chihli...........	24	26	55	15	50
III Fukien..........	3	31	32	5	20
IV Honan..........	9	33	51	..	52
V Hunan..........	2	1	5	..	11
VI Hupeh..........	1	6	4	..	38
VII Kansu..........	5	0	..	..	..
VIII Kiangsi..........	..	5	26	..	29
IX Kiangsu.........	21	16	12	..	70
X Kwangsi.........	1	..	..	..	2
XI Kwangtung.......	..	..	9	..	9
XII Kweichow........	..	..	..	..	8
XIII Nganhui.........	1	7	12	..	36
XIV Shansi...........	70	40	28	5	25
XV Shantung........	195	19	31	18	96
XVI Shensi...........	31	21	11	6	33
XVII Szechuan........	6	69	12	..	6
XVIII Yunnan..........	..	..	..	..	3
Unknown...............	50	94	63	9	58

IX. WU

(a) *Origin*

Account 1:

"Wu is the ancient name of modern Suchou city (Kiangsu). T'ai-pei and Chung-yung were both the sons of T'ai-wang of Chou, and elder brothers of Chi-li. When Chi-li had born the saintly son, Ch'ang (the founder of the Chou dynasty), T'ai-wang wanted to make the youngest son (Chi-li) the heir-apparent so that Ch'ang could carry on the reign.

"The two elder sons, having discerned the intention of their father, escaped to Wu (Suchou), which was at that time occupied by Chin-man, a southern barbarian, so that the secret wish of their august father might be fulfilled without embarrassment. . . . Later on their descendants founded a state among the barbarians and called it 'Wu.' This was confirmed by the royal house of the Chou dynasty. . . . After Wu was conquered by Yüeh, in 448 B.C., the descendants thereafter took 'Wu' as their surname. . . ." (*Chêng Ch'iao*, quoted, book 77, page 1.)

Account 2:

"Wu Shen's ancestors were Nüchens (the Tungus tribe which occupied North China between 1115 and 1235 A.D.). His surname was derived from the original form, Wu-ku-lun. Their original home was in Lin-t'iao. The great grandfather of Wu Shen was an officer of the Kins (the Nüchen dynasty referred to above) at T'en-yang; ever since his time, his descendants made their home at T'en (Yen-chou-fu, Shantung)." (*History of the District T'en*, quoted, book 77, pages 1, 2.)

Conclusion: Wu is of dual origin. The main stem is traceable back to the Yellow Emperor; the exotic element of the Nüchen began to appear in the eleventh century A.D. The origin of the main stem, unlike the others, was located in the Yangtze Valley.

(b) *Centres and Migrations*

Account 1:

"The main centres of Wu were Yen-lin (Kiangsu); Po-hai (Chihli); and Po-yang (Shantung)." (*Liao Yung-hsien*, quoted, book 77, leaf 1.)

Account 2:

"The first appearance of Wu in Szechuan was in the T'ang dynasty, beginning with a military officer whose great grandson served Ch'ien-shu (901–926 A.D.)." (*History of Szechuan*, quoted, book 77, page 1.)

Account 3:

". . . In the Ming dynasty there were many centres of Wu . . .; those of Lü-ling (Kiangsi), Chin-chao (Honan), and Yü-chang were especially eminent. . . ."(Preface to the *Genealogy of the Wus of T'ai-Yüan*, by Wang Tao-Kun, quoted, book 82, page 20.)

Conclusion: The accounts do not give enough information for a reconstruction of the migratory route of the family of Wu. But there is one feature which needs to be especially noticed: the date at which the Wus began to appear in Szechuan (cf. Chang). Detailed information about their migration has to be deduced from the next section.

TABLE 60

PERIODICAL AND PROVINCIAL DISTRIBUTION OF WUS

Provinces	Periods					
	C	D	E	F	G	H
I Chekiang	3	4	5	13	2	26
II Chihli	..	..	8	1	4	5
III Fukien	..	..	1	44	5	49
IV Honan	5	..	5	4	1	7
V Hunan	..	..	1	3	..	4
VI Hupeh	..	..	..	5	1	33
VII Kansu	..	..	..	..	..	0
VIII Kiangsi	17	1	4	4	9	31
IX Kiangsu	1	..	4	6	2	52
X Kwangsi	..	..	..	..	..	1
XI Kwangtung	..	..	..	6	1	6
XII Kweichow	..	..	..	..	..	4
XIII Nganhui	..	..	..	12	..	31
XIV Shansi	..	1	..	8	1	8
XV Shantung	3	5	..	1	1	22
XVI Shensi	..	..	1	4	..	5
XVII Szechuan	..	..	..	2	..	0
XVIII Yunnan	..	..	..	..	..	5
Unknown	11	7	5	21	3	4

X. YANG

(a) *Origin*

Account 1:

"There were six Yangs: (1) the descendants of T'ang Shu-yü; (2) the descendants of the son of Chou Hsüan-wang (827–783 B.C.); (3) the descendants of Chou Ching-Wang (543–521 B.C.); (4) the descendants of a branch of the house of Chin; (5) the descendants of Yang Tu; (6) the descendants of Mo-hu-lu, who substituted the surname Yang for their original tribal name. . . ." (Revised edition of *Wen-hsien-t'ung-k'ao*, by Wang Ch'i, quoted, book 225, page 1.)

Conclusion: Two major divisions exist, among the Yangs. The main stem was from the royal house of Chou; the other came in with the Tobas.

(b) *Centres and Migrations*

Account 1:

". . . When the territory of Yang-shê-shih was appropriated, the descendants of Shu-hsiang escaped to Hua Shan and made their home at Hua-ying (Shensi). One of them, Yang Chang, had three sons: Pao, Long, and K'uan. Pao later became a military officer of Han and founded a line in Ho-nei (Honan); Long who served the state of Ch'in founded the Feng-i line (Shensi); K'uan also served the state of Ch'in, and his descendants later on centered in Fu-feng (Shensi), Ho-chung (Shansi), and Yüan-wu (Honan)."

Conclusion: The later migration of the Yangs is unascertainable. The early migrations, like most of the others, are limited to those provinces north of the Yangtze River.

TABLE 61

PERIODICAL AND PROVINCIAL DISTRIBUTIONS OF YANGS

Provinces	Periods					
	C	D	E	F	G	H
I Chekiang	..	..	1	14	..	24
II Chihli	..	6	3	8	4	12
III Fukien	..	..	2	9	..	15
IV Honan	5	..	13	11	2	14
V Hunan	..	..	..	2	1	9
VI Hupeh	1	..	..	3	0	12
VII Kansu	2	9	1	1	2	1
VIII Kiangsi	..	1	2	7	2	10
IX Kiangsu	3	1	2	21	2	21
X Kwangsi	..	..	..	..	..	0
XI Kwangtung	..	2	1	..	..	1
XII Kweichow	..	..	..	..	..	12
XIII Nganhui	..	..	1	2	2	12
XIV Shansi	1	2	1	15	6	20
XV Shantung	0	..	4	14	5	14
XVI Shensi	11	59	30	4	4	17
XVII Szechuan	9	2	2	26	..	13
XVIII Yunnan	..	..	..	0	1	9
Unknown	13	69	39	31	6	14

TABLE 62

A Summary of the Documentary Accounts Showing the Origins of the Ten Surnames

Surname	Founder: real or fictitious	Period of the 1st appearance	Founder's group
Chang 1	the 5th son of Shao-hao	A period	D. Y. E. (Descendants of the Yellow Emperor)
Chang 2	Chieh-chang	B period	D. Y. E.
Chang 3	?	D period	Ch'alo (Tungus)
Ch'en 1	Emperor Shun	A period	D. Y. E.
Ch'en 2	Pai	D period	?
Ch'en 3	Liu	C period	D. Y. E.
Ch'en 4	Hou-mo-ch'en	D period	Tungus
Chu 1	the 5th son of Lu Chung	A period	D. Y. E.
Chu 2	Ko-chu-hun	D period	Tungus
Chu 3	K'o-chu-hun	D period	Tungus
Hu 1	State Hu	B period	D. Y. E.
Hu 2	He-ku	D period	Tungus
Kuo		B period	D. Y. E.
Li 1	Chuan-yü	A period	D. Y. E.
Li 2		?	Khitan
Li 3	Nan-t'o-sun-p'o-lo	E period	Ngansi
Li 4		?	Korean
Li 5	Chi-ah-tieh	?	
Li 6	Chu-hsieh	E period	Shato
Liu 1	Shih-hui	B period	D. Y. E.
Liu 2	Yao	A period	D. Y. E.
Liu 3	Wang Chi	A period	D. Y. E.
Liu 4	?	C period	Hiungnu
Liu 5	Lou	C period	?
Wu 1	T'ai-pei	B period	D. Y. E.
Wu 2	Wu-ku-lun	F period	Nüchen
Wang 1	Chou dynasty	B period	D. Y. E.
Wang 2	Emperor Shun	B period	D. Y. E.
Wang 3	Tzu	B period	D. Y. E.
Wang 4	K'o-pin	D period	Tungus
Wang 5	Kan-er	D period	?
Wang 6	Korean		Korean
Wang 7	A-pu-ssu	F period	Nüchen
Wang 8		F period	Nüchen
Yang 1	Shu-yü	B period	D. Y. E.
Yang 2	Chou Hsüan-wang	B period	D. Y. E.
Yang 3	Chou Ching-wang	B period	D. Y. E.
Yang 4	Mo-hu-lu	D period	Tungus

The summary table shows clearly the diversity of the origins of the ten surnames. The formative period of the surnames as an institution is decidedly B. All the surnames which originated in this period, with one exception, are in one way or another related to the Yellow Emperor. The State of Ch'u is presumably also related to the Yellow Emperor, but was considered as Southern Barbarian at that time, and is according to some sinologue's contention, the ancestor of the Shan. Later on we shall see that they form a really important element in the formation of the earliest stratum of the Chinese population. The Hsiung-nu infiltrated in period C; the Tungus in period D; the Turks in period E; the Nüchêns in period F. The date for the beginning of the Korean infiltration cannot be stated with certainty. Classified ethnographically, we may reduce the five main sources to three. The Turks have been identified on some grounds with the Hsiung-nu; the Nüchen and Khitans are definitely Tungus. The three major fountain sources of these surnames are therefore the Yellow Emperor, the Hiung-nu (Turk), and the Tungus. This of course leaves the Korean out of consideration, although their influence, it must be stated, is by no means negligible. It may be asked why there is a remarkable absence of Mongol sources, as the Mongols gave a dynasty to China. The answer will be seen later on. But a curious instance may be mentioned here. The biographical sketches attached to the surname Kuo give the description of a man in Yüan known as Kuo-Yung; he is said to be a Mongol. This example serves to show that there were Mongols who had adopted Chinese surnames even in the Mongol Dynasty. Our data furnish scanty information in this respect. But it must be remembered that only ten surnames have been studied. These ten, while typical of the nature of the surnames as a whole, by no means cover the whole field. It is very probable that the Mongols have adopted a different set of Chinese surnames. In the annals of the history of the Ming dynasty, in the third year of the Hung-wu era (1370 A.D.), an ordinance issued by the emperor has been fully recorded. It explicitly ordered all the Mongols to retain their original tribal names; the reason being that many Mongols, after the change of dynasty, desiring intensely to become assimilated, adopted Chinese surnames; but the emperor (T'ai-Tsu—1368 A.D.–1398 A.D.) wanted to see them as they were; hence this ordinance. To what extent this ordinance was effective cannot be ascertained, but it proves that there were a large number of Mongols who remained in China proper after the downfall of the Mongol dynasty. We have no other evidence to show that they were not assimi-

lated later on. The presence of the Mongol element in the We-group
by the end of the Ming dynasty (1644 A.D.) is therefore only a question
of degree.

A diagram showing the evolution of the We-group may be constructed
on the basis of the above study. But the relation of the southern aboriginals to the We-group is not definitely indicated by these data; this
will be studied further on.

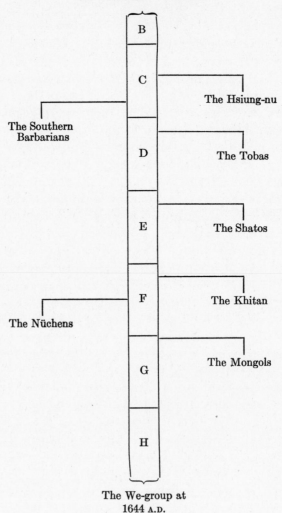

Descendants of the Yellow Emperor
The Earliest We-Group

The Hsiung-nu

The Southern
Barbarians

The Tobas

The Shatos

The Khitan

The Nüchens

The Mongols

The We-group at
1644 A.D.

TABLE 63

Showing the Recorded Movements of the Main Stems of the Ten Surnames According to the above Documentary Accounts

Periods	Surnames									
	Chang	Ch'en	Chu	Hu	Kuo	Li	Liu	Wu	Wang	Yang
A	....	....	....	....	....	....	....	In Kiangsu	In Honan, Shansi	....
B	....	....	Intra-provincial movements in Honan	....	From Shansi to Shensi, Shantung	From Honan to Kansu, Chihli	From Shensi, Kansu to Honan, Kiangsu	....	To Shantung, Shensi	From Honan, Shansi to Shensi, Kansu
C	From Shensi, Shansi to Honan, Szechuan	....	From Honan to Kiangsu	....	....	From Kansu to Shansi, Chihli		....	From Shansi to Shensi; from Shensi to Kansu	
D	(1) Cross the Yangtze; (2) to Kwangtung	From Honan to Kiangsu	....	....	To Nganhui	....	....	....	From Shantung to Kiangsu, Hunan	....
E	From Kwangtung to Szechuan	From Honan to Nganhui	From Kiangsu to Nganhui	....	....	....	....	To Szechuan	To Fukien	....
F	....	From Honan, Nganhui to Fukien	From Nganhui to Fukien	....	....	....	....	....	From Fukien to Kwangtung	....
G	....	....								
H	....	....	....	From Nganhui to Shantung						

The above summary shows only the recorded movements of these ten families. There are undoubtedly many missing links. If we analyze it period by period, we may get a general idea of the trend of migration. Beginning with period B, the movements are of a fluttering type; they are eastward to Shantung and Chihli and westward to Shensi and Kansu from Honan and Shansi. The only exception is the family of Liu, which takes a southeastward direction. But this occurred only in the very late part of period B. In period C, the major movement is in a southward direction; this itself may be divided into two branches: (a) to Szechuan, (b) to Kiangsu; the fluttering type still lingers in this period. The movement in period D assumes altogether a different form. It belongs to a dashing type. The general aim is to cross the eastern part of the Yangtze River. The frontier line already reaches as far south as Kwangtung. The movement as a whole is perhaps the most important in Chinese history. It continued toward the period E with no less intensity. But in the E period there also appeared a new element: that is, inter-provincial movement south of the Yangtze River. This inter-provincial movement south of the Yangtze becomes even more pronounced in the F period. Although in the record we have no evidence to show that the movement in period F is as important as that in period D, actually it is so. To realize this, it is only necessary to refer back to Chen b, account 2, once more. Our knowledge about the movement of the We-group in G and H is practically nil, according to the table. But there is no reason for us to conclude that the population in this period was static, as we shall see later. To study the movement more in detail, let us turn our attention back to the distribution table.

It will be observed that the period distribution given in the previous table does not go much beyond the C period. This limitation is set up by the nature of the data. But in the early period, we have more information from the documentary accounts, which become insufficient concerning the last two periods. The dynamic aspect of the distribution table, which gives full accounts of the G and H periods, is therefore exactly supplementary to the documentary accounts. The following 62 maps are constructed on the distributional data. The rules of construction are:

(1) For each surname in each period, the five provinces are mapped out that give birth to the greatest number of men of that surname on record. The mapping does not go beyond period D. There are thus five periodical maps for each surname, and thus fifty maps are constructed. The five are chosen on an empirical basis. (Maps 14–63.)

(2) The first five provinces of each period are compared with those of the succeeding period. A summary map showing the probable migratory direction for each surname is constructed on the basis of the results of these comparisons. The assumptions here are: (a) The centres of settlement of a certain surname produce more men of prominence of that surname than places which are not its centres; (b) While the fact that the absence of men of prominence in any region does not necessarily indicate that there are no settlements of that particular surname, it is not likely that this settlement can be compared in importance with those places where a large number of men of prominence of that particular surname are recorded; (c) So it is to be inferred that the shifting of centres of men of prominence of any surname is correlated with the shifting of the centres of settlement of that particular surname; (d) By a study of the change of centres of the men of prominence of any surname from one period to its succeeding period, the direction of the interperiod movement of any group of a particular surname is determined. It is hardly necessary to say that these four assumptions cannot be easily proved, nevertheless, hardly any practical argument seems to exist against them. We should like to discover more solid ground, if the data are capable of offering it. But at present this seems to be the only basis that we can find. Maps 64–73 showing the migratory routes of the ten groups are thus constructed. It may be worth while to go into detail with one of these groups. The Chang group may be taken for illustration; the first five provinces of each period that produced the greatest number of Changs of prominence are (cf. Maps 14–18):

D	E	F	G	H
Chihli	Chihli	Chihli	Chekiang	Chekiang
Kansu	Honan	Honan	Chihli	Chihli
Kiangsu	Kiangsu	Kiangsu	Honan	Kiangsu
Shansi	Shansi	Nganhui	Kiangsi	Shansi
Shensi	Shantung	Shantung	Shantung	Shantung

Table 64 (page 162) shows the disappearance, persistence, and appearance of provinces among the first five when compared interperiodically.

Considered together with the geographical contiguity of the different provinces, the above table suggests the following probable movements: (1) from Kansu and Shensi to Honan and Shantung in the D and E periods; (2) from Shansi to Nganhui by way of Honan in the E and F periods; (3) from Kiangsu and Nganhui to Chekiang and Kiangsi in the F and G periods, and (4) from Honan and Kiangsi to Shansi and Kiangsu in the G and H periods.

A further interpretation is necessary. The actual number of the men of prominence for each province in different periods must be compared with each other. In other words, the fluctuation of this number in the successive periods in any province, if we push our logic here consistently, must also serve as an index of the migration. This will be true whether the province disappears or persists among the first five. For, if the number of the men of prominence should fluctuate, it must, on the assumption that has been advocated here, be considered as a sign of give and take in itself, despite the fact of disappearance, persistence, or appearance of the said province among the first five.

TABLE 64

	Provinces that disappeared	Provinces that persisted	Provinces that appeared
From D to E.....	Kansu Shensi	Chihli Kiangsu Shansi	Honan Shantung
From E to F.....	Shansi	Chihli Kiangsu Honan Shantung	Nganhui
From F to G.....	Kiangsu Nganhui	Chihli Honan Shantung	Chekiang Kiangsi
From G to H.....	Honan Kiangsi	Chekiang Chihli Shantung	Kiangsu Shansi

Hence Chihli has persisted among the first five ranking provinces as far as its rank goes: but the actual numbers in the successive periods are: 78 (D), 53 (E), 37 (F), 22 (G), and 54 (H). This shows, according to the above assumption, that Chihli has been giving off to the neighboring provinces in D–E, E–F, and F–G. And it has been taking in from the neighboring provinces in period G–H, although its relative rank in the succeeding period does not seem to show it. On this basis, the exact direction of the movements of any of the ten groups may be determined, while the inter-period comparison of the centres as a whole serves to indicate the *general direction* of the movement.

The following table shows the inter-period fluctuations of all the provinces that have been ranked among the first five regarding the production of prominent Changs. The comparisons are on a percentage basis. (Cf. p. 135.)

TABLE 65

Provinces	Inter-periods			
	D–E	E–F	F–G	G–H
Chekiang	+	+	+	−
Chihli	−	−.	+	−
Honan	+	+	−	+
Kansu	−	+	+	−
Kiangsi	+	+	+	−
Kiangsu	−	−	−	+
Nganhui	+	+	+	−
Shansi	+	−	−	+
Shantung	+	+	+	−
Shensi	+	−	−	+

So while both Chihli and Shantung are among the first five ranking provinces in E and F, we may nevertheless infer from the above table that there is a movement from Chihli to Shantung, as shown by their opposite directions in this period. The synthetic maps of the migrations of all the surnames are constructed on this basis. (Maps 64–73.)

Before we can introduce the final synthetic map, however, we must explain the principles of grouping that are to be utilized all through. The principles are these:

(1) Other things being equal, any inter-provincial movement of population, when it occurs, occurs only between neighboring provinces.

(2) So when two provinces, A and B, which are neighbors, show opposite fluctuation in their numbers or rank; and a third province, C, which is separated from these provinces by others, also shows fluctuation, the movement to be inferred from these fluctuations is between A and B, not A and C, or B and C.

A concrete case will suffice to illustrate these principles. The "Changs" in the D and E period decrease in: Kansu, Chihli, and Kiangsu; and increase in: Shensi, Shansi, Honan, Shantung, Nganhui, Chekiang, and Kiangsi. The direction of the movement to be inferred in this case is from Kansu to Shensi; from Chihli to Shansi, Honan, and Shantung; and from Kiangsu to Nganhui, Chekiang, possibly also to Shantung and Honan. This leaves out only Kiangsi, whose source of increase may be traced back to Kiangsu — then to Nganhui and Chekiang. All the arrow-points of maps 64–73 are so determined.

(3) If, instead of considering the movements of the ten surnames as ten separate groups, we combine them into a united whole to show the trend of the movement of the We-group as represented by these ten surnames on the plan explained above, we find the data combined in the following tables and may construct maps 74–77.

TABLE 66

Provinces	Periods				
	D	E	F	G	H
I Chekiang	15	21	152	32	239
II Chihli	234	197	190	82	232
III Fukien	4	54	277	27	294
IV Honan	47	132	188	27	294
V Hunan	3	19	31	4	81
VI Hupeh	18	18	33	4	228
VII Kansu	57	29	5	7	5
VIII Kiangsi	19	18	148	40	299
IX Kiangsu	265	83	96	18	302
X Kwangsi	1	..	5	1	6
XI Kwangtung	2	11	38	10	99
XII Kweichow	..	..	..	..	54
XIII Nganhui	9	34	84	14	195
XIV Shansi	120	75	123	29	181
XV Shantung	223	60	105	55	302
XVI Shensi	130	110	49	23	165
XVII Szechuan	35	107	93	4	59
XVIII Yunnan	..	1	..	3	37

TABLE 67

REDUCED TO PERCENTAGES

Provinces	Periods and Interperiods								
	D	E	F	G	H	D–E	E–F	F–G	G–H
I Chekiang	1.27	2.17	9.40	8.42	7.96	+	+	−	−
II Chihli	19.79	20.33	11.75	21.58	7.72	+	−	+	−
III Fukien	.33	5.57	17.13	7.11	9.79	+	+	−	+
IV Honan	3.97	13.62	11.63	7.11	7.49	+	−	−	+
V Hunan	.25	1.96	1.92	1.05	2.70	+	−	−	+
VI Hupeh	1.52	1.86	2.04	1.05	7.59	+	+	−	+
VII Kansu	4.82	2.99	.31	1.84	.16	−	−	+	−
VIII Kiangsi	1.61	1.86	9.15	10.51	9.95	+	+	+	−
IX Kiangsu	22.42	8.56	5.94	4.74	10.05	−	−	−	+
X Kwangsi	.08	...	.31	.26	.20	−	+	−	−
XI Kwangtung	.17	1.13	2.35	2.63	3.30	+	+	+	+
XII Kweichow	...	...	...	...	1.80	−	−	−	+
XIII Nganhui	.76	3.51	5.19	3.68	6.49	+	+	−	+
XIV Shansi	10.15	7.74	7.61	7.63	6.03	−	−	+	−
XV Shantung	18.87	6.19	6.49	14.47	10.06	−	+	+	−
XVI Shensi	11.00	11.35	3.09	6.05	5.49	+	−	+	−
XVII Szechuan	2.96	11.04	5.75	1.05	1.96	+	−	−	+
XVIII Yunnan	...	.10	...	.79	1.23	+	−	+	+

(4) Finally the movement between two neighboring provinces at any particular period may be in one direction only or in both. Map 78, based on Maps 64–73, shows the general inter-provincial relationship regarding the movement of the We-group among the various provinces.

A FINAL STUDY OF THE GENERAL DIRECTION OF THE MOVEMENT

The last five maps may be taken up first for this purpose. In the D–E inter-period, at the outset it is a centripetal movement from three directions (Map 74); but Map 78 shows that the southern provinces are of no great importance in any period, so it may be concluded that D–E represents a southward, southeastward, and southwestward movement. The E–F inter-period (Map 75) shows a distinct southeastward direction; there is no question here. The F–G movement (Map 76) cuts both north and south. Finally, G–H shows a southwestward movement from two directions (Map 77). Combined with the summary of the documentary accounts, this final summary of the movements of the We-group as a whole may be reached:

Periods	Direction of Movement
A	(?)
A–B	(?)
B	Fluttering north of the Yangtze; beginning of S. E. movement.
B–C	Fluttering.
C	Southward movement in E; southward movement in W.
C–D	(?)
D	Southeastward movement.
D–E	Southward; southeastward; southwestward.
E	Southward; southeastward; southwestward; fluttering south of the Yangtze.
E–F	Southeastward movement dominant.
F	Southeastward movement.
F–G	Southward; northward.
G	(?)
G–H	Southwestward.
H	(?)

The above summary shows the following features: (a) The movement before period C (206 B.C.) was limited to the north of the Yangtze; (b) the southeastward movement was the dominant current up to the end of period F (1280 A.D.); (c) the southeastward currents were especially dominant in period D (265 A.D.–618 A.D.), and the E–F and F periods (906 A.D.–1280 A.D.); (d) the southwestward movement began faintly at C and became dominant only in the G–H period. Finally, it may be assumed that in A and A–B the movement began with a faint fluttering north of the Yangtze which found its full expression in the B period, while in the H period it was a continuation of the G–H type, namely, southwestward.

But it is still questionable whether the resultant direction of the movement of these ten groups can represent the general movement as a whole. I propose to apply a special test in order to ascertain the value of the above results. Since the directions of the movements are determined by relative density of distribution of the members of the ten groups, it is evident that if the relative density of the distribution of these members in any period is indicative to a reasonable degree of the general distribution, the direction thus determined for these groups will also be reliable as an index of the movement at large. But to find out the total distribution of the whole group in any period is an unnecessary task, more elaborate than can be performed within the present limits. So a partial test may be applied. Eight surnames of fairly common occurrence are chosen at random, and the distribution of the members in the H period is determined. The results compared with the ten groups that we have studied are as follows:

TABLE 68

Types of Surnames	The distribution of the Members of the ten test surnames in the H period		The distribution of the Members of the eight surnames chosen at random in the H period	
Provinces	Number	Percentage	Number	Percentage
I Chekiang	239	7.96	93	11.4
II Chihli	232	7.72	35	4.30
III Fukien	294	9.79	94	11.5
IV Honan	225	7.49	28	3.43
V Hunan	81	2.70	35	4.30
VI Hupeh	228	7.59	77	9.43
VII Kansu	5	.16	1	.12
VIII Kiangsi	299	9.95	58	7.11
IX Kiangsu	302	10.05	72	8.22
X Kwangsi	6	.20	5	.61
XI Kwangtung	99	3.30	36	4.41
XII Kweichow	54	1.80	16	1.96
XIII Nganhui	195	6.49	85	10.41
XIV Shansi	181	6.03	48	5.88
XV Shantung	302	10.06	104	12.74
XVI Shensi	165	5.49	14	1.71
XVII Szechuan	59	1.96	9	1.10
XVIII Yunnan	37	1.23	6	.73

The following table shows the rank of density of different provinces:

TABLE 69

Provinces	I	II	III	IV	V	VI	VII	VIII	IX	X
Ten Test surnames	5	6	4	8	13	7	18	3	2	17
Eight Surnames chosen at random	3	10	2	12	10.5	5	18	7	6	17

Provinces	XI	XII	XIII	XIV	XV	XVI	XVII	XVIII
Ten Test surnames	12	15	9	10	1	11	14	16
Eight Surnames chosen at random	9	13	4	8	1	14	15	16

The table shows a remarkable correspondence of the relative ranks regarding the density of distribution. It therefore proves that the movement of the ten test surnames we have studied represents quite a normal tendency and can serve faithfully as an index of the trend of the movement of the We-group as a whole in historical time.

RACIAL ASPECT OF THE DISTRIBUTION

Two features should be recalled here: (1) there are two major foreign elements which settled in China proper, the Hsiungnu-Turk and the Tungus, in different periods; (2) all those branches of the ten families which crossed the Yangtze River in different periods trace back their ancestry direct to the Yellow Emperor. Could it be proved that at the end of H (1644 A.D.) the Chinese population north of the Yangtze was a mixture of three elements, and that south of the Yangtze the population was a mixture of the Descendants of the Yellow Emperor and the indigenous population (of which more anon)? This, at least, should be the beginning of the whole question.

To answer this question, another set of data concerning the surnames may be studied. There is a group of surnames which the Chinese genealogists call the "strange surnames" — strange because they, like bastard children, know not who were their forefathers. They are strange also because they are of very unusual occurrence. These facts, added to the one that no Chinese would ever change his name without a good reason, make possible the inference that these names are of foreign origin. There are more than 1000 of these, of which 802 can be definitely located in the H period.

TABLE 70

DISTRIBUTION OF STRANGE SURNAMES IN THE H PERIOD

Provinces	No.	%	Rank	Provinces	No.	%	Rank
I Chekiang	16	2.00	16.5	X Kwangsi.....	20	3.5	15
II Chihli.......	84	10.47	2	XI Kwangtung ..	39	4.86	9
III Fukien	32	4.00	12.5	XII Kweichow....	6	.75	18
IV Honan.......	49	6.10	4.5	XIII Nganhui.....	42	5.23	7
V Hunan.......	26	3.23	14	XIV Shansi.......	94	11.72	1
VI Hupeh.......	37	4.61	10	XV Shantung	75	9.35	3
VII Kansu.......	32	4.00	12.5	XVI Shensi.......	41	5.11	8
VIII Kiangsi......	46	5.73	6	XVII Szechuan	35	4.36	11
IX Kiangsu	49	6.10	4.5	XVIII Yunnan......	16	2.00	16.5

The most significant feature of this table is that it shows quite a different type of distribution from those we have studied. All the northern provinces rank very high, and I take this as a clear indication that those strange surnames are of foreign origin; and the foreign elements (as opposed to the Descendants of the Yellow Emperor) are more dominant north of the Yangtze. The question will be made clearer by a study of the evolution of the You-group. But, before we do this, we shall study more fully the migration of the We-group in the historical period.

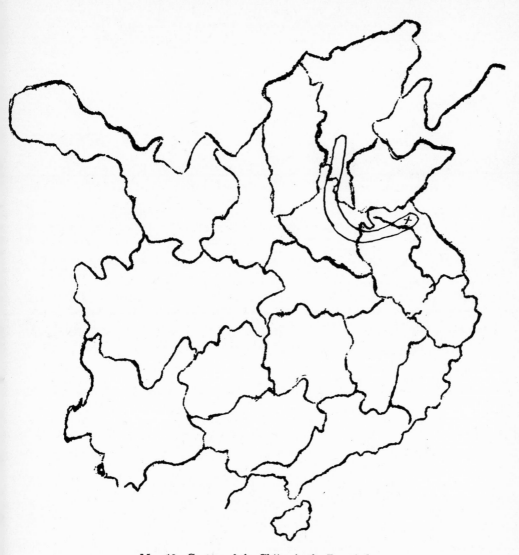

MAP 19. Centres of the Ch'êns in the D-period

169

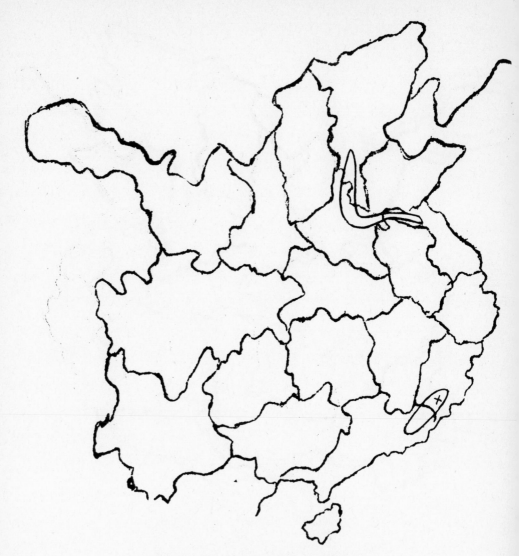

MAP 20. Centres of the Ch'êns in the E-period

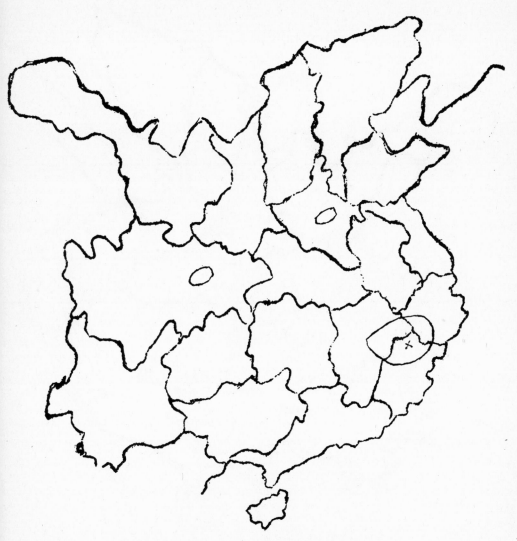

MAP 21. Centres of the Ch'êns in the F-period

171

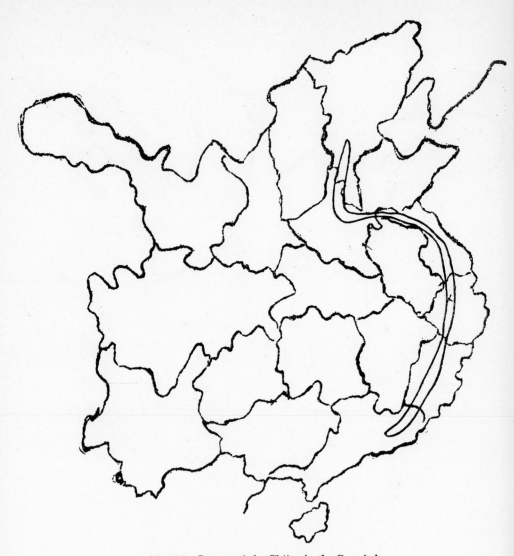

Map 22. Centres of the Ch'êns in the G-period

172

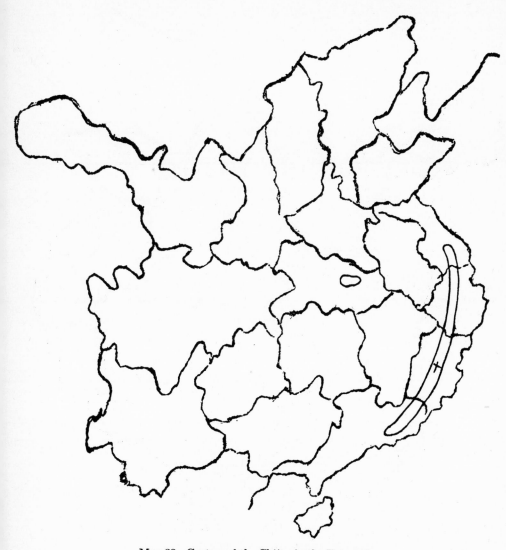

MAP 23. Centres of the Ch'êns in the H-period

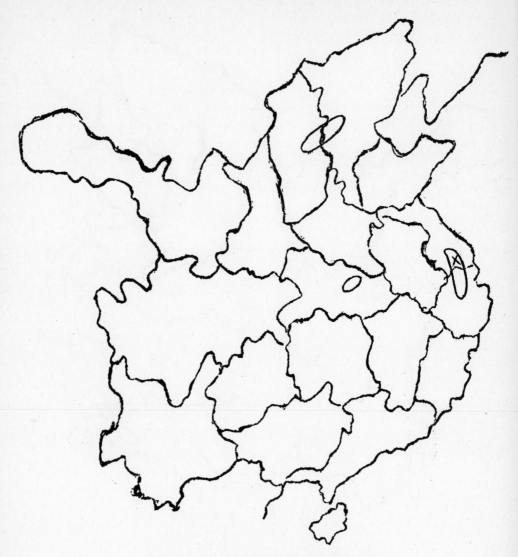

MAP 24. Centres of the Chus in the D-period

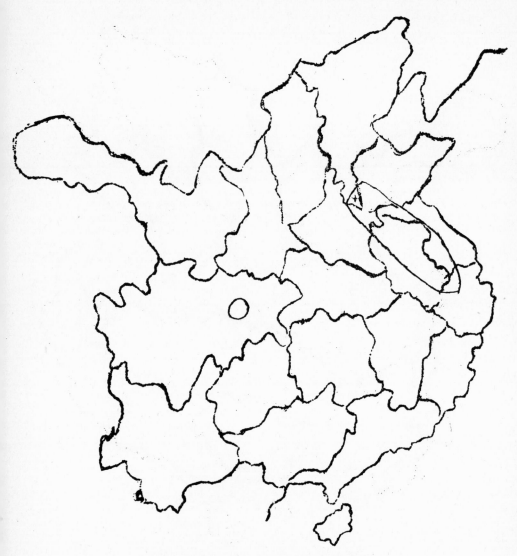

Map 25. Centres of the Chus in the E-period

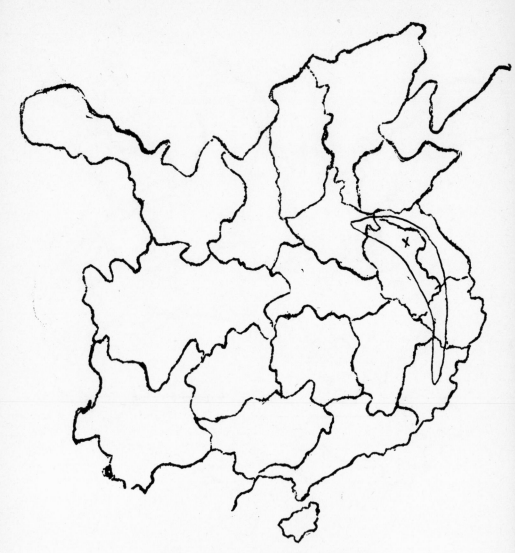

MAP 26. Centres of the Chus in the F-period

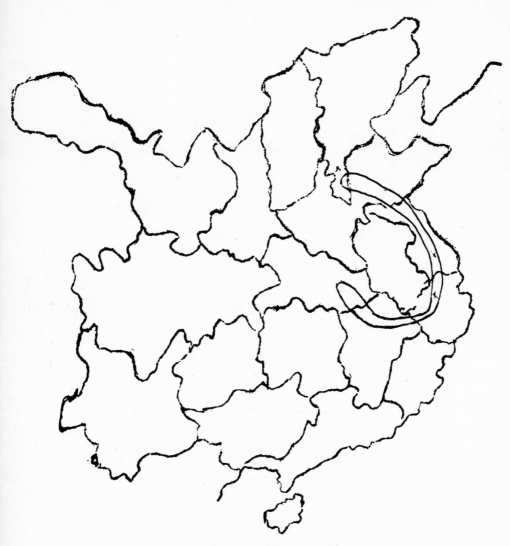

MAP 27. Centres of the Chus in the G-period

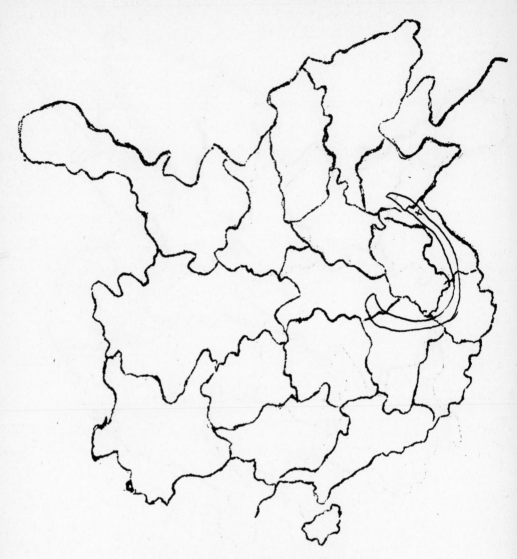

MAP 28. Centres of the Chus in the H-period.

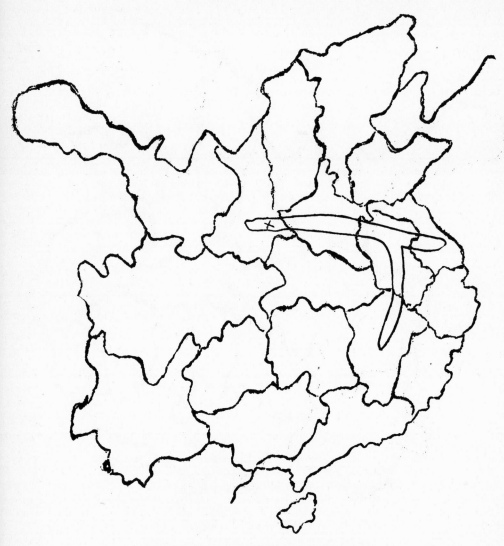

MAP 29. Centres of the Hus in the D-period.

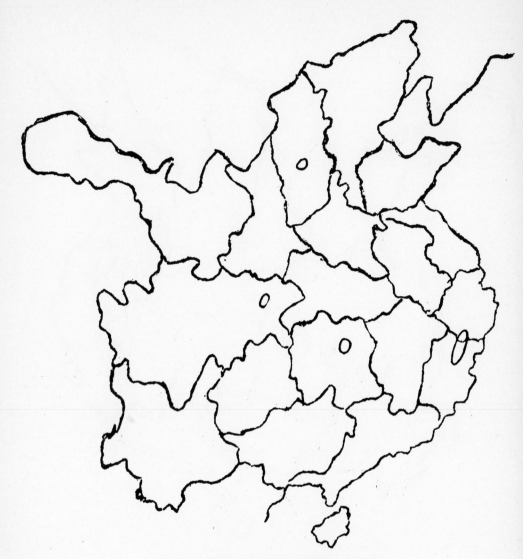

MAP 30. Centres of the Hus in the E-period

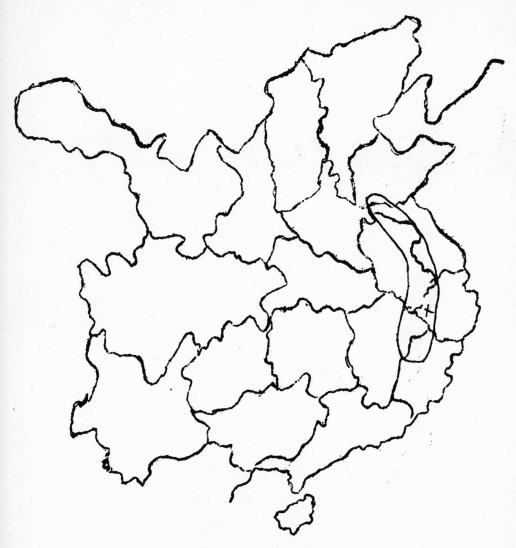

MAP 31. Centres of the Hus in the F-period

181

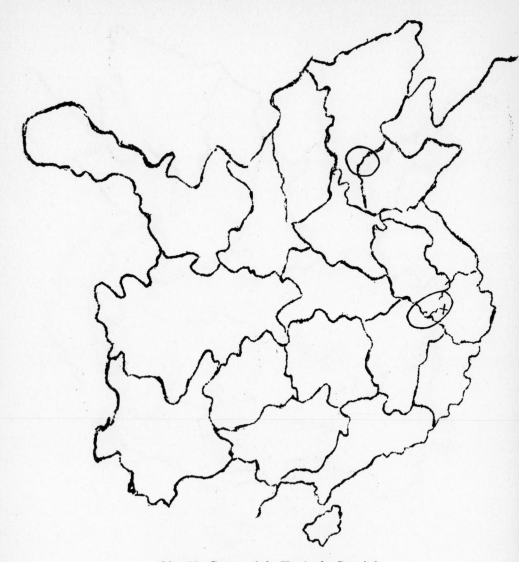

MAP 32. Centres of the Hus in the G-period

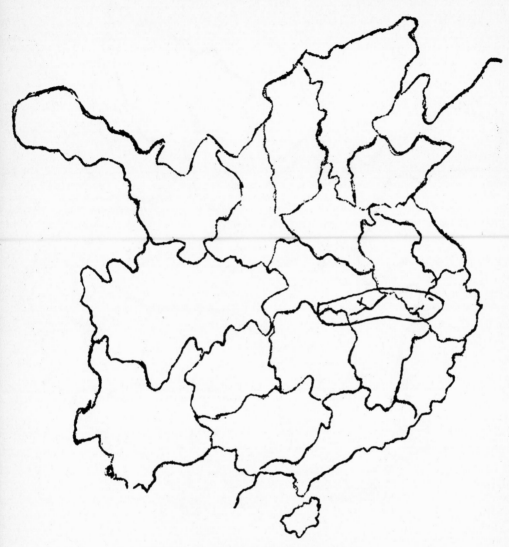

MAP 33. Centres of the Hus in the H-period

183

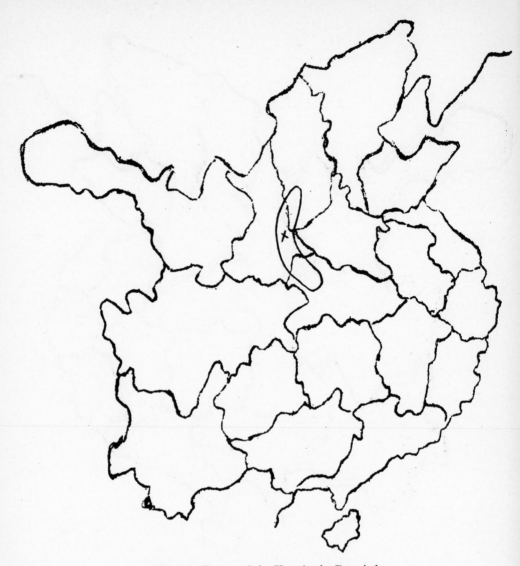

MAP 34. Centres of the Kuos in the D-period

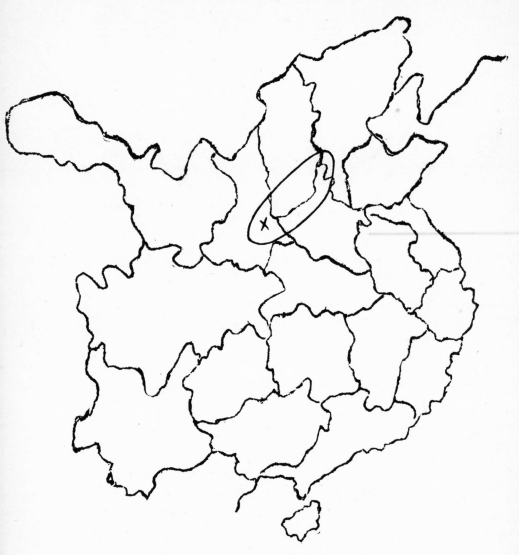

MAP 35. Centres of the Kuos in the E-period

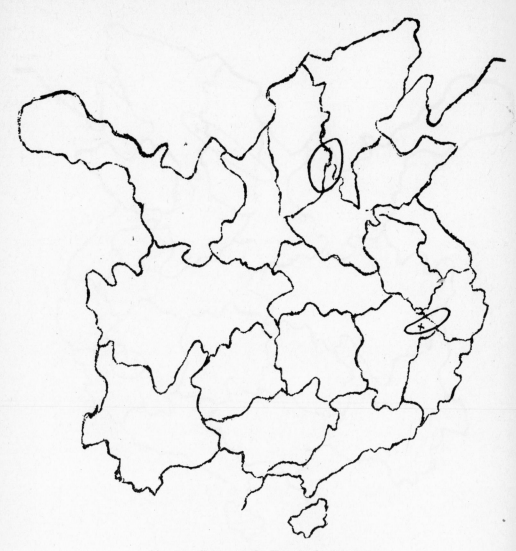

MAP 36. Centres of the Kuos in the F-period

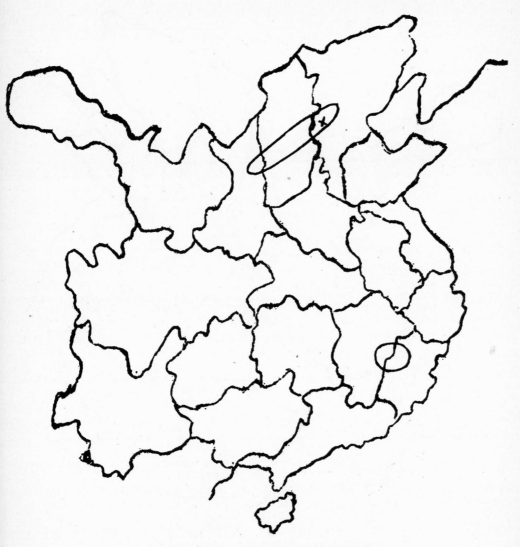

MAP 37. Centres of the Kuos in the G-period

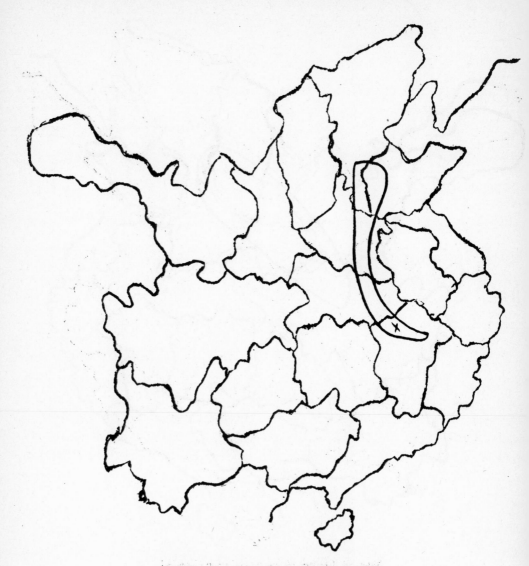

MAP 38. Centres of the Kuos in the H-period

188

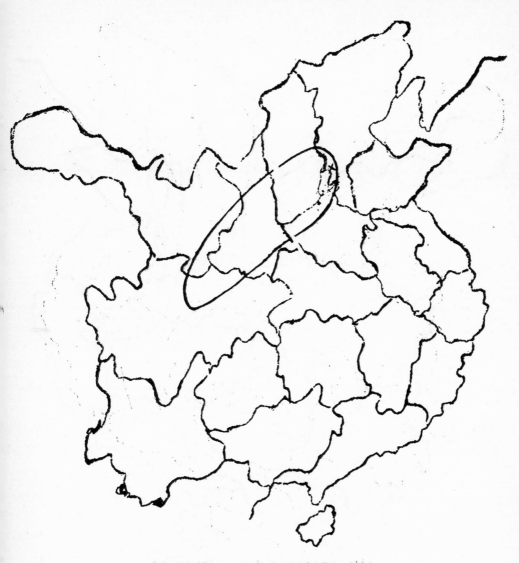

MAP 39. Centres of the Lis in the D-period

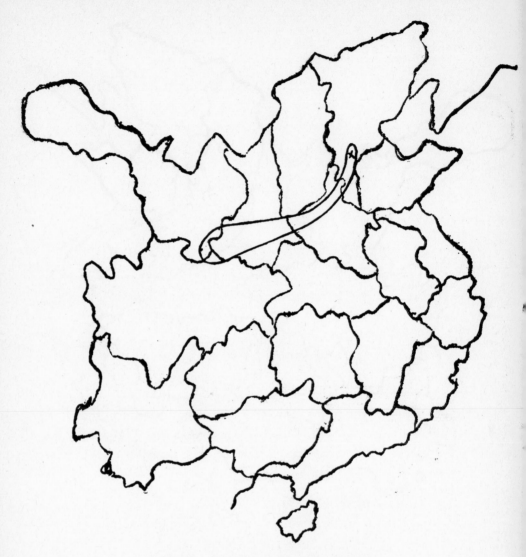

MAP 40. Centres of the Lis in the E-period

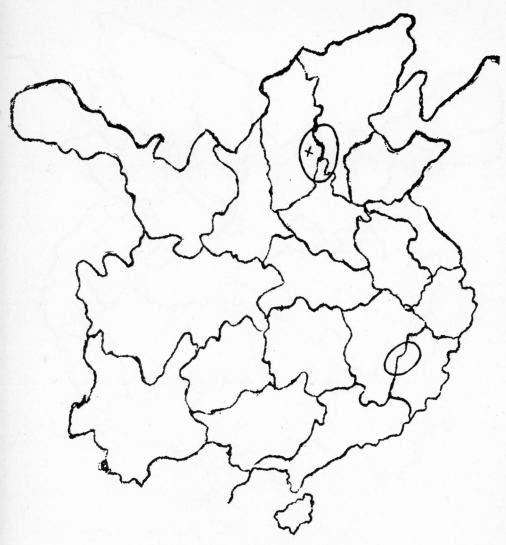

MAP 41. Centres of the Lis in the F-period

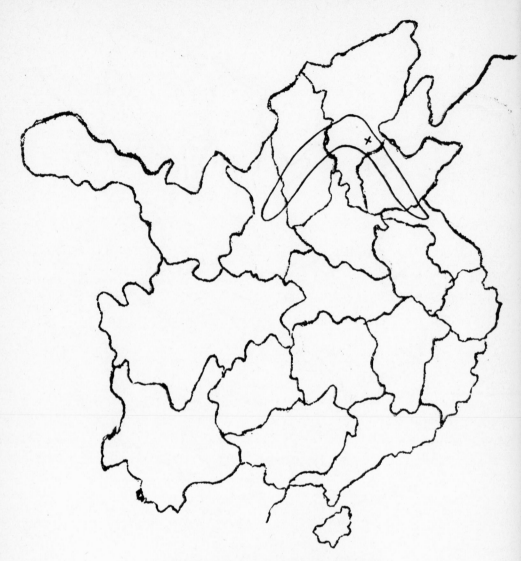

MAP 42. Centres of the Lis in the G-period

192

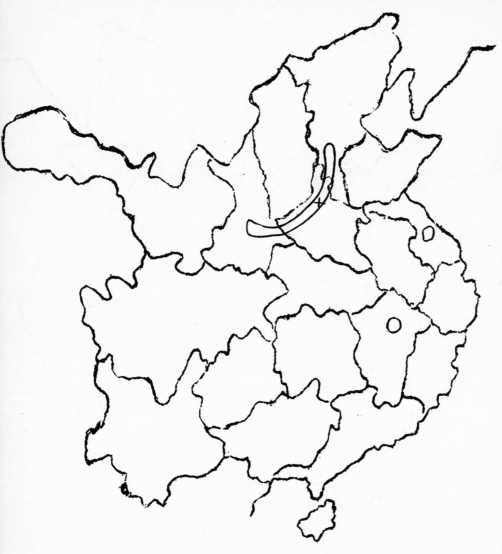

MAP 43. Centres of the Lis in the H-period

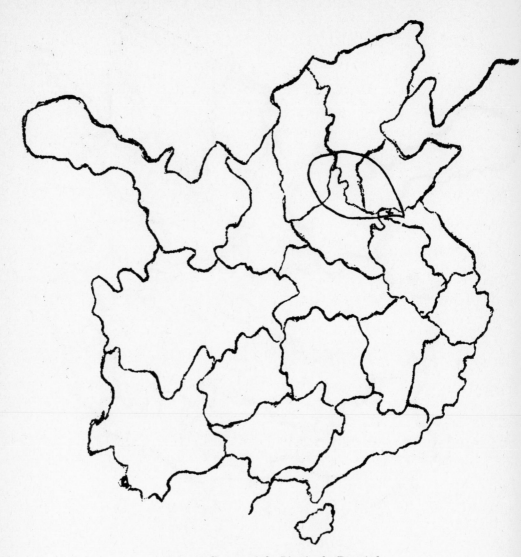

MAP 44. Centres of the Lius in the D-period

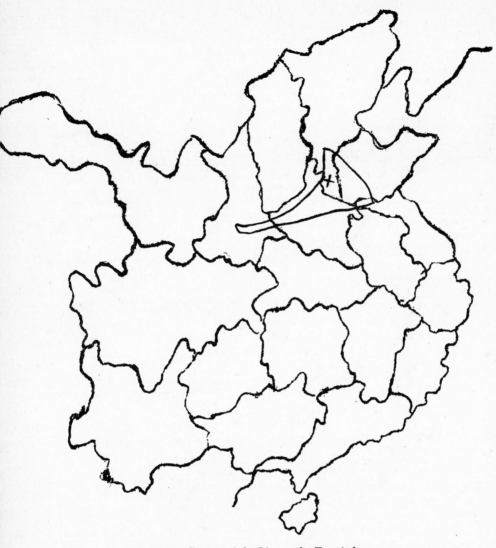

MAP 45. Centres of the Lius in the E-period

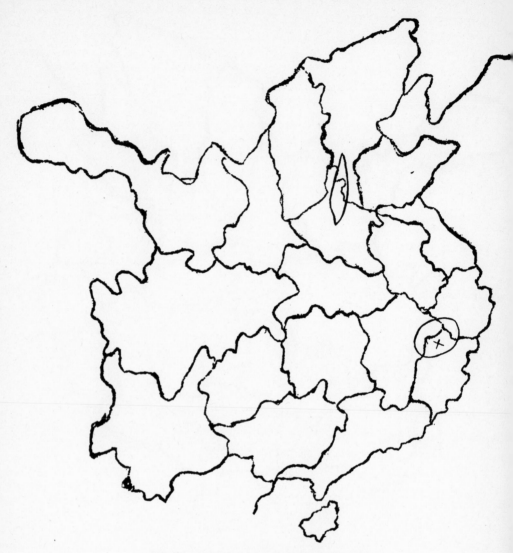

MAP 46. Centres of the Lius in the F-period

196

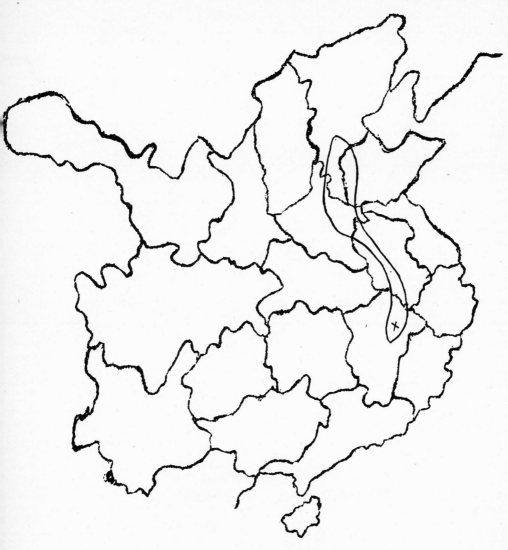

MAP 47. Centres of the Lius in the G-period

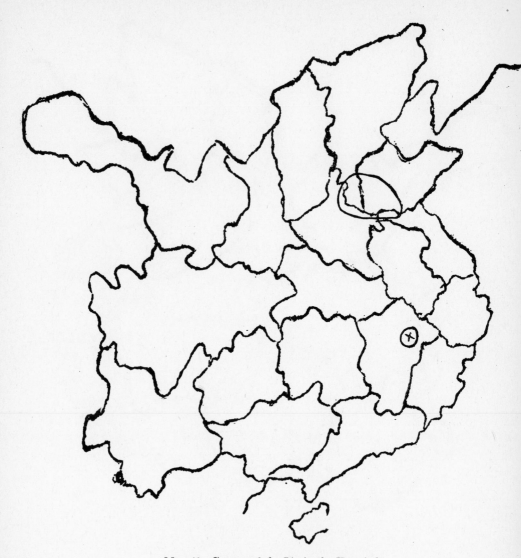

MAP 48. Centres of the Liu in the H-period

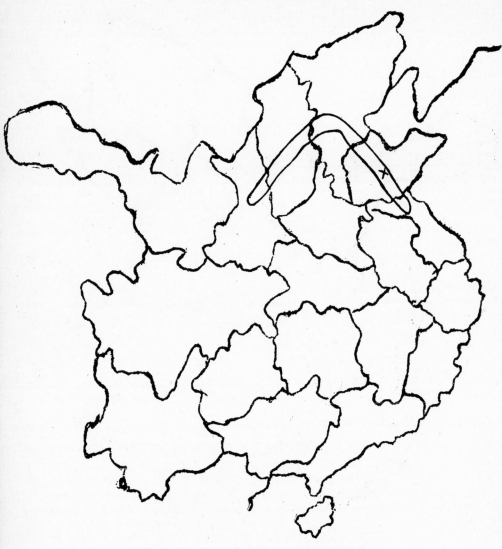

MAP 49. Centres of the Wangs in the D-period

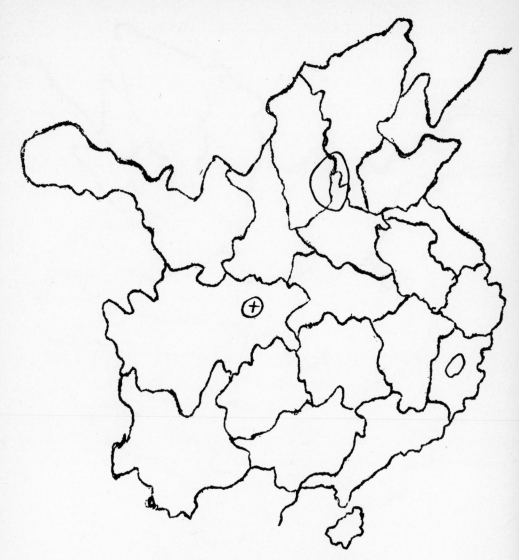

MAP 50. Centres of the Wangs in the E-period

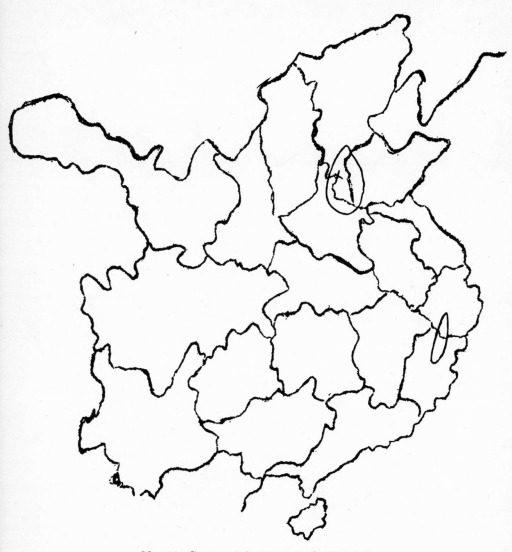

MAP 51. Centres of the Wangs in the F-period

201

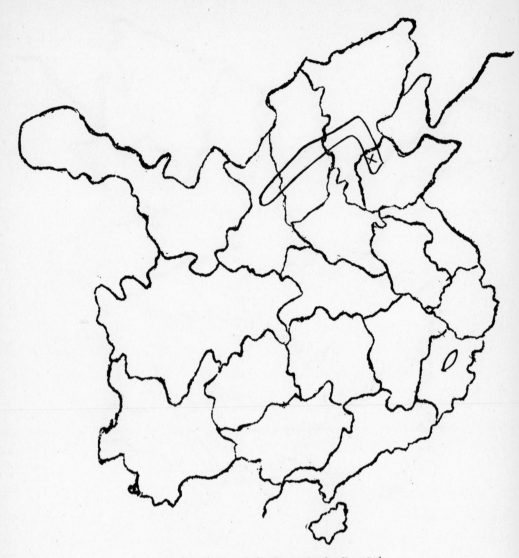

MAP 52. Centres of the Wangs in the G-period

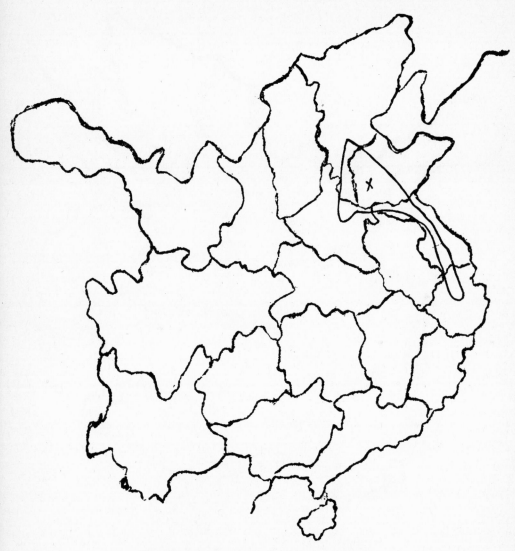

MAP 53. Centres of the Wangs in the H-period

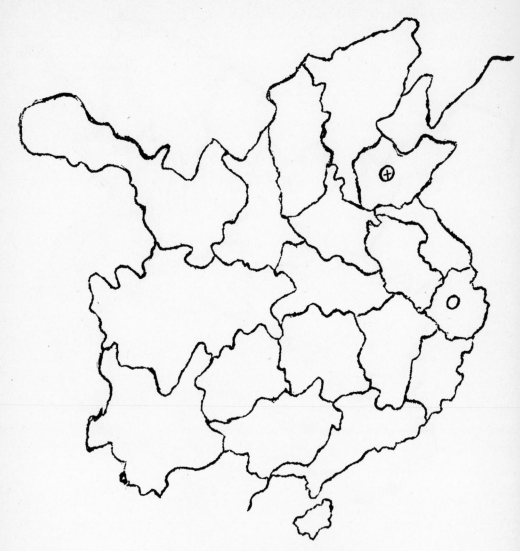

MAP 54. Centres of the Wus in the D-period

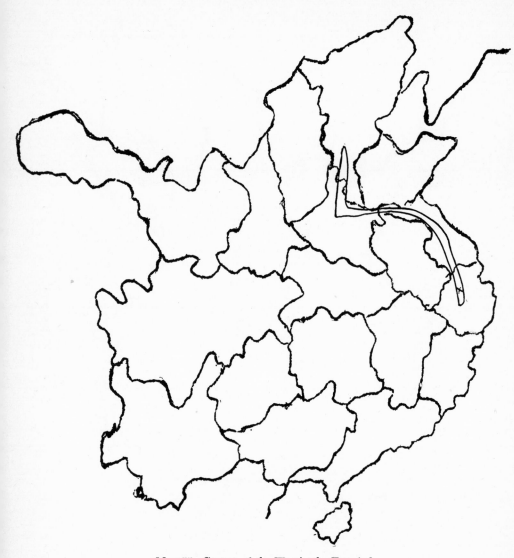

MAP 55. Centres of the Wus in the E-period

205

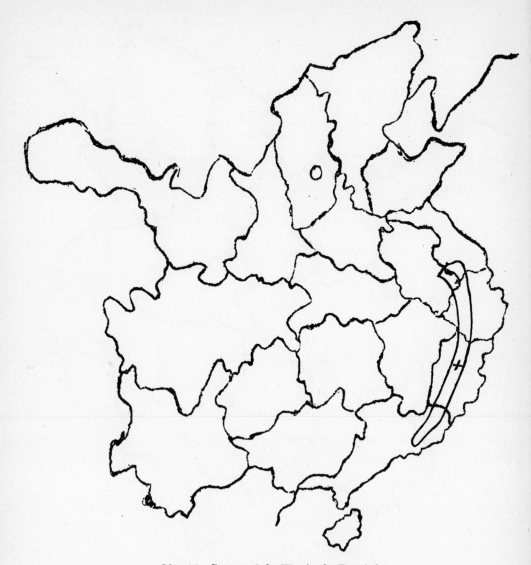

MAP 56. Centres of the Wus in the F-period

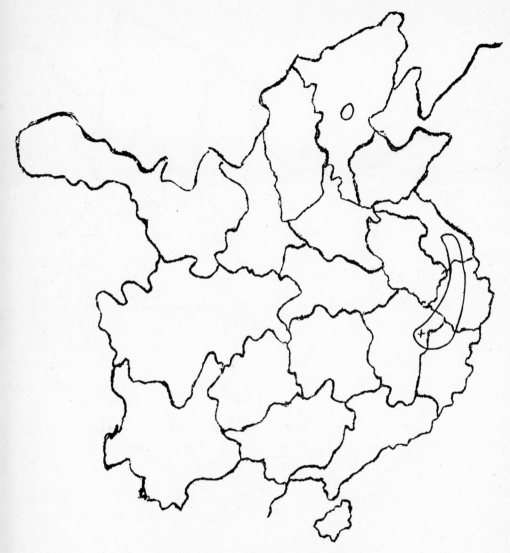

MAP 57. Centres of the Wus in the G-period

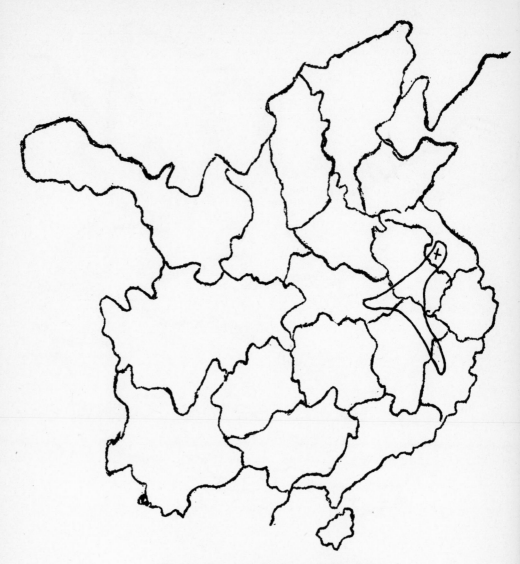

MAP 58. Centres of the Wus in the H-period

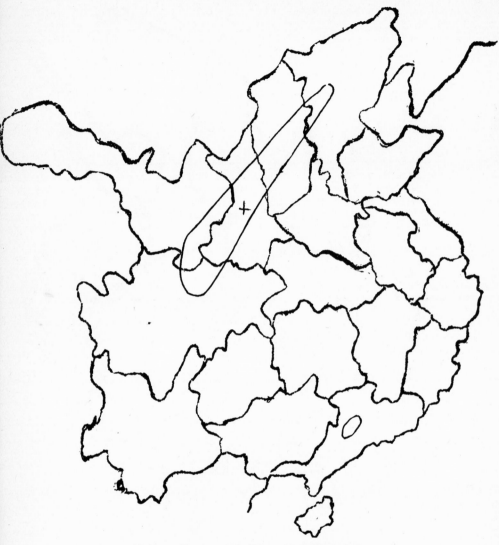

MAP 59. Centres of the Yangs in the D-period

209

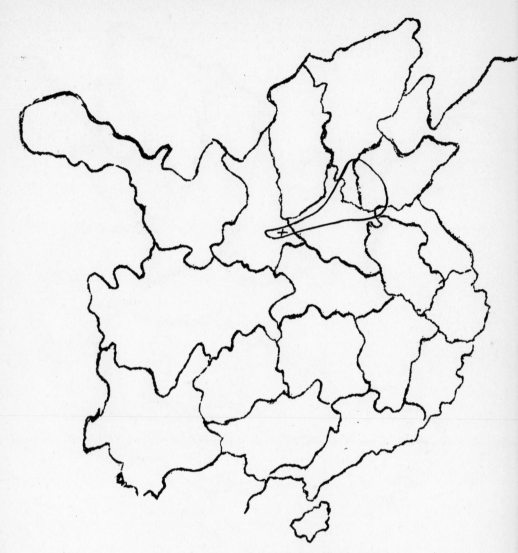

MAP 60. Centres of the Yangs in the E-period

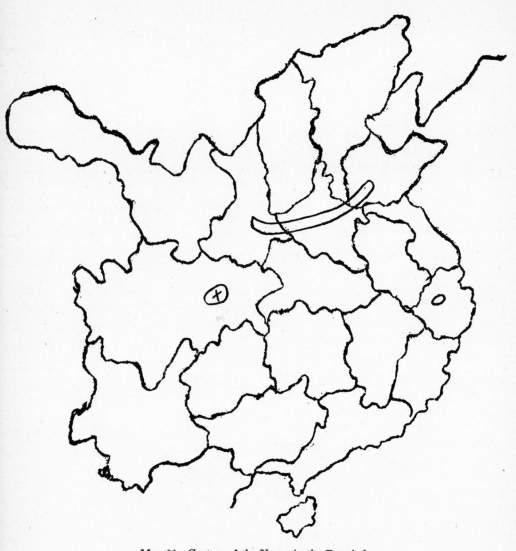

Map 61. Centres of the Yangs in the F-period

211

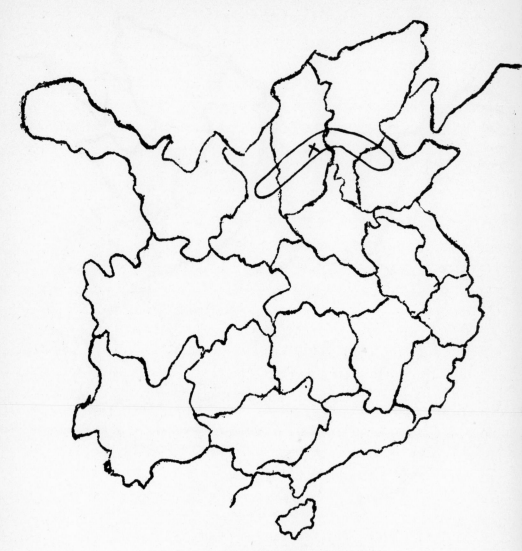

MAP 62. Centres of the Yangs in the G-period

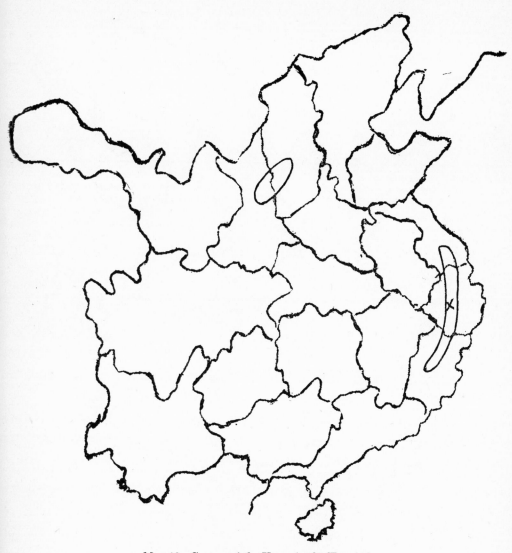

MAP 63. Centres of the Yangs in the H-period

213

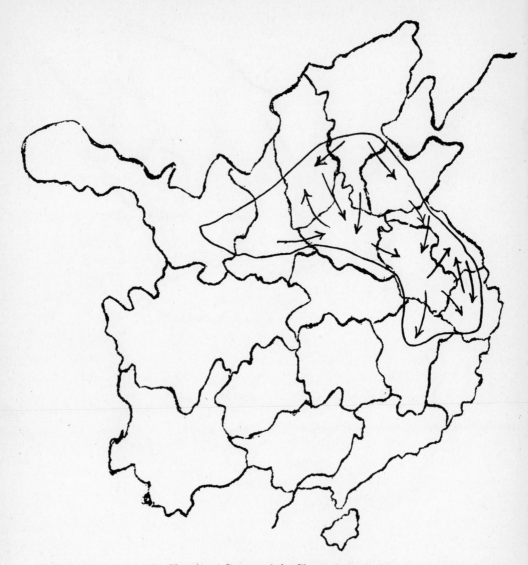

MAP 64. Directions of the Changes of Centres of the Changs from the D-period to the H-period

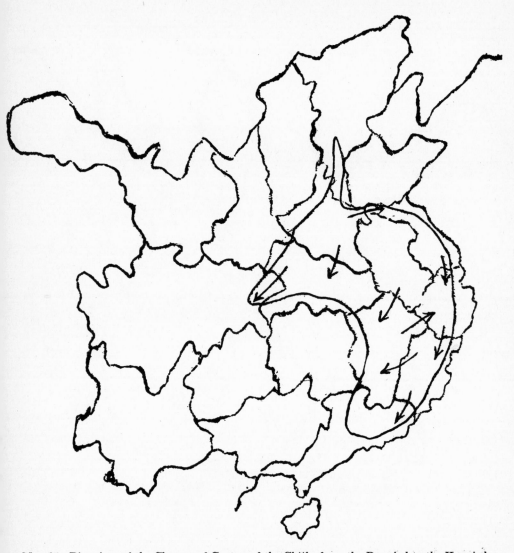

MAP 65. Directions of the Changes of Centres of the Ch'êhs from the D-period to the H-period

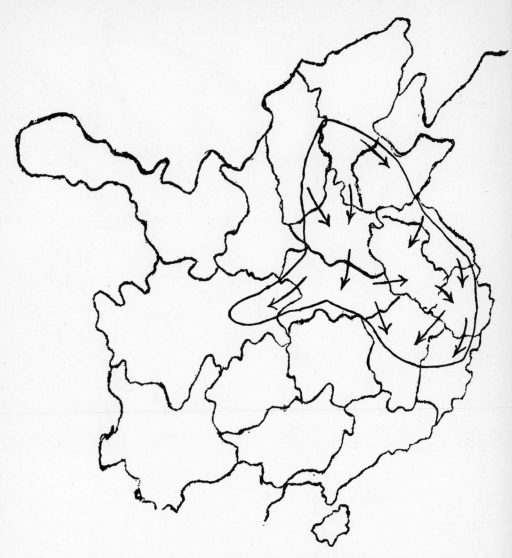

MAP 66. Directions of the Changes of Centres of the Chus from the D-period to the H-period

216

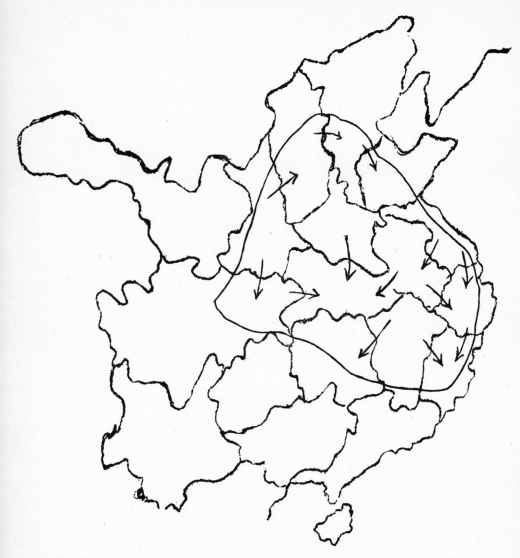

MAP 67. Directions of the Changes of the Centres of the Hus from the D-period to the H-period

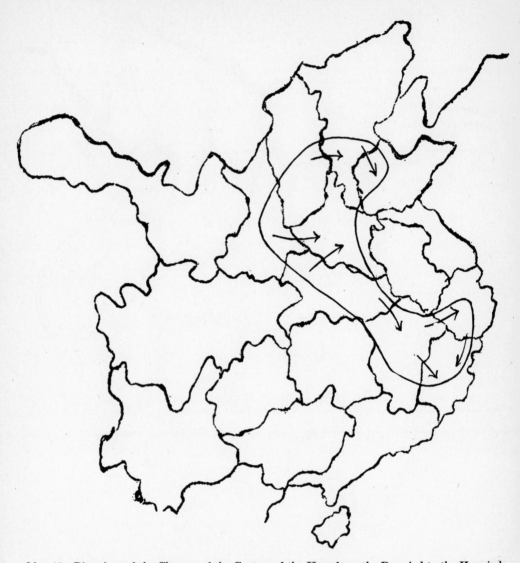

MAP 68. Directions of the Changes of the Centres of the Kuos from the D-period to the H-period

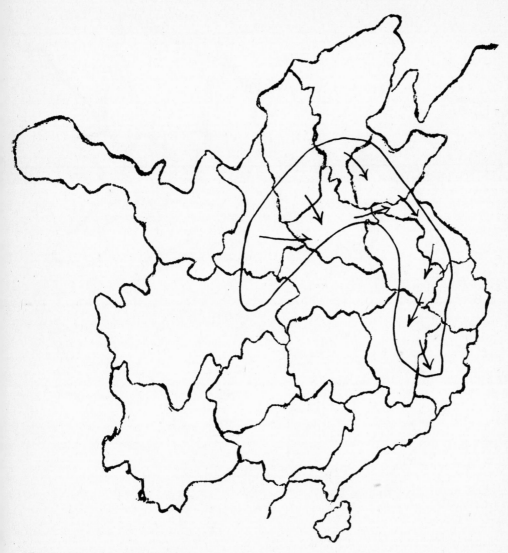

Map 69. Directions of the Changes of the Centres of the Lis from the D-period to the H-period

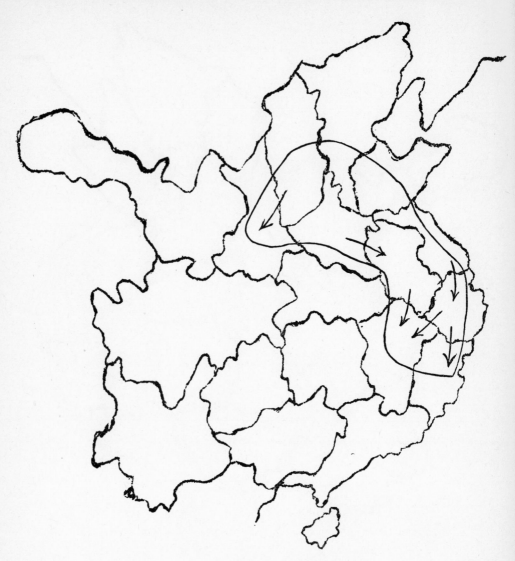

MAP 70. Directions of the Changes of the Centres of the Lius from the D-period to the H-period

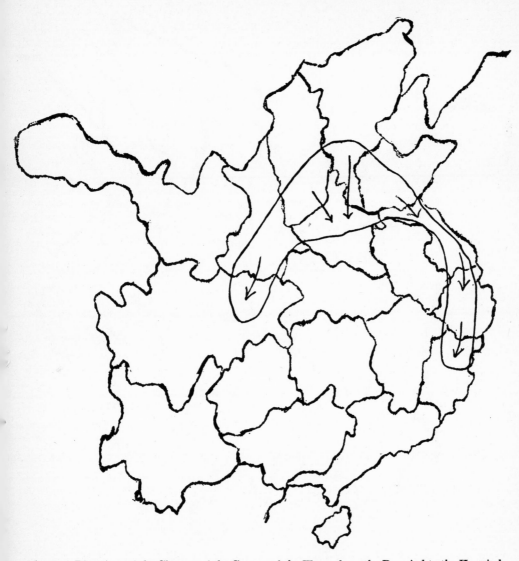

MAP 71. Directions of the Changes of the Centres of the Wangs from the D-period to the H-period

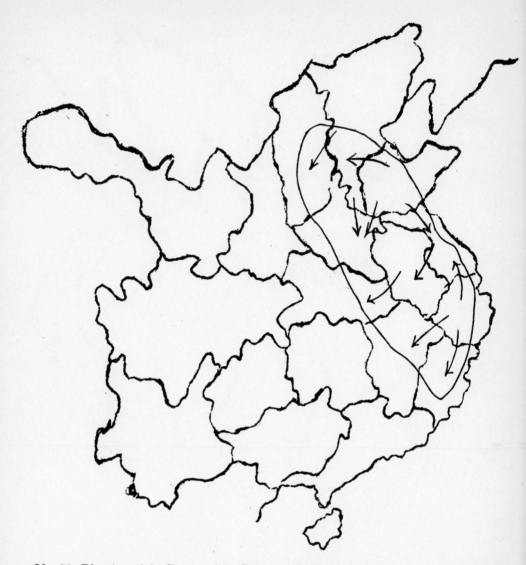

MAP 72. Directions of the Changes of the Centres of the Wus from the D-period to the H-period

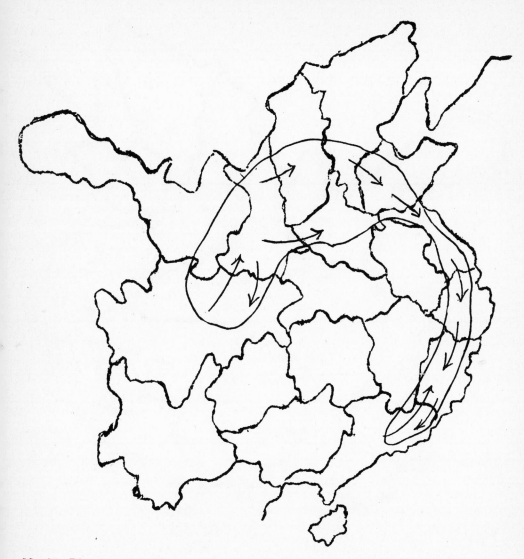

MAP 73. Directions of the Changes of the Centres of the Yangs from the D-period to the H-period

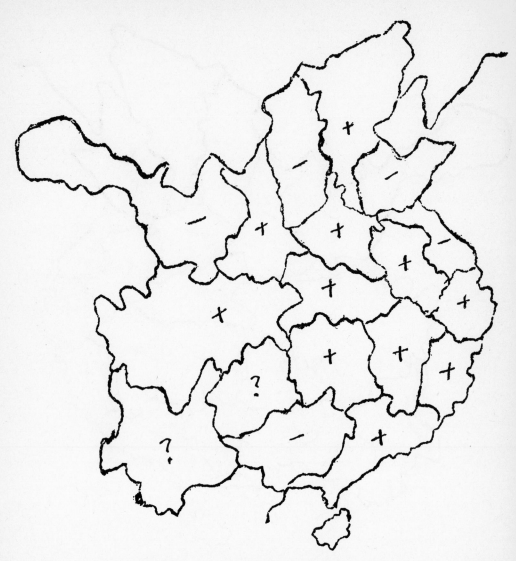

MAP 74. Directions of the Changes of the Centres of the Ten Surnames from the D-period
to the E-period

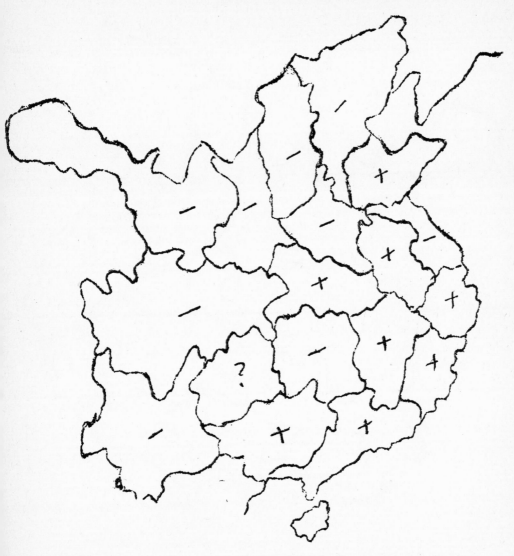

MAP 75. Directions of the Changes of the Centres of the Ten Surnames from the E-period
to the F-period

225

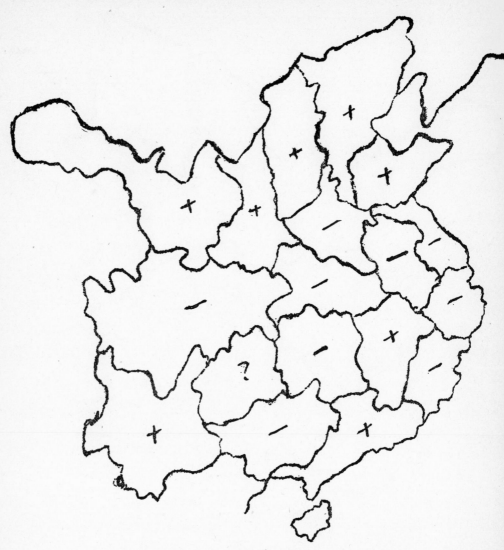

MAP 76. Directions of the Changes of the Centres of the Ten Surnames from the F-period
to the G-period

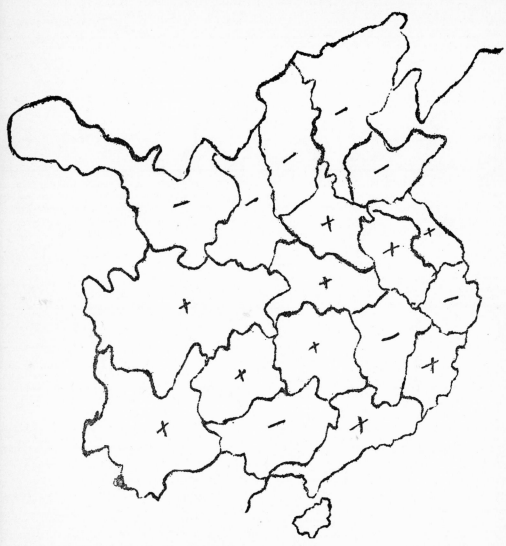

MAP 77. Directions of the Changes of the Centres of the Ten Surnames from the G-period
to the H-period

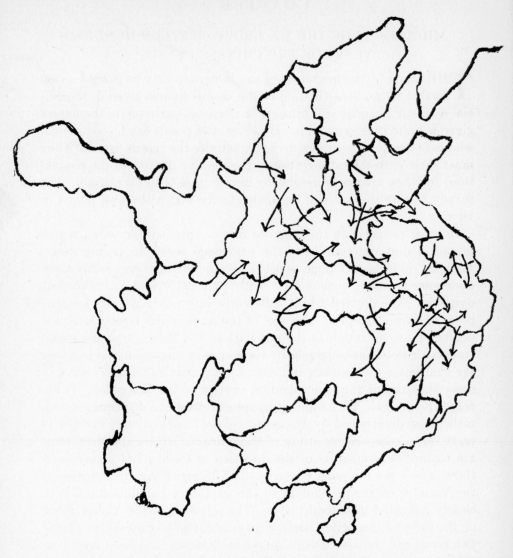

MAP 78. Inter-provincial Movements of the Chinese Population between 256 A.D. and 1644 A.D. as indicated by the Changes of Centres of the Ten Surnames

CHAPTER V

MIGRATIONS OF THE WE–GROUP: FIFTEEN HUNDRED YEARS OF THE CHINESE CENSUS

THE study of the migration of the We-group may be carried a step further by an investigation of the census figures given in the official dynastic histories of China. The degree of accuracy of the figures given is quite indeterminable. However, two points can be postulated, whatever degree of accuracy may characterize the census figures. They must show with tolerable certainty the relative density of the population, and they always represent the distribution of the We-group. The survey in this chapter will be made chiefly with these two points in view.

In order to translate these figures into comprehensible terms, a geographical unit different from the provincial seems to be necessary. Regional divisions of China, as it has been pointed out previously, have undergone changes concomitant with political evolution. Different dynasties have divided China differently into political units for purposes of administration. The size of the units varies largely with the degree of concentration of the population, and the centres of concentration are determined largely by the routes of migration. So in a way the changes in the number and size of the political units may serve to show the drift of the concentration centres of the We-group. It becomes plain, then, that some geographical divisions determinative of, rather than determined by, the centres of drift are necessary in order to carry out a comparative study of these drifts. Rivers and mountains are natural determinants of the direction of the drift of peoples. Of these, rivers are the most effective. In Chapter Four, the influence of the Yangtze on the psychology of the migratory population has been clearly indicated in several places. The influence of the Yellow River on the early Chinese civilization is an established historical fact. These two rivers are the arteries of Chinese civilization, and have been constant factors associated with all the great historical movements of the Chinese. On these natural boundary lines, China may be divided into these following five divisions (Map 79):

(1) North-eastern Section (N. E.): North of the eastern bend of the Yellow River, corresponding to modern Chihli and Shansi.

(2) Central Eastern Section (C. E.): South of the eastern bend of the Yellow River and north of the eastern half of the Yangtze River;

the boundary on the west is an imaginary line extended from the eastern bend of the Yellow River (the modern Honan-Shansi-Shensi border point) to the Yangtze River. This region corresponds to Shantung, Honan, and almost the whole of Hupeh, Nganhui, and Kiangsu.

(3) Northern and Central Western Section (N. C. W.): The whole region south of the Yellow River, west of the Central Eastern Section, and north of the Yangtze, corresponding to modern Shensi, Szechuan, and a large portion of Kansu.

(4) North-western Section (N. W.): That little portion of Kansu which is outside of the Yellow River.

(5) Southern Section (S.): The whole region south of the Yangtze including Chekiang, Fukien, Kiangsi, Hunan, Kweichow, Kwangtung, Kwangsi, and also a portion of Kiangsu, Nganhui, Hupeh, and Yunnan.

The distribution of the population in different dynasties may now be given in terms of these five sections. All the data are extracted from the *Twenty-Four Histories* — 1739 edition.

TABLE 71
FIGURES

Periods	C		D		E	F	G	H
Regions	2 A.D.	140 A.D.	280 A.D.	590–613 A.D.	740 A.D.	1102 A.D.	?	1491 A.D.
N. E.	13,080,331	10,009,175	759,200	3,144,223	13,874,184	5,335,164	3,691,496	6,287,071
C. E.	307,666,883	21,086,688	733,865	3,002,698	14,576,920	9,136,746	4,005,901	14,519,010
N.C.W.	8,781,027	50,916,624	365,920	1,634,314	5,954,353	8,346,626	?	58,611,215
N. W.	4,219,859	142,773	30,700	28,728	283,102	....	?	....
S.	4,613,301	10,405,607	605,400	703,485	12,666,266	15,112,619	4,962,463	25,607,426

TABLE 72
PERCENTAGES

Periods	C		D		E	F	G	H
Regions	2 A.D.	140 A.D.	280 A.D.	590–613 A.D.	740 A.D.	1102 A.D.	?	
N. E.	22.68	21.45	30.42	36.03	29.3	14.06	?	12.02
C. E.	53.33	45.11	29.41	39.03	30.78	24.08	?	27.77
N. C. W.	15.22	10.90	14.66	17.57	12.57	{ 22.01	?	11.23
N. W.	.74	.31	1.23	.31	.59		?	
S.	8.08	22.26	24.26	7.52	26.75	39.85	?	48.98

The table shows that the Chinese population was concentrated mainly in the northeastern and central eastern region at about the beginning of the Christian Era. Less than 25 per cent were found in the other parts of China. The southern region was sparsely populated at that time in relation to its size. Since that period, there has been a steady decrease in both the northeastern and central eastern region, and a parallel increase south of the Yangtze, which is almost phenomenal. This increase south of the Yangtze must not be taken as a simple local multiplication: there must have been a stream of immigrants pouring down from the northwest where in the same span of time (138 years) the population decreased from almost 430,000 to a little over 140,000. During this time the south was the only region that had gained in population, while all the other regions decreased. But the loss in the other regions is in no way as serious as that in the N. C. W.; so the chief source of increase must be located in the N. C. W., although the other regions must also have made contributions. This exactly corroborates what has been discovered in the last chapter, in which it has been stated that the southeastward movement started about the end of period B and continued for over 1000 years. Since 140 A.D. there had been a steady increase in the S. region with only one exception which occurred in the D period. This is a paradox that needs detailed explanation. It is a paradox because as a result of our study of surnames, we should expect another phenomenal rush to the Southern region in this period; but the tables show a decrease as phenomenal as the increase in period C. It is the decrease in percentage that specially needs explanation. Can it mean that the other regions (N. E., N. C. W.), which have gained in percentage during this period, increased at the expense of this region? The following remarkable document published in 299 A.D. on "The Necessity of Excluding the Jung and the Ti from China proper," by Chiang T'ung, illuminates the whole situation:

"... In the time of Ch'in Shih Huang-ti (who first unified China — 246–222 B.C.) there were no barbarians in the Middle Kingdom. Then the Han Dynasty began and chose Ch'ang-ngan (Shensi) as the capital city, which was named as the Three Metropolises at that time (Sanfu). ... When the T'zu-Mei rebellion was suppressed (27 A.D.), all the regions around this western capital (Chang-Ngan, Shensi) became desolated, and the inhabitants of that region partly died and partly migrated. ... In the middle of the Chien-wu era (40–41 A.D.) Ma Yuan, who was appointed the administrator of Lung-hsi (Kansu), subjugated the rebellious Ch'iangs, and moved the rest of the tribes inside of the boundary of China proper, who populated the empty places in Kuan-Chung (Kansu and Shensi), thus mixing with the Hua Jen (meaning the genuine Chinese population at that time). . . . Ever since, this element has been a constant source of trouble. . . . At present (299 A.D.) the population in Kuan-chung (Shensi, Kansu, Szechuan) is more than 1,000,000 — half of them are the descendants of these barbarians. . . .

"The Hus of Pin-Chou (Shansi) are the descendants of the ferocious Hsiungnu. . . . They submitted to the Chinese sovereign power in the Chien-wu Era (26 A.D.–55 A.D.). . . . Since that time they have increased their numbers on several occasions. . . . Now their number amounts to several ten thousands and exceeds that of the western Jung.

"The Kou-Li (Koreans) of Yüng-yang were originally found in Liao-Tung (South Manchuria). In the time of Chêng-Shih (240–249 A.D.) the administrator of Yu Chou (Chihli), Wuchiu Chien, after having conquered them, moved a few hundred of them inwards; and now they have increased to thousands. . . .

"China proper is not the place for these barbarians — they should therefore be ordered back to their original home, so that the grounds of future trouble may be nipped. . . ." (Translated from the *Biography of Chiang T'ung*, book 56, *History of Chin* (1739 A.D. edition).

This memorandum was written for the consideration of Emperor Hui-ti (290–306 A.D.), but it produced no effect. In less than ten years the trouble with these tribes began which culminated in the extremely tragic Yüng Chia era (307–312 A.D.).

From these documents, the following facts are important for our present consideration: (1) Half of the population in N. C. W. at 299 A.D. were not Chinese; (2) several thousands of Hsiung-nu descendants were found in the Northeastern area together with several thousand Koreans. The disturbance of North China, caused by the Tungus tribes, began at the opening of the fourth century A.D., and lasted for three centuries. The effect of this disturbance was the ascendancy of these tribes in North China and the migration of the genuine Chinese population across the Yangtze River. The disturbances of these three centuries, however, were not limited to the region north of the Yangtze; they occurred all over China. Thus the devastating effect was universal, and consequently there was a general decrease of population. It is probable that in these three centuries the sturdy tribes of the north, newly emerged from barbarism, bred at a faster rate than the long and highly civilized Chinese who had migrated southward. It is also possi-

ble that the northerners had small households, and so these two figures
are not comparable even in terms of percentages. It is not impossible
that there was a backward wash; but it is improbable. Of the censuses
in the D period, one was taken just before the disturbances began, and
the other at about the end of them. The change in the percentage distribution in these two periods may be explained in any of the above ways.
But before this statement is to be positively affirmed, there are two
other sets of figures to be considered.

The first southern dynasty that succeeded Chin was Sung (420–479
A.D.). The territory of this dynasty included all the Southern region,
a large portion of the Central Eastern and a small portion of the North
and Central Western region. The census taken in this period may be
compared with the 280 A.D. census as well as the 590 A.D. census.

	280 A.D.	464 A.D.	590 A.D.
C. E.	733,865	1,545,063	3,602,698
N. C. W.	365,920	354,712	1,634,314
S.	605,400	2,970,883	703,485

The 590 A.D. census, it must be remembered, is given in terms of
households. I am unable to determine the numerical relationship between the household and the actual number of population, as I have
found that it not only varies with dynasties, but also in different regions. But the relative proportion of these numbers should at least
have some significance. From 280 A.D. to 464 A.D., the increase of
population south of the Yangtze was more than fivefold. If we take
5.3 members [1] to each household as our basis of calculation, then from
464 A.D. to 590 A.D. there was little increase south of the Yangtze. So
the D period may clearly be divided into halves, so far as the population south of the Yangtze is concerned. The first half shows a phenomenal increase, owing to the disturbances that have started in the North:
this half lasted, let us say, until 464 A.D. From this time onward, the
migration practically ceased, and local increase was kept in check by
the continual civil war in that region which lasted up to the beginning
of the T'ang Dynasty (618 A.D.). It must be observed that there is
another reason to support the theory that the increase of population
south of the Yangtze, during the first half of the D period, was due to
migration rather than natural increase. For the occurrence of war in
this region in the first half of period D is almost as frequent as that in

[1] This is based on the result of ten calculations: [1:4.8 (2 A.D.)]; [1:4.9 (51 A.D.)];
[1:5.8 (75 A.D.)]; [1:5.8 (88 A.D.)]; [1:5.7 (105 A.D.)]; [1:5.+ (125 A.D.)]; [1:5.+ (144
A.D.)]; [1:5.+ (145 A.D.)]; [1:5.1. (146 A.D.)]; [1:6.5. (280 A.D.)]. Average equals 1:5.3.

the second half, and the population could not have increased so enormously if it had not been for the immigration from the Northern region. If still more evidence is necessary, the following texts from the geographical account of Sung may be cited:

1. "... At the beginning of the barbarian disturbance (beginning of the fourth century A.D.), the territory of Sze (N. E. and C. E.), Chi (N. E.), Yang (N. C. W.), Liang (N. W.), Ching (C. E.), Pin (C. E.), Yeng (C. E.), Yü (C. E.), Zu (N. E.), Ping (N. E.) were all lost. ... The Chinese inhabitants of these regions moved southward in great numbers; thus temporary offices were set up in new regions in order to facilitate administration. ..." (*Geographical Account, History of Sung,* book 35, page 1.)

2. "... During the time of the three Kingdoms (221 A.D.–265 A.D.), the territory between Chiang (Yangtze) and Hui (the river that divides a large portion of C. E.) was a battle ground for many years; and the region was entirely depopulated during that period. People began to return home during the reign of Chin. Then came the barbarian invasion. Most of the people south of Hui thus came south of the Yangtze. ... During the rebellion of Su-Chün (326 A.D. and since), the immigrants across the Yangtze became still more numerous. ..." (*Ibid,* page 4.)

3. "... In 329 A.D. ... Shih Chien, one of the ministers in the Cabinet, made all the homeless people south of Hui settle in the Yangtze basin. ..." (*Ibid.*)

4. "... In the beginning of the Chin dynasty, when the barbarian invasion was devastating all North China, the inhabitants of Yung and Ch'in (Shensi, Kansu) who had survived mostly came to Fan and Mien (Hupeh) .... But not until the time of Emperor Shao Wu (373 A.D.–396 A.D.) were they properly cared for. ..." (*Ibid.*)

The intensity of the southward movement of the Chinese at this time is vividly described in all these accounts. But I can find no description for the second half of the D period. I take this as a clear substantiation of what has been discussed above.

After the D period, the gain of population in the south is a very steady one, until at the end of the fifth century 48.98 per cent is reached. In order to analyze these movements more closely, we need to go into more detailed figures. The following table shows the number of districts having more than 10,000 population, for each province south of the Yangtze at different periods. These are calculated according to the 280 A.D., 464 A.D., 740 A.D., 1102 A.D., and Yuan (the Mongol) censuses.

TABLE 73

Periods	280 A.D.	464 A.D.	740 A.D.	1102 A.D.	
Provinces	D	D	E	F	G
Chekiang.............	4	19	56	66	80+
Fukien..............	0	2	9	40	58
Hunan..............	7	14	39	43	69
Kiangsi.............	2	12	33	66	81
Kwangsi............	..	8	5	$\left\{\begin{array}{c}794{,}734 \\ \text{House-} \\ \text{holds}\end{array}\right\}$	39
Kwangtung...........	..	8	24	..	42
Kweichow...........	..	..	..	..	..
S. Hupeh............	1	4	7+	7	8
S. Kiangsu...........	3	41	20	20	16+
S. Nganhui...........	1	2	14	21	34
Yunnan..............	2	2	?	?	?

One outstanding feature that characterizes this table is the steady increase in the course of time of the number of 10,000 population districts, in each province south of the Yangtze; there is only one exception, S. Kiangsu in the D–E period. This can be easily explained. The southern dynasties of the D period had their capital at Chien K'ang (Kiangsu), whose neighboring districts (South Kiangsu) survived the barbarian invasion in that period. This temporary crowded condition, however, could not have lasted very long, especially as there was plenty of room in the south for expansion. So when the more restful time of the E period came, the expansion took the normal course, and Chekiang, hitherto rather scarcely populated, became the natural receptacle for most of the northern immigrants; thus the number of districts with more than 10,000 population increased from 19 to 56 in less than three hundred years.

Contemporaneous with the settlement of Chekiang was the movement of the We-group into Kiangsi and Hunan. I have reason to believe that those were two independent movements. The physical geography along the Yangtze Valley shows three separate points south of this great river which furnish the least resistance to the movement of population: these may be characterized by the Tunt'ing Lake, North of Hunan; Poyang Lake, north of Kiangsi; and T'ai Lake, south of Kiangsu. The first two lakes are directly connected with the Yangtze River, while the last is not very far separated from it. The regions around these three lakes are all less than two hundred meters above sea-level, while separating them are two mountain systems [1] whose altitude averages between 500 and 1,000 meters.[2] These three points, therefore, form the most natural outlets for the southward expansion.

The independence of these three movements is also illustrated by the above table. In the E period, Hunan, Kiangsi, and Chekiang, as we have noted, all show a phenomenal expansion: this was the natural extension of the Tungt'ing, Poyang, and T'ai movements respectively. There were, however, some differences in their extensions. While the T'ai line scarcely goes beyond Chekiang, and the Poyang line is confined within Kiangsi in this period, the Tungt'ing line follows its course all through Hunan, crosses the northeast border of Kwangsi, and stops only at the mouth of the Pearl River (Kwangtung). The T'ang dynasty gave rise to the beginning of the Kwangtung and Kwangsi settlement. The Kwangtung and Kwangsi districts are to be aligned with the Tung'ting, rather than the Poyang, line again for geographical reasons. Kiangsi, which has a longer borderline with Kwangtung than Hunan has, is, however, separated from its coastal neighbor by a very high mountain range (Ta-Yüling, 1000–4000 meters and above), which forms quite a formidable barrier to southward drift along the Poyang line. This barrier extends all along the borderline between Hunan and Kwangtung; but Hunan maintains, nevertheless, quite a free intercourse with Kwangtung by way of Kwangsi. All the five districts with 10,000 population in Kwangsi in this period are found in its northeast corner; most of the twenty-four 10,000 population districts are found in conjunction with these five districts. The continuity of these, therefore, shows clearly the line of extension.

The figures for the F period and the G period have to be studied together, although they are the results of many complicated factors which should be separated. The figures in the F period are based on the census taken in 1102 A.D., just twenty-four years before the Ching K'ang disaster (1125 A.D.), when the Kin Tartars captured the capital (K'ai-fêng-fu, Honan) of the Sung dynasty and the whole of North China, an event as serious in its consequences as the Yüng-Chia catastrophe of the D period. The movement of population which resulted has already been forecast in the previous chapter on the study of surnames. But it

[1] The Huan Shan system south of Nganhui, and the Yüan-Shan system on the Kiangsi and Hunan border.

[2] According to the Physical Map of Cheng Kao-Chi, published by the Commercial Press, Shanghai, 1917, third edition.

must be noted that the loss of K'ai-fêng by the Sung dynasty by no means started any new southward movement; it only intensified the old one that had been going on for several hundred years. The result of the Yüng-chia movement in the D period was the gradual settlement of Chekiang, Kiangsi, and Hunan in the T'ang dynasty. The result of the Ching-K'ang intensification was the definite occupation of Kwangtung, Fukien, and Kwangsi by the We-group during the Mongol period.

This leaves two provinces south of the Yangtze—Yunnan and Kwei-chow—unanalyzed. Unfortunately, the census figures of the Ming dynasty are quite incomplete. But we are on safe ground in saying that the beginning of the occupation of these two provinces by the We-group occurred in this period.

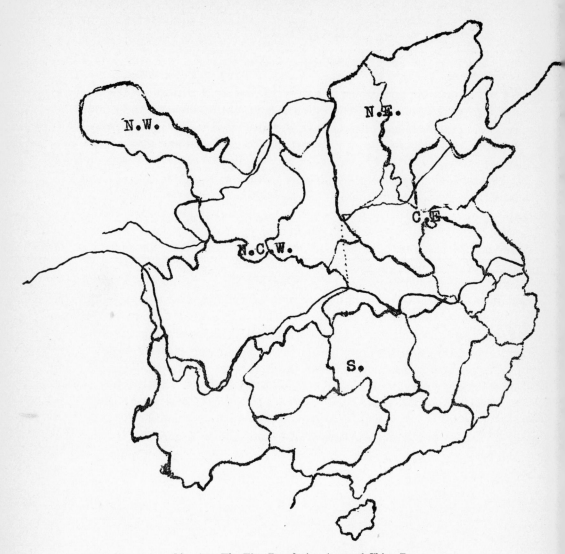

MAP 79. The Five Population Areas of China Proper

CHAPTER VI

THE SOUTHERN YOU–GROUP

THE southern You-group will be considered first mainly for chronological reasons. It is the older of the You-groups within China proper. The problem concerning this group, like that of the We-group, presents two aspects: i. e., its size within China proper and its constituents.

Presumably the size of the southern You-group should vary with that of the We-group within the boundary of China proper. In other words, the northern frontier of the southern You-group should retreat in the same way in which the southern line of expansion of the We-group moves. (Cf. the maps at the end of the third chapter.) This might be true, if it were not for these possibilities: (1) that there may be uninhabited places between the territory of the We-group and that of the southern aborigines; (2) that there may be neutral zones ethnographically under the influence of the We-group, but actually a part of the You-group or vice-versa. These two possibilities have to be inquired into before the territorial extension of the You-group can be defined.

The second point may be taken up first, as its solution will also indirectly solve the first. The evolution of the size of the We-group and the provincial ages studied in chapter III shows that it is in the following provinces in the successive periods that the line of contact between the We-group and the southern You-group may be found:

(1)	Yunnan	(6)	Kwangsi
(2)	Hunan	(7)	Kwangtung
(3)	Kiangsi	(8)	Fukien
(4)	Szechuan	(9)	Kweichow
(5)	Chekiang		

Consequently, in the above order, province by province, the nature of the relationship between the We-group and the southern You-group may be studied. Since this study must be based largely on the historical material, it may be noted that the accuracy of knowledge on the part of the We-group about the You-group depends to a large extent upon the degree of contact between these two groups. The less intimate their contact, the less accurate would be their knowledge about each other;

inversely, an accurate knowledge of the other group in any period would tend to show a close relationship at this time. If the following order is to be adopted instead of the above, it is largely for this reason.

I. Southern Barbarians in Early Times

Ethnographical study of the southern You-group by the Chinese historians is not marked with definiteness until the Han dynasty (period C). Therefore, little previous to this period will be considered here. Nevertheless, there is one document worth recording.

In the year 316 B.C. there took place a debate, of whose consequences the debaters were perhaps scarcely conscious, in the court of the State of Ch'in (one of the seven contending states of that period), between Chang I, one of the two most eminent diplomats of that period, and Ssŭma T'so, an able general. The state of Ch'in, corresponding to modern Shensi and Kansu, was at that time pursuing an aggressive policy towards her neighbors. The two advisers differed in their opinions regarding the most advantageous line of advance. Chang I thought it best to send a military expedition to Han (Honan); Ssŭma T'so, on the other hand, advised the king to conquer Shu (Szechuan) first. Each submitted his point of view for the king's consideration; hence the debate. The speech of Ssŭma T'so began in a very heroic fashion:

"I have heard that when a king desires to enrich his country, he must enlarge his territory; when he desires to strengthen his army, he must enrich his population; when he desires to become an emperor, he must make himself virtuous. Having achieved these three, the empire inevitably follows. Now, your Majesty's territory is small (Shensi and a part of Kansu); your people, poor. With such a start, the career of conquest must be begun with the one that best promises success. The condition of Shu seems to be such that it will offer the least resistance against our expedition. It is situated in the westernmost part of the Middle Kingdom (hence standing all alone); the chieftains are Jung and Ti (barbarians) and, therefore, should be conquered. The country is, moreover, in a very chaotic condition. It would be much like a wolf's invasion into a flock of sheep, if we should send an expedition there. Whereas, etc. . . ." (Translated from *Tactics of the Contending States,* Chan-Kuo T'zê, p. 7, Japanese edition.)

It must be added that Szŭma T'so was sent on this expedition, and that he finished his task with a magnificent flourish. The state of Ch'in was enriched, and this made it possible for Ch'in Shih Huangti to unify China later on.

The important point in this connection is, however, not the conquest, but rather the fact that Szechuan, according to this account, was inhabited by a people, known as Pa and Shu, who were considered at that time as barbarians. They were not incorporated into the We-group until after 316 B.C. *The History of the Later Han Dynasty* (220 A.D.) gives a more detailed version regarding the origin of the barbarians of Szechuan. "The Mans of Pa Ch'un," according to this account, "originally consisted of only five surnames: Pa, Fan, Shen, Hsiang, and Chêng, and all were indigenous to the Chungli Mountain of Wulo (Szechuan). There were two caves in the mountains; one black and one purple. The children of Pa were born in the purple cave and the children of the other four surnames were born in the black cave. They had no chief at that time, and all worshipped spirits. Then they decided to elect a leader by throwing swords at the cave. By agreement the one who could hit the target was to be elected. The son of Pa, Wu-hsiang, won the prize and was consequently chosen for the post; so he became their chieftain. When he died, he was incarnated in a white tiger. Thus human sacrifice was practised to satisfy the earthly demand of the tribal founder. . . ." (Translated in part from *Hou Han Shu* [*History of the Later Han Dynasty*], book 116, p. 5.)

Another account regarding a cognate tribe of this region (Pan-têng Man) says that they were fond of dancing, singing, and fighting. They were the first tribe who knew how to make an arrow out of white bamboo. When the founder of the Han dynasty fought for his imperial throne, some of his best fighters came from this tribe. Their dancing steps were officially adopted by the Han Court. Among the chieftains, seven surnames were eminent. It is not clear, however, to what extent these two tribes were related to each other.

These were not the only tribes that were found in Szechuan. In the history of Toba Wei dynasty (period D) the Liao tribe, extending from Shensi to the south of Szechuan, was shown to be of an entirely different ethnographical character:

". . . They (the Liao) are divided into many tribes, and all dwell among the caves and valleys. They have no surname or clan organization. Nor do they have any personal names. The children are named according to their rank. They build their houses in the trees and call them Kan-lan. The size of the Kan-lan varies with that of the household. Sometimes they elect a chieftain whose power, however, is limited. The succession to the chieftainship is patrilineal as in the case of the nobility of the Middle Kingdom. Each chieftain has a pair of horns and a pair of drums, which are blown and beaten by his male children. They are fond of murdering each other, and hence afraid of travelling afar. They can kill with a sword fishes at the bottom of the water, and eat them as food. They drink through the nose. The dead are buried in a perpendicular coffin. They behave simply, like beasts. When out of temper, father and son kill each other. Should the son kill the father, he would run away and ask forgiveness of the mother by presenting a dog. The mother would forgive the son on receipt of the dog. If the murder is due to retaliation, the dog must be killed. The common plundering is limited to the stealing of dogs and pigs. Neighbors and relatives sometimes sell one another into slavery. If the one sold should try to escape, he would be pursued like a fugitive. When he was captured, he would be bound hand and foot. This would serve as the first sign of submission. He would then be satisfied with the status of slavery, and not dare attempt to escape again. When the children die, the parents cry only once, and then forget them immediately.

"They know the use of the shield and lance, but have no knowledge of the bow and arrow. They make reed-pipes out of bamboo and play in a crowded gathering. They make bright clothes. A big dog may be used to buy a cow. They are afraid of spirits and worship many of them. Human sacrifice is practised. If the victim has a full beard and mustache, the skin is preserved on a bamboo frame, and is called "Kwei" or "Spirit," after it has dried up. This "Kwei" is also prayed to by them for blessing. Sometimes brothers, wives, slaves are sold as victims for sacrifice. Having sold all, the seller will offer himself for this purpose. They make out of bronze a utensil which has a big mouth and a wide belly and is called T'ung-Ch'uan. It is thin and light and is excellent for purposes of cooking. They began to make trouble in Szechuan in the Chien-Kuo era (371–377 A.D.)." (*History of Wei* [386–549 A.D.], book 101, page 10.)

The fact that the "Lias" had no knowledge of the bow and arrow in the fourth and fifth centuries A.D., while the Pan-Têng-man was the inventor of bamboo arrows, makes it unlikely that they were related to each other ethnographically in spite of their common practice of human sacrifice. Moreover, the Liao had no surnames, while both the Pa-Man and the Pan-Têng-man did. This important ethnographical distinction serves well to show at least two independent types of aborigines in Szechuan. Of course, there may have been more; and there actually were, as will be seen. But at any rate Szechuan became a part of the territory of the We-group as well as every other province north of the

Yangtze River at the end of the second century A.D., in spite of these aboriginal tribes; for we learn from history that one of the Three Kingdoms succeeding the Later Han dynasty had its capital in this province. The line of contact in Szechuan was therefore not the type of "either I kill you or you kill me." The We-group and the You-group have co-existed up to the present time.

Eastern Hunan may be taken next, because here another important tribe, ethnographically well defined in the *History of the Later Han Dynasty*, is found. The text shows a half-mythical and half-ethnographical description of the P'an-hu race. But the mythical account is by no means of less importance than the ethnographical, since it will serve as an important link in grouping many of the other unrecognizable tribes in other provinces. The time element again needs special consideration. This tribe did not find a place in the *History of Ch'ien Han Shu*, written in the first century of the Christian era. It is evident that Hunan, where this tribe was originally found, was little known previous to the Later Han dynasty. The contact of the We-group and the You-group in Hunan, therefore, cannot be set earlier than this period. In this period the contact became close; the proof is that the following account of the main aboriginal tribe in this province was written by the historian of this dynasty.

II. ACCOUNT OF THE P'ANHU TRIBE

"The Emperor Kaohsin (in the mythological age) was greatly disturbed by the invasion of Chüan-jung. Several expeditions sent to subjugate this barbarian tribe had been quite ineffective. A chieftain of this tribe, Wu, was especially invincible. The Emperor then proclaimed a prize to be given to anybody who could cut off the head of the chieftain; this prize consisted of ten thousand households, and his youngest daughter for a wife. After this proclamation one of the pet dogs of the emperor, remarkable because of its variegated coat and known as P'an-hu, brought to the emperor's throne a man's head, which to the astonishment of all the ministers proved to be actually that of the enemy. Intoxicated with joy, the Emperor was, however, at a loss to know how to reward the faithful hound, as it was inconceivable to marry this animal to his daughter or give it any title. The princess having become aware of all that had taken place was of the opinion that the Emperor should under no circumstances forfeit his provinces and volunteered to marry the dog, so that the Emperor could not be accused of a breach of faith, even with reference to an animal. Not knowing how to refute her argument, the Emperor consented. The princess thus married P'an-hu. P'an-hu, having attained a wife, carried her on his back to a stone house in the Nan-Shan (Shenchou District, Hunan), a mountain full of dangerous precipices and absolutely devoid of any human trade. This girl also changed her mode of living. Stripping off all her clothes, she made a Puchien (unintelligible) coiffure and wore Tuli (unintelligible) clothes. Meantime the Emperor felt greatly distressed at the loss of his daughter. Several messengers were sent to look for her; but they were all turned back by winds, rainstorms and fogs. Three years after the marriage, twelve children were born to this dog father and princess mother: six boys and six girls. P'an-hu died. The children married among themselves, and multiplied. They made bark clothes and ornamented them with various grass juices. The fashion and cut of the clothes always left a tail at the end. The mother then returned to the Emperor and told everything to her father. The grandchildren were summoned to the court; their clothes were all variegated and their speech unintelligible. Fond of living in high altitudes and averse to plains, they were allowed to pursue their instinctive happiness in the spacious mountains. Their descendants multiplied and ever since have been known as Man-i. They are inwardly cunning, but have a silly appearance. They are conservative and love to stay at home. Because of the service and nobility of their progenitors, they have always been exempted from taxes of all kinds. They have villages, and chieftains who are usually given by the government a seal together with a hat made of the skin of otter. The chieftains are known as Chin-fu, and they call each other Hang-tu. The Men of Wuling at Changsa are a branch.[1] ..." (Directly translated from *Hou-han-shu*, the *History of the Later Han Dynasty*, book 116, pp. 1, 2.)

The P'an-hu tribe, according to the history of the Southern dynasty as well as that of Toba-wei and Liu-Sung (both in the D period), crossed the Yangtze about the beginning of the fourth century and were subsequently found in Hupeh, Szechuan, Honan, Northern Kiangsu, and Shensi. The same movement took place in the case of the Laio tribe originally found in Szechuan. They spread northeastward and were scattered through Hupeh, Nganhui, Kiangsi, and South Honan. This movement is significant in that it introduced an important complicating factor in the strata of population of the northern provinces. It will be considered more fully later on.

Kiangsi, Chekiang, Fukien, and to a certain extent Kiangsu and

---

[1] Y. Colquehoun, A. R. — Among the Shans — p. xlv.

Nganhui were in the beginning of the Han dynasty occupied by a group of people collectively known as the Tung-ou and Ming-yüêh. Unlike the other aboriginal tribes named, however, they have been in more or less intimate contact with the We-group from the beginning of period B. This is at least true with regard to the inhabitants of Ming-yüêh. But still they were described in the middle of the second century B.C. (138 B.C.) as "cropping the hair, tattooing the body, possessing no towns or villages, living among bamboos and valleys, experts in fighting on the water, but impotent on land; having no cars or horses, or bows or arrows." (*Ch'ien-Han Shu*, book 64, *Biography of Yen-Chu.*) A part of the inhabitants were moved by imperial order of the energetic Emperor Wuti, to the north of the Yangtze and south of Hui, as a result of a military expedition in his region. (*Ibid.*, book 95.)

Here, for the first time in Chinese history, tattooing is mentioned among the Chinese aboriginal tribes. Hence, ethnographically they are altogether different from any that have been hitherto described. But again this is not the only type of aboriginals prevalent in this region at about this period. In the history of the Three Kingdoms (San-Kuo-Chih), the people of Tan-Yang (Nganhui-Kiangsu border) are said to be fond of fighting, expert mountain climbers, making their own armor from the copper and iron found in their region. They were subjugated by Chu-Ko-Ko. That they were one of the You-group is attested by the name "Jung," given to them in the memorandum of Chu-Ko-Ko to the Emperor of Wu at 226 A.D. What is almost more interesting is that among the captives taken among these defeated barbarians there were many dwarfs. On page 7, book 54, of the *Official of the Liang Dynasty* (502 A.D.–556 A.D.), this account occurs:

"... A merchant of Ta-t'sin (Roman Orient) whose name was T'sin-lun, came to the Chiao-Chih (Tung-King); the prefect (T'ai-Shou) of Chiao-Chih, Wu-miao, sent him to Sun Ch'üan (the Wu Emperor), who asked him for a report on his native country and its people. T'sin-lun prepared a statement and replied. At the time Chu-Ko-Ko chastised Tan-yang they had caught *blackish-colored dwarfs*. When T'sin-lun saw them, he said that in Ta-t'sin these men are rarely seen. Sun Ch'üan then sent male and female dwarfs, ten of each, in charge of an officer.[1] ..."

The term "blackish-colored" is, however, a mistranslation. The original terms are meant to denote the geographical names of the region where these dwarfs were found. Professor Hirth made this correction

---

[1] Hirth, *China and Roman Orient*, p. 48.

on page 306 in his book. But whether black or not, the dwarf element was found in this region in the third century A.D. I have been unable to find any other official account of this period to corroborate and verify this statement. The question immediately arises whether these dwarfs were Negrito remnants such as are now found in Cochin China, the Malay States, Andaman Islands, Philippine Islands, and Formosa. I have found no reason to believe that they were not. For a people that can be captured and transported as an object of curiosity must belong to a very low order of humanity. If they were Negritoes it would show that in the southeast of China proper there were at least two distinct types of the You-group: the tattooed and the dwarfs.

Southward towards Yunan, Kweichow, Kwangsi, and Kwangtung, the problem of the You-group becomes vastly more complicated. The quadripartite division of China's south and southwest began only in the Ming dynasty (H). Previous to this period, the region was divided politically into only two or three units and sometimes less. In the T'ang dynasty (E), the entire Yunnan province formed an independent kingdom, the conquest of which, aimed at by the existing Emperor, was the main cause that led to the downfall of the dynasty in the first decade of the tenth century A.D. From a historical point of view, the more natural way is to divide this whole region into two unities instead of four; namely, Kwangtung and Yunnan.

The accounts of the barbarians of the southwest by Ssŭma Ch'ien and Pan-Ku, made accessible to Europeans by Wylie, relate chiefly to the tribes of modern Southern Szechuan, Yunnan, and Kweichow. Concisely, Pan-Ku described these tribes in the following terms: "Among the barbarians of the south, there were several tens of Chiefs, the largest of their domains being the Yailang. To the west of that were the Me-Mo tribes, several tens in number, the largest domain being that of Teen. To the north of Teen were several tens of Chiefs, the largest domain being that of K'eung-too. . . . All these tribes *bound up their hair in a knot, cultivated the ground, and congregated in towns.* Beyond these to the west, from Tung-sze eastward, and north as far as Yeh-Yu, all were included under the name of Suy and Kween-Ming. *These people plaited their hair and removed their dwellings for the convenience of pasturage, having no fixed residence. They had no chiefs and their land might be estimated at several thousands of square li.* Northeast from Suy, there were several tens of Chiefs, the largest domains being those of Se and Tsotoo. Northeast from Tso there were some tens of chiefs, Yeng and Mang being the largest of the domains. *Some of these tribes cultivated the ground, and others led a migratory life.* On the west of Shu, and northeast from Mang, were several tens of Chiefs, the greatest being that of Pih-Ma. These all belong to the Tê race. . . ." [1]

The accounts further show that the actual contact of these barbarian tribes with the historical We-group began at this period. For, further on, the account continues:

"At first in the time of Wei, the King of T'soo (Ch'u) (339–329 B.C.), the general Chwang Keau was sent up the Keang with troops to settle the boundaries of the several tribes from Pa and Teen-Chung westward. Chwang Keau was a descendant of Chwang, the King of Tsoo (613–591 B.C.). On reaching the Tien marsh (Yunnan) he found it three hundred li square bordered by rich level land for some thousand li; of which the inhabitants, whom he overawed by his military strength, were attached to the Kingdom Ts'oo. . . ."

The beginning of the influence of the We-group over Yunnan, therefore, may be set at this period (339–329 B.C.).

Among the further information given in the *History of the Later Han Dynasty* concerning the barbarian tribes of the southwest, the following items are significant:

(1) The Yai-lang tribe eat breadfruit and have surnames, the most eminent of which are Lung, Yün, Tung, (Yunnan).

(2) The Ngai-Lo tribe carve their bodies (puncture method) with a dragon design; wear clothes having tails; live in villages; have bamboo boats, a dragon myth, chieftains; pierce the nose; elongate the ear — the King three inches below the shoulder, the commoners only to the shoulder; have mulberries, silkworms; wear bark clothes; — the bark clothes first used to cover the dead body and then worn; have copper, iron, tin, lead, gold, silver, and bright beads, pearls, and so forth.

(3) The Chung-Tu (Yunnan) are licentious, fond of singing; have chieftains; are rebellious; make poisonous wine.

(4) The Tso-tu have long hair, and button their coats on the left side.

(5) Yuen-Pang (W. Szechuan) consists of six Yi, seven Chiang, and nine Ti; the chieftains read and write; the laws are strict; woman's position is high; descent is matrilineal; cremation is practised. The region is cold in winter, hence the people work as servants in Shu (Szechuan) in the winter quarter and go back in summer to their stone houses, which are often very high; they have no cereals except wheat; the hornless ox (Yak) is native there; the people make blankets, and so forth (Tibetans?).

In the case of Kwangtung, Ssŭ-ma Ch'ien is again to be our au-

---

[1] Wylie's translation in *History of the Southwestern Barbarians* J. A. I., vol. 9 (1880), pp. 55, 56.

thority. In book 103, *The Biography of Wei-to, Chieftain of Nan-Yüeh* (*Kwangtung and Kwangsi*), the beginning of the colonization of Kwang-tung is set forth in unmistakable terms:

". . . After Ch'in Shih Huang-ti had unified China (221 B.C.), he began to conquer the territory of Yang and Yah (Chekiang, Kiangsi, Fukien) and set up three administrative areas: Kweiling, Nanhai, and Hisang-Chün (Kwangtung, Kwangsi, Yunnan, Kweichow) in the south, where the criminals were exiled to live among the 'Yüehs.' . . ."

Wei-to, the chieftain of Nan-Yüeh at the beginning of the Han dynasty, called himself "Man and I." Some quarrel had occurred between this chieftain of the Man I and the court of Han because the Empress Dowager of Han (187–180 B.C.) had forbidden her merchants to sell any iron tools to the barbarians. Other than this no other reference to the ethnographical character of the Yüeh can be found. For a more detailed account, a considerably later period has to be referred to.

These early accounts of the southern barbarians shows that practically all the provinces south of the Yangtze and Szechuan were excluded from the influence of the historical We-group as late as the beginning of the Christian era. About this time, however, the influence of the We-group began to extend to the south of the Yangtze among the various indigenous tribes. The following table gives a summary of the approximate dates of the beginning of the influence of the We-group in the various provinces, and also the various indigenous tribes as recorded by the historians of the C and D periods.

TABLE 74

Provinces	Beginning of the influence of the We-group	Indigenous tribes as recorded by the historians of the C and D period
Szechuan	316 B.C.	Pa, Shu, Pantung, Liao
Hunan	47 A.D.	Pan-hu
Kiangsi	138 B.C.	Tung Yüeh
Chekiang	138 B.C.	Tung Yüeh
Fukien	138 B.C.	Min-Yüeh
Kwangtung	221 B.C.	Nan-Yüeh
Kwangsi	221 B.C.	Nan-Yüeh
Yunnan	330 B.C.	Tê, Ngailo, etc.
Kweichow	330 B.C. (?)	Yailang- (?)

FORMS OF RELATIONSHIP

Once the contact had begun, it may be assumed that there were only three possible forms of this relationship between the two groups. In the course of time the You-group is either (1) assimilated, or (2) annihilated, or (3) in constant conflicts with the invading We-groups. I have evidence to show that all of these relationships have obtained, except the process of annihilation. Conflict, especially, has been the most conspicuous and tenacious. The prevalence of any one form depends largely on circumstances, but also to a certain extent on the inherent nature of the particular You-group and their attitude toward the culture that the We-group brought with them.

In the 82d Book of the *History of the Sui Dynasty*, the southern barbarians were described collectively as declining. Cropping the hair and tattooing were the two traits noticed by the We-group in regard to these barbarians. But, according to these accounts, they mixed with the northern immigrants and enjoyed the same civil rights as they did. The statement is of course a little vague, and offers no light as to the extent to which the You-group was assimilated. It is significant, however, to notice that the two groups mixed quite freely, and there was no political discrimination. This period, as we may remember, was feeling the full effect of the Yünchia movement, which had its sphere of most intensive activity in Hunan, Kiangsi, Chekiang, and Fukien. Bearing these two points in mind, the passages on the ethnography of these provinces in this period become significant reading.

"In Yanchow (including Chekiang, Kiangsi, Fukien, Kwangtung, and Kwangsi at this period), the people are mostly hunters and fishers. They do not save. . . . They are superstitious and believe in many ghosts. Father and son often maintain independent households. In some parts (N. Kiangsi), women work in the market like a man and go so far as to support their husbands. . . . In others (Kiangsi, Fukien) the people cultivate Ku.[1] . . ." (Book 31, *History of Sui*.)

These are, however, the descriptions not of the new immigrants but those of the half assimilated You-group. I base this conclusion on two facts: (1) that some of the ethnographical characters are contrary to the practise of the We-group—for instance, the independence of the son and the following of a profession by the women; and (2) that some survive later on only among the barbarians, not in the typical We-group. This is especially true in the case of the Ku culture.

Since the D period, there have been found no barbarians in the provinces of Chekiang, Fukien, and Kiangsi, as far as the official history goes. This, of course, would not indicate that there have been actually none of the You-group remnant in this region. There actually are. The fact that they were willing to live as the We-group made it

[1] The cultivation of a poisonous insect to murder strangers.

unnecessary for the later historian to call them barbarians. Those who were unwilling to adapt themselves have, as we shall prove later, migrated southwestward to Kwangtung.

Those who were unwilling to adapt themselves were, of course, barbarians. The form of their relationship with the We-group was that of a perennial conflict. The conflict naturally could not take place where there was no trace of the We-group. But the minute the contact with the We-group begins, the conflict necessarily follows. In the following table (cf. Map 80) I have compiled a list of conflicts between the We-group and the You-group in the different parts of the younger provinces from the earliest times up to 1644 A.D. It is based upon the material extracted from the same section of the Encyclopedia in which the dates of the wall-building are found.

TABLE 75

Districts	Periods						
	B	C	D	E	F	G	H
I. Szechuan:							
1. Ch'êntu..................	..	2	1	..	6	..	3
2. Chungchou..............	..	..	..	..	23	..	..
3. Yachou.................	..	..	..	..	3	..	..
4. Tatuho.................	..	..	..	..	14	..	..
II. Hunan:							
1. Shenchoufu.............	5	20	18	2	88	3	8
2. Paochinfu..............	..	..	..	8	24	3	8
III. Kwangsi:							
1. Kweilingfu..............	..	..	..	1	1	..	18
2. Liuchou.................	..	..	..	..	2	..	15
3. Ch'inyüanfu.............	..	..	..	..	37	2	35
4. Sze-enfu................	..	..	..	..	..	..	29
5. Pinlofu.................	..	..	..	..	1	2	23
6. Wuchou.................	..	2	..	1	..	..	8
7. Hsünchou...............	..	..	..	..	10	..	18
8. Nanlingfu...............	..	..	..	11	..	1	6
9. T'aip'ingfu.............	..	..	..	..	..	..	7
10. Szemingfu..............	..	..	..	..	..	..	25
11. Chenganfu..............	..	..	..	..	..	..	17
12. Szecheng...............	..	..	..	..	..	..	17
IV. Kwangtung:							
1. Chaoch'ingfu............	..	..	..	..	..	..	10
2. Kaochoufu..............	..	..	..	..	..	..	10
3. Lienchoufu..............	..	2	3	5	2	2	13
4. Ch'ünchoufu............	..	2	..	4	21	15	19
V. Yunnan.................	1	3	3	53	..	7	2
VI. Kweichou...............	..	..	..	..	..	..	91

The above table is instructive in several respects. It not only gives the time order in which the conflicts followed in different parts of these provinces, but it may be safely assumed that in those places where the conflicts occur late in time there could have been no presence of the We-group previous to those occurrences. The conflicts are, in other words, a natural sequence of the southward expansion of the We-group. If the order of the conflicts is viewed in the light of its temporal setting, as well as the direction of their extension, both the line of retreat of the You-group and the line of agression of the We-group will find a clear symbolic expression. It may be discussed province by province.

Chekiang, Fukien, and Kiangsi in this respect are conspicuous by their absence from this historical struggle. This, as I have tried to show, is a clear indication of the ready adaptation to the incoming culture on the part of the You-group in these provinces, and there are historical evidences to confirm this interpretation. This, however, is not meant to exclude the migratory possibility. A part of these indigenous tribes could have migrated southward and southwestward to Kwangtung, Kiangsi, Yunnan, and Indo-China. Topographical consideration shows no difficulties in the way of this expansion, especially as many of these people are reputed to be hill-tribes. So far as I can judge at the present stage of our knowledge about these tribes, this is about the case.

In Hunan, where the P'an-hu tribes were found originally, there were two points of constant conflict. Both of them are located in the western part of this province. The conflict was most severe in the F period (Sung dynasty), and, as may be expected, it began on the north (Shenchowfu) far back in the Chou dynasty (period B). But it diminished phenomenally in the two succeeding periods.

In Szechuan, the points of conflict were located in the west and the south; and, as in Hunan, the struggles began in the Sung dynasty, when no less than forty-two took place.

In Kwangtung the places of conflict were again in the south and the west. The Island of Hainan seems to have been coveted by the colonizers as early as the Han dynasty; so was Lienchou, one of the west coastal districts of this province. The western inland districts, Chaoching and Kaochow, had a peaceful existence until the H period. This shows clearly that the migratory route chosen by the We-group after they had reached Kwangtung was first along the seacoast, by which they also moved northward into Kwangsi by way of Lienchow.

This is proved by the fact that in Kwangsi all the four quarters had

offered resistance; the line was first broken at Wuchow (C) a city on the
West River, and then at Nanling and Kweiling (E). In Chapter V it
has been shown that there is a line of migration from Hunan southward
across the northeast border of Kwangsi to Kwangtung. This easily
explains the Kweiling and Wuchow conflicts in the early period. It
may of course also explain the early conflict at Nanling, since this is a
district situated on a branch river which flows into the West River.
But it is also possible that the Nanling conflict was a result of the incoming immigrants who had followed the Kwangtung coastal line.
Kwangsi's drama, however, was fully staged only in the Ming dynasty;
and this contest, one may safely infer, ramified from these three points,
since there could be no possible source from Kweichow.

In Kweichow, nothing occurred until the Ming dynasty. The ninety-
one conflicts in the Ming dynasty show conclusively that in this period
a large number of immigrants must have come into this province.

Last of all, in Yunnan the conflicts began early and ended late. This
province offers the most puzzling problem. The climax of the struggle
came in the T'ang dynasty, during which the famous Nanchao Kingdom ruled this province. So the struggles occurring in this period can
hardly be interpreted as the southward push of the We-group, inasmuch as the Nanchao Kingdom was often on the offensive side.
Undoubtedly there were immigrants in this period. But the degree of
intensity of the movement cannot be determined either by the frequency of the struggles or the degree of activity of the wall-building.
All in all, Yunnan seems to be the most complicated problem. What is
more is that in Yunnan, at the end of the Ming dynasty, the greatest
number of barbarian tribes were found.

As a result of this survey a few points need to be emphasized before
we proceed with the classification of the aborigines and their migrations.

A fourth line of the southward migration of the We-group to Szechuan must be added. Since the conflict between the We-group and the
You-group in this province goes as far back as the Han dynasty, and
the point of conflict is found in the western part (Ch'ên-tu) of the
province, it shows that there was probably a great settlement of the
We-group in the eastern part previous to this period, the beginning of
which, as previously noted, is to be dated in the fourth century B.C.
I say "probably" quite advisedly. And this for the reason that a large
part of this settlement might have been the result of the assimilation of
the barbarian tribes. In this case, it could only indicate the spread of
the culture of the We-group instead of their actual migration. But even

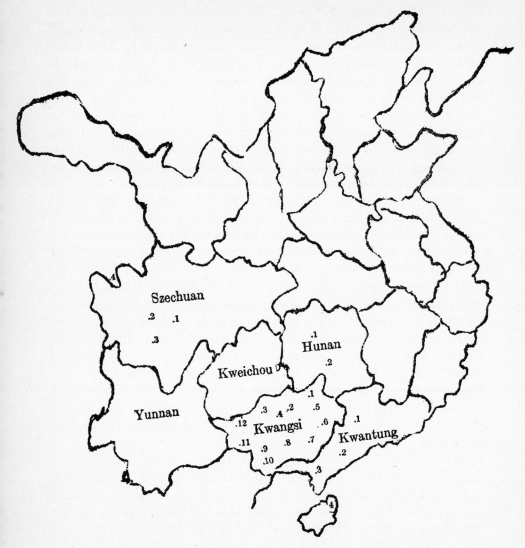

MAP. 80. Conflicting Districts between the We-group and the You-group in the Southwestern Provinces, Numbers indicating the different Districts (cf. Table 75)

253

then a total absence of migrations to this province cannot be confirmed. As it is, this line of migration also proves to be the earliest. This line continued southward to Yunnan.

This survey also furnishes additional evidence for the establishment of the conclusion about the Hunan-Kwangtung migration, the Kiangsi migration, and the Chekiang migration. What is especially new is the revelation of the westward thrust of the We-group in the Sung dynasty, which is shown both in the case of Szechuan and Hunan; the northward migration of the southern tribes is also an important addition to our knowledge of the migration of peoples.

III. Classifications and Migrations

In the absence of any available physical data, linguistic classification forms the only basis for the grouping of these tribes. Unfortunately, however, even in the way of philological classification, hardly anything final can be said. The pioneer work initiated by Terrien de Lacouperie [1] has not found many successors. De Lacouperie's work is inaccurate in many respects and he often mistook many perfectly good Chinese vocabularies for those of aborigines.[2] The main difficulty in the way of classification of these tribes on a philological basis lies in the excessive multiplication of small communities and the apparent minute divisions based on local appellations of extensive tribes. Moreover, the ancient sounds of the Chinese language are not yet fully reconstructed, and the grammatical structure of the Chinese written language is quite misleading as a basis of philological study. The work of Lacouperie based entirely on historical documents would be, in the nature of the case, necessarily inaccurate and incomplete, even if he had read the original documents faithfully.

A recent work [3] by Major H. R. Davis has made a great advance along this line. For one thing the material is collected entirely in the field. Barring the personal equation, his classification is more satisfactory, although on the whole the system does not deviate much from that of Lacouperie. Dr. V. K. Ting,[4] so far as I know, is the last person who has attempted anything in this field. Neither Davis nor Ting is

---

[1] *The Language of China before the Chinese.* London, 1897.

[2] The study of the vocabulary of Nanchao is one example. On page 60 of the above book the words: tsong-so, tchi-jen Kuan, tu-to, are all Chinese words which he took for those of Nanchao. There are many other examples of this kind.

[3] *Yunnan.* Cambridge, University Press. 1909.

[4] Anatomical and Anthropological Association of China, *China Medical Journal,* 1921.

a trained philologist. Since Ting's work is based on that of Davis with modifications, Ting's system is taken here as a starting point for tracing the historical migration of these tribes.

V. K. Ting's Classification of the Languages of Yunnan

After Major Davis with Modifications

A.	Mon–Khmer:	(*a*) Miao-Yao branch.	(1) Miao
			(2) Yao
		(*b*) Wa-Palaung.	(1) Wa or K'awa
			(2) La or Kala
			(3) Puman
			(4) Palaung
			(5)
			(6) Chisi
B.	Shan:	Shan Group.	(1) Pa-yi, including Lüjen, Nun-gen, Shajen, Chengchia, T'ulao, Mengwu, Lamao
			(2) Minchia, or Nama
C.	Tibeto–Burman:	(*a*) Tibetan Group.	(1) Tibetan or Kutsang
			(2) Hsifan
			(3)
			(4) Lutzu
			(5) Chintze
		(*b*) Lao Group.	(1) Lolo
			(2) Liso
			(3) Woni
			(4) Lahu
		(*c*) Burmese group.	(1) Achang
			(2) Maru
			(3) Lashi
			(4) Zi
		(*d*) Kaishin.	(1) Kaishin

D. The Negritos

These, it must be noted, represent the modern southern tribes in China and they are limited to the province of Yunnan. Whether or not they are comprehensive enough for the purpose here will be seen in the course of time. It will be convenient, however, to trace the movement of these tribes up to 1644 A.D. on this basis.

A. *The Mon-Khmer group:* The Miao-Yao branch of this group had never been represented in Yunnan up to 1644 A.D. Of more than 60 tribes described in book 1515 of the Encyclopedia only "Puman" may be taken as representing the Mon-Khmer group in this province. But this tribe with three of its cognates is found all over the southern border of Yunnan from K'aehua in the southeast to Yün Ch'ang in the south-west. It is significant to notice that K'aihua is a district bordering

Kwangsi where the Miao-Yao are found throughout. The same is true with Kweichow, except that the Miaos are more especially preponderant. In Kwangtung they are found as far east as Kwangchou, and northward up to the southern border of Shaochow. The two western districts of Hunan-Shenchou and Yüan-Chou were the homes of the Yaos, in the Han dynasty (period C), and they were flourishing in the Ming period in spite of the western thrust of the We-group in Sung time (period F). The southeastern border of Hupeh and the northern border of Kiangsi and Hunan are the earliest homes of the Miaos. It is necessary to remember that the Miaos are the first of the You-group that disturbed the We-group. They figured the most prominently in the *Book of History*. It is possible that their original home might even have been north of the Yangtze, although there is no actual proof of this.

If the Mon-Khmer group is taken as a whole, its migration may be said to begin on the northern border of Kiangsi and Hunan in the B period. It was probably pushed southwestward to the western border of Hunan during the B–C period. On this border it remained for a long time and ramified subsequently in all directions except toward the east. Its northward movement in the D period has already been noted. The southward movement must have taken place long before the eleventh century A.D., for in 1172 A.D. Fan Ch'ên-ta, a resident at Ch'in-Chiang, the modern Kuei-lin, in northeast Kwangsi, found them already in a flourishing state. The date of the westward movement to Kweichow is uncertain; but it could not have been earlier than the D period. In the T'ang dynasty (period E), none of the subject races of the Nanchao Kingdom had any Mon-Khmer affiliation, so the people speaking these languages must have moved from Kwangsi to Yunnan between periods F and H. Presumably they must also have branched off eastward to Kwangtung. There is good reason to set this movement in the F period, because in this period the second southward movement of the We-group took place. It is conceivable that the Tungting line of the We-group had forced the Mon-Khmer group in Kwangsi both eastward and westward. In the east, however, it was stopped at Kwangchow by another line of the We-group from Fukien, the continuation of the T'ai line. As a result of this set-back, its west flank was much consolidated and so it was enabled to wedge into Yunnan continuously up to the end of the Ming dynasty — 1644 A.D.

B. *The Shan Group:* The modern representatives of the Shan are the Siamese, Laos, and so forth, found directly south of Yunnan. One of its most typical ethnographical traits is tattooing.[1] This trait so far as I know is associated neither with the Mon-Khmer group nor with the Tibeto-Burmna group in China proper. So unless there is still a fourth branch which uses tattooing as a means of beautifying the body, it is safe to assume that the traces of tattooing in China may serve to indicate the traces of the Shan Group. The following aborigines of South China, besides those noticed previously, are said to tattoo their body:

(1) The Chuachia of Yunnan in the Ming dynasty. Encyclopedia, Book 1515.

(2) The Wennen of Yunnan in the T'ang dynasty. Encyclopedia, Book 1515.

(3) The Pa-pei-hsi-fu of Yunnan in the T'ang dynasty. Encyclopedia, Book 1515.

(4) The White-footed Pa-Yi of Yunnan in the T'ang dynasty. Encyclopedia, Book 1515.

(5) The Langs of Linchow, Kwangsi in the Ming dynasty. Encyclopedia, Book 1410.

(6) The Li-Jen of Hainan in the Ming dynasty. Encyclopedia, Book 1391.

(7) The Atayals of Formosa. Davidson, J. W., *The Island of Formosa: Past and Present*. London, 1903.

It may be recalled that the southwestern barbarians described in the *History of the Later Han Dynasty*, all belonged to the Tê race (Tibetan group). They were found all over Yunnan and Kweichow. If the sundry tribes in this region during the Han dynasty all belonged to the Tibeto-Burman group, there could have been no contemporaneous trace of the Shan-speaking group in the same region, or at least none known to the historians of the We-group. On the other hand, in the C period, the tattooing people known as "the Ou" and "the Yüeh" were found all through the southeastern provinces — Chekiang, Kiangsi, and Fukien. Whether the people of Kwangtung and Kwangsi of this period were in any way related to the tattooing people or not can only be left to conjecture. But the fact that they were called the Yüeh of the South, while the tattooing people were known as the Yüeh of the East, indicates a possibility of their being related to each other. Besides, there was at that time the Ngai-lao in south Szechuan, a tattooing and Shan-speaking people. The evidence taken as a whole seems

---

[1] *Amongst the Shans.* A. R. Colquhoun, London, 1885, pp. 206–213.

to indicate that in the Han dynasty the Shan-speaking people were found all over southern China except in Yunnan and Kweichow.

The historical accounts again show that in the middle of the T'ang dynasty (period E) the southwestern barbarians of the C period were replaced by the famous Nanchao Kingdom. This kingdom was constituted of six small principalities. Of these six, five, at least, according to Lacouperie's identification,[1] were Shan-speaking, while one (Yueh-hsih, the progenitor of Moso) belongs to the Tibeto-Burman group. Apparently the authority of the Tibeto-Burman (the Tê of Han) declined considerably from period C to F, and the Shans, who were unknown in this region about the beginning of the Christian era, assumed complete ascendency in the course of six hundred years. Bearing these historical facts in mind, the migration of the Shan-speaking peoples can be traced comprehensively.

The condition that necessitated the movement of the Shans was undoubtedly the southward pressure of the We-group which began about the B–C period and intensified in the Yüng-Chia era. There has been occasion, previously, to point out that the T'ai line of the We-group was the most intense at this time, and this must have served as the efficient cause of the movement of the Shan-speaking aborigines to the southwest. Their sudden gain in authority in the T'ang dynasty in Yunnan shows that they must have moved en masse. This, of course, does not mean that they left no remnants behind; on the other hand, there are reasons for believing that a good portion of them were assimilated by the We-group. There are, for instance, the Lang-S'en of Kwangtung, found at the end of the Ming dynasty, who still practised tattooing; the Atayals of Formosa and the Li-jens of Kwangtung may be also considered as their branches in this area. In this case, however, more evidence is needed in order to establish their connections.

After they had reached Yunnan, the Shans evidently determined to make a last stand against the northern invading group, although they kept on their southward migration and gave rise to the modern Siamese. At the end of the Ming dynasty, they were still found all over the province of Yunnan; but not, however, outside of this province.

C. *The Tibeto-Burman group:* The movement of this group within China proper seems to be simpler than that of either of the above. They were found all over Yunnan and Kweichow and the western part of Szechuan in the Han dynasty. They are still found in this part now,

---

[1] *Ibid.*, p. 60.

except in Kweichow. But the incoming current of the We-group undoubtedly caused much disturbance. Since the Tibeto-Burman is itself not a homogeneous group, its intra-group movements may also be safely assumed. But, taken as a whole, the Tibeto-Burman group shows little significant movement within China proper, from the Han dynasty to the Ming, except its withdrawal from Kweichow province.

D. *The Negrito problem:* That there is a negrito problem in South China cannot be denied. Besides the reference to dwarfs in the period of the Three Kingdoms, I have found one more clear-cut historical reference. Among the Yunnan tribes referred to in Book 1515 of the Encyclopedia there is one tribe known by the name of Hala. Unfortunately, they are not definitely located except that they live on the mountains. Here I translate the whole description:

"Hala: Live in the mountains; men wear a breech-cloth, while women wear a deep-black loin girdle made of red and black creepers. The children are carried in a bamboo frame. . . ." (Book 1515.)

The term "hala" is also interesting. The "Luchiang" or "Angry River" (known as the "Black River" in the *Book of History*) of Yunnan has its source in Tibet where the Tibetans call it Halawusu. According to T'zŭ-Yüan, a Chinese Dictionary,[1] "Hala" in Tibetan means "black" while "Wusu" means "river"; hence "Hala-wusu" — "black-river." So in plain terms — "Hala" means no more, no less than "the black."

The description of the Hala given by the Encyclopedia, brief as it is, corresponds almost exactly to that of the modern Sakai as given by Skeat and Blagden.[2] If they do have any affiliation, it would be more appropriate to call them Negroid rather than Negrito. Modern writers[3] on Szechuan and Kansu have found traces of both the Negroid and the Negrito in China. None, however, has found any pure type.

As the black people of Yunnan are known to the Chinese by the Tibetan term, the Tibetans must have known them intimately before the Chinese. This must be due to the fact that the black folk were in Yunnan in a very early period when the Tibetans were still dominant there. This would place them at least as early as period C and very probably earlier. Since dwarfs were found in the south of Nganhui at that time, it may, perhaps, be inferred that traces of the Negroid (or Negrito?) peoples were found all over south China as late as the second

[1] *T'zŭ-yüan.* Commercial Press.
[2] *Pagan Races of Malay Peninsula.* 2 vols., London, 1906.
[3] Bonifacy and Farrer.

century A.D., provided, of course, there was a continuity in the distribution of this race. And this is as much as can be said regarding the problem of "the blacks" in China.

Yunnan, therefore, is the centre of all the historical converging migratory movements in China proper. The Chinese, the Mon-Khmer, the Tibeto-Burmans, the Shans, and the Negroids all had a share in the make-up of the Yunnanese at the end of the Ming dynasty. To what extent these tribes have intermarried is at present quite indeterminable. But that they have intermarried is unquestionable. It is due to this crossing and inter-crossing, I take it, that so large a number of varieties of the aborigines were found at the end of the Ming dynasty.

The intermingling of the different races, as cited above, occurs also in other provinces besides Yunnan. Broadly speaking, the Shans are the most assimilable, and the Mon-Khmer the least, while the Tibeto-Burman occupies an intermediate position. There is probably none of the Negroid element assimilated in the We-group; their intermingling, if there is any, has been largely limited to that with the other aboriginals.

That the Shan-speaking people are the most adaptable of all may be readily shown by the fact that the Yüeh, of all southeast China, have seldom taken a persistently stubborn attitude toward the invading We-group. Their remnants in Yunnan were sometimes called Pê-jen. The Chinese word for Pê is made up of two radicals, one superimposed upon the other; the upper one "Chi" means "bush" and the lower radical "Jen" means "man." Taken together they mean "man under the bush." The origin of the name is due to the fact that in contrast with the Mon-Khmer-speaking people, who are fond of living among the mountains and are known sometimes as the cave-men, the Shan-speaking people have a natural disposition for lower places. They may be aptly described as water people, living among the valleys where plants and berries are found in abundance. They have the reputation of being, among all the aborigines, the most cordial towards the We-group, according to various Chinese writers in the sixteenth century.

On the other hand, the Mon-Khmer-speaking folk are invariably hostile towards the We-group. Most of the conflicts that have been recorded of the We-group in the south were with the Miaos, the Yaos, the T'ungs and the Liaos — all of whom, philologically speaking, belong to the same stock. The Tibeto-Burman-speaking branch, perhaps, has not been much more friendly towards the We-group. Their influ-

ence has been confined more or less to a corner; so their chance of showing hostility towards the We-group in the southeast has been similarly
limited.   As the Shan-speaking branch, who were friendly disposed
towards the We-group, were able to dominate them in the T'ang
dynasty, their hostility towards the We-group would not have added
much to their chance of survival in China proper even if they had had
more occasion to try it.

CHAPTER VII

THE THREE GREAT NORTHERN INVASIONS
PREVIOUS TO 1644 A.D.

WITHIN the boundary of China proper, the barbarians of the north are, comparatively speaking, late comers. The more definitely historical parts of the Chinese documents on the northern You-group have been translated and summarized by E. H. Parker in his "A Thousand Years of the Tartars," which has served up to the present time a useful purpose for many an anthropologist who wished to talk about man, past and present, with reference to Central Asia. There are, of course, problems about the northern You-group previous to that thousand years, and there are problems after the end of that period. But, on the whole, these one thousand years (approximately from the beginning of the Christian era to 1000 A.D.) are perhaps more important than any other period from the point of view of the formation of the modern Chinese. It is, however, beyond my scope here to go into history in detail. My task here, again, is limited to three aspects: the chronology, the extent of invasions, and the ethnographical impression made by the northern You-group on China proper.

The three aspects of each of these three great northern invasions are to be studied: (a) the Hsiung-nu-Hsüen-pei invasion; (b) the Khitan-Nüchên invasion; (c) the Mongol invasion.

To introduce these three great invasions, the remarkable document of Tsiang-tung on the exclusion of the Jung and the Ti (northwest barbarians) written in the third century and partially quoted in Chapter V may be translated here more at length:

". . . As the Government of the Royal House of Chou began to become effete, its sovereignty was violated everywhere by its feudal principalities, of which the larger swallowed the smaller, and the stronger annihilated the weaker. As a consequence, the defensive line on the border was gradually weakened. The feudal lords thus having no unity of purpose, the "Jung" and the "Ti" took this opportunity to sneak into the Middle Kingdom. Some of them were induced to come in by some of the feudal lords to serve in their armies. . . ."

"In the time of Ch'un-Ch'iu (722 B.C.–481 B.C.) I-Ch'ü and Ta-Li were found in the State of Ch'in and Chin (Kansu, Shensi, and Shansi);

Lu-hün and Ying-Jung settled between the river Yi and the river Lo (Honan); the tribe of Shou-man invaded the region east of the river Chi, in the states of Chi, Sung, Han, and Wei (Shantung and Honan); thus the barbarians of the north and the barbarians of the south both invaded the Middle Kingdom at the same time. . . ."

"After the period of Ch'un-ch'iu, when the contending states (481 B.C.–221 B.C.) were in the prime of their power, these inland barbarians were gradually conquered by the various states. . . . Until the time of Ch'in-Shih Huangti, who (in 221 B.C.) unified China into one empire and conquered the Hundred Yüehs of the south and drove the Hsiung-Nu outside of the Great Wall. This great achievement will be ever celebrated in spite of the fact that it involved the loss of millions of lives. At this time there were no barbarians within the domain of the Middle Kingdom."

"The Royal House of Han (206 B.C.–220 A.D.), when it came to power, chose Chang-Ngan (Shensi) as the capital city. For that reason the districts of Kuan chung were called 'The Three Metropolises' (Sanfu). . . . Sanfu was entirely devastated after the upheaval of the period between the two Hans; the inhabitants of this region partly died and partly migrated."

"In the middle of the Chien-wu era (40–41 A.D.), Ma Yuan was appointed the administrator of Lung-hsi (Kansu). He conquered the rebellious Ch'iangs (Tibetans) and moved their tribal remnants to Sanfu, left empty since the devastation about twenty years before, where they settled amidst the Hua-Jen (the We-group). A few years after this forced migration, the Ch'iangs multiplied at a tremendous rate and formed a strong factor in this region. As they became conscious of their 'fatness and great numbers' they began to seek means of expressing their resentment against the oppression of Hua-jen. In the beginning of the Yüng Ch'ie era (107–113 A.D.) Wang Hung was commissioned to take a number of these Chiangs to Hsi-yü (Chinese Turkestan). This gave them cause for alarm. They rebelled and extended their influence southward of Shu-han (Szechuan) and east-ward to Chao and Hsi. . . . It took almost a hundred years to quiet them down again. . . . While the causes of this long and disastrous disturbance may have been many, there is no question that the main one was that they were in the midst of the Middle Kingdom." . . .

"There were still remnants left even after the second conquest. Wherever there was an opportunity, they brought about disturbance. Added to this, the revolution at the end of the Han dynasty devastated

Kuan-chung again. . . . Wei-Wuti (the founder of the Kingdom of Wei in the period of the Three Kingdoms) once made the fatal mistake of moving the tribes of Wutu [1] (South Kansu) to Ch'in-Ch'uan [2] (Kuan-Chung), Shensi, and Kansu) with the purpose of fortifying his own defense and weakening that of the enemy, which might have been a wise plan for that moment but was certainly injurious in its consequences. The evil effects are already beginning to unfold. . . ."

"The soil of Kuan-chung is rich; the products are abundant; the farming lands are classified as the most superior. . . . It is a natural place for Emperors and Kings. Certainly I have never heard that barbarians should be permitted to settle here. They do not belong to our race, and are therefore inscrutable. . . . As they were forced to settle here in the time of their weakness, constantly injured and insulted by the civilians, their resentment must be deeply rooted in the marrow of their bones. They would naturally revolt after they have reached large numbers. Under such a condition and with such a history, disturbance is bound to come if it is not averted in time. . . ."

The author argued further, with a wealth of historical evidence supporting his thesis, the advisability of excluding the barbarians from Chinese soil. He showed that of the total population of Kuan-chung, more than 1,000,000 in number, about half were of "Chiangish" extraction. Then he continued:

"The Hu of Pinchow (East Shensi, Shansi) are the descendants of Hsiungnu, a ferocious northern tribe of old. In the time of Han-Hsüanti (73–49 B.C.) the tribe was broken, suffering hunger and cold and all kinds of privations. It was then divided into five units, which again were united into two. The Hu-han-hsieh Zenghis being weak, lonely, and in isolation, unable to rule the tribe any further, came to the northern border and submitted. In the Chien-wu Era, the Zenghis of the south followed suit; they were (for the first time) allowed to live south of the northern border. But being treacherous by nature they began to make trouble after a few generations. . . . At the end of the Later Han dynasty, when civil war was going on all over China, these Hsiungnu remnants also took the opportunity to plunder as far south as modern Honan. . . ." (Cf. E. H. Parker, pp. 56–94.)

"The number of these tribes now exceeds several ten thousands, and is greater than the Jung of the west. . . ."

"Then there are the Kou-li of Yüng-yang, who were originally the

---

[1] Wutu is on the border of the Kingdom of Chu (modern Szechuan and S. Kansu).
[2] Ch'inchuan belongs to the Kingdom of Wei.

inhabitants of Liao-tung (Manchuria), but now number thousands in this place (Chihli). . . ." (Book 56, *History of Chin.*)

This remarkable document would be worth translating in its entirety if space permitted. But all the essential features have been excerpted here. It gives a historical sketch of the northern invasions from 722 B.C. down to the end of the third century A.D. in the most succinct form. Aside from the masterly fashion in which he handled the historical materials, the author has also portrayed the contemporary condition of the alien population in China's most fertile region. But it must be remembered that China's troubles on the north were in these one thousand years chiefly outside of the Great Wall and our author's task is entirely limited to the forces that have come within. The chronology of these events needs to be specially remembered. The entrance of the Chiang into China proper may be dated in 40 A.D.; that of Hsiung-nu also 40 A.D.; of the Koreans (Kouli), 245 A.D.

This document was written just about ten years before the first great eruption of the northern barbarians took place. If it had been heeded by the reigning emperor to whom it was submitted, the course of events might have been quite different. However that may be, the three great invasions may now be described in the way that has been outlined in the beginning of the chapter.

A. Chronology and Extent, of the Three Northern Invasions

The political chronology and extent of the three northern invasions are well-known historical facts. They may be conveniently summarized, as in Table 76 (page 266).

From a purely historical point of view, the three great northern invasions may be dated respectively as (*a*) 304–580 A.D., (*b*) 907–1235 A.D., and (*c*) 1280–1368 A.D. It is possible to consider the second and the third as one continuous period; it is also reasonable to divide the second period into the Khitan and the Nüchên periods, as their territories in China proper varied considerably. But, on the whole, these are the best chronological divisions. They indicate more faithfully the duration of the political powers of these various You-groups within China proper than any other event, and they serve well as a background for a survey of the ethnographical impressions that these various tribes have left behind as a result of their political ascendancy.

TABLE 76 [1]

Names of the States	Capital	Period of Reign	Group Affiliation
Ch'ien Chao.............	Pin-yang (Shansi) Chang-ngan (Shensi)	304–329 A.D.	Hsiungnu
Pei Liang...............	Chang-I (Kansu)	397–439 A.D.	Hsiungnu
Hsia....................	T'ung-wan (Kansu)	407–432 A.D.	Hsiungnu
Hou Chao...............	Hsiang-Kwo (Chihli)	319–352 A.D.	Hsiungnu
Ch'en..................	Ch'en-tu (Szechuan)	302–347 A.D.	Paman
Ch'ien Ch'in...........	Chang-ngan (Shensi)	351–395 A.D.	
Hou Liang.............	Ku-chang (Kansu)	386–403 A.D.	Te
Hou Ch'in.............	Chang-ngan	384–417 A.D.	Te
Ch'ien Yen.............	Lingchen (Inner Mongolia)	349–370 A.D.	Ch'iang
Hou Yen...............	Chung-shan (Chihli)	384–408 A.D. ⎫	
Nan Yen...............	Kwang-ku (Shantung)	398–410 A.D. ⎪	
Hsi Yen...............	Chung-shan	384–396 A.D. ⎬	Tungus
Hsi Ch'in.............	Wan-chuan (Kansu)	385–432 A.D. ⎪	
Nan Liang.............	Lo-tu (Kansu)	397–414 A.D. ⎭	
Hou Wei...............	P'ing-ch'en (Shansi) ⎫	386–557 A.D.	Tungus
Yüan Wei..............	Loyang (Honan) ⎭		
Pei Ch'i..............	Po (Chihli)	550–557 A.D.	Tungus
Pei Chou.............	Chang-ngan	557–580 A.D.	Tungus
Liao...................	Ling-huang (East Mongolia)	907–1003 A.D.	Khitan
Hsia..................	Ning-hsia-fu (Kansu)	1032–1228 A.D.	
Kin...................	Ta-hsin (Chihli)	1115–1235 A.D.	Nüchen
Yüan..................	Ta-tu (Chihli)	1280–1368 A.D.	Mongol [1]

[1] This table is based largely on the one given in the book on "Methods of Chinese Historical Research." by Liang Ch'i Ch'ao; published by the Commercial Press, 1921. The original table is found on pp. 171–172.

B. Their Ethnographical Effects

It is necessary to keep in mind the distinction between the political domain and the ethnographical domain each of which has its own definition, although to a certain extent related to each other. The task of defining the ethnographical domain may be begun with these questions.

How many of the members of these You-groups settled in China proper during these periods? What were their social relations with the We-group? Were there remnants left over after they were politically excluded?

1. *Hsiung-nu Hsüen-pei Period*

In the first part of this chapter it was shown that according to the estimate of Chiang T'ung in the end of the third century of the Christian era:

(1) About five millions of the population of Shensi and Kansu were Changs.

(2) Several ten thousands of Hsiung-nu were found in Chihli and Shansi and to a certain extent in Shantung.

(3) Several thousands of Koreans were in Chihli.

These served as the starting point of the ascendency of the You-group in North China from the third to the sixth century. The above table shows that in these three hundred years the Hsiung-nu tribes gave rise to four dynasties with Chihli, Shansi, Shensi, and Kansu respectively as their centres of radiation. Aside from overlapping, the period of their ascendancy began at 304 A.D. with Pinyang (Shansi) as the capital and ended at 439 A.D. with Chang-i (Kansu) as the capital. The total duration is thus 135 years; their centres shift gradually westward from Shansi-Chihli to Shensi-Kansu.

Te and Ch'iang were cognate tribes who were the joint ancestors of a part of the modern Tibetans. Their political ascendancy in this period began at 351 A.D. and ended at 403 A.D.; the sphere of their influence was limited to Shensi and Kansu.

The Paman were supreme in Szechuan for thirty-five years (302–347 A.D.). They were a cognate tribe of the Shans.

Most important of all, were the various Hsüen-pei States in North China during this period. For almost two centuries, nearly the entire territory of China proper north of the Yangtze was under their rule. Their influence began at 349 A.D. and ended at 580 A.D.; their greatest centre was Loyang (Honan); their migration began in Inner Mongolia, then spread to Chihli, Shantung, Kansu, Honan, and finally dispersed to Chihli and Shensi again.

Historical materials, so far as I have been able to discover, offer no data for a further estimate of the number of Ch'iangs and Hsiung-nus. So we must, for the moment, rest contented with Chieng T'ung's figure. Nor is a definite estimate of the number of the Tungus tribe in this period ascertainable. What is known is that there were 120 clans of this tribe which migrated to China proper after 220 A.D. (*History of Wei*, book 113). But the process must have been very slow at first for almost seventy years after the beginning of the movement, Chiang T'ung in his memorandum did not yet consider their migration as a menace. In 459 A.D., when the Tungus dynasty was at the height of its power, this imperial edict was recorded in the history:

"All the people who have followed the royal house to Loyang are commanded to bury their dead right in Honan. They shall not move the coffins northward." (*History of Wei*, book 7.)

The historian commented that since that time all the men who had come from Tai-pei (Inner Mongolia) became natives of Honan. About fifty years later, after several devastating wars, the Tungus population of the district of Honan was estimated to be 14,715. (*History of Wei*, book 106.) This it must be remembered was in the last days of the dynasty.

It cannot be wholly true, however, that the Tungus settlement was limited to Honan. Since the political domain of this group had covered practically all of the provinces north of the Yangtze River, their settlement must have been more or less free within this domain. But there is no conceivable way of determining their relative proportions. They had, moreover, adopted wholesale the way of the We-group, including the monosyllabication of their surnames (which took place in 495 A.D.). After the close of the fifth century, ethnographically there is almost no appreciable difference between the Tungus You-group and the We-group north of the Yangtze. Intermarriage between the two groups may be proved by the fact that in the list of the empresses of this dynasty at least two surnames are undoubtedly of the We-group origin. The first invasion as a whole may be said to have ended definitely at 580 A.D., the first year of the reign of the Sui dynasty. In this period of almost three hundred years, the Hsiung-nu tribes moved from Chihli-Shansi to Shensi-Kansu; the Chiang-Tê prospered for a while in Kansu and Shensi, but apparently never moved eastward. The Tungus, the latest comers, dominated North China the longest and also covered the largest area; with Loyang as their capital, their influence permeated everywhere within their domain.

2. *The Khitan-Nüchên Period.*

The Khitan territory was essentially Mongolian and Manchurian and the dynasty was synchronous in the main with the Northern Sung dynasty. Its influence in China proper was limited to the northern part of Chihli and Shansi, and began in 936 A.D. whenS hih Chin-t'ang[1] conceded 16 districts in this part to the Khitans as an award for the military aid that had been given to him in his campaign; it ended in the same year when the Northern Sung dynasty ended — in 1125 A.D., the year when the Nüchên (the Kins, or the "Golden Tartars") made

[1] *History of China*, Wang Fêng Chou, book 27, leaf 10.

a definite step towards their later domination over North China. During these 190 years, the Khitan settlement in the northern part of Shansi and Chihli is almost certain, but there is uncertainty regarding its intensity.[1]

With the advance of the Golden Tartars (Nüchên) the change of racial composition worked in North China can be stated in more definite terms. The provinces of Shantung, Chihli, Shansi, Honan, Shensi, and the southeastern part of Kansu were included in their territory approximately from 1126 A.D. until the days of Kublai Khan, 1235 A.D. The period thus lasts 110 years. In 1180 A.D., the proportion of the candidates for civil administration was fixed as 16 of Hanjer (men of the Middle Kingdom) to 15 of Nüchên. It shows that in spite of the royal affiliation of the Nüchêns their number was inferior in the realm of officialdom to those of the group whom they conquered, and this must have been due to their rather small number as compared with the "Men of Han." (*History of Nüchên*, book 3.)

The economic history of the Nüchen dynasty (book 47, *History of Kin*) has a more significant story to tell regarding the settlement of this group in the interior of China. In 1156 A.D., eleven officials were appointed by the Court of Nüchên to inspect the agricultural land in Ta-Hsin (Chihli), Shantung, and Chenting (Chihli) for the explicit purpose of allotting the uncultivated and the official parts of them to the two Nüchen tribes, "Mungan" and "Mou-k'ê," who had travelled from three to four thousand "li" (a little over 1000 miles) to settle in this newly conquered territory. There were evidently difficulties in the way of these nomadic tribes' settling down and becoming sedentary. Stories of their laziness and incompetency were related in official reports. They often, by virtue of their noble affiliation, compelled the "poor" men to till the land for them, while they enjoyed the benefit of the crop without due labor. They utilized their leisure to drink and work havoc. Wherever they went they are said to have pillaged the land of the poor quite shamelessly. Finally, the immorality of these "nobles" had reached such a degree that some reform measures were deemed necessary by the "Royalties." Prohibition, which has been considered as a twentieth-century supreme achievement of democratic America, was

---

[1] *The History of Liao* (Khitan) gives 232,000 and 157,300 households in the northern parts of Chihli and Shansi respectively (book 35), but it is not clear whether they were the original inhabitants of these regions. The administration of this dynasty consists of two sets of officials; one for the Khitans and the other for the people of the Middle Kingdom. This indicates that quite a large portion of the population of the Khitan domain were apparently of the We-group origin. (Book 47.)

actually enforced for some time among these "nobles" in order to lessen the opportunity for their misbehavior. The efficacy of this measure is unknown. But their lawlessness was reported in Shansi and Honan in later times. In 1183 A.D., the total population of Nüchên was estimated to be 6,306,888, of which 1,391,856 were the slaves of the rest. (*History of Kin*, book 47.) Unfortunately, their distribution is not given in detail. The relative distribution, however, may be inferred from a later report which states that in 1221 A.D. the "militant population" south of the eastern bend of the Yellow River alone (Honan and Shantung) was about 400,000.

On the whole it is quite impossible to estimate the exact number of the Nüchên that came into China proper in this period. Even if there were a definite number given, it would be hazardous to infer that it was a number which remained constant. So after all the exact number is not important. One fact, and the only important one in this connection, to my mind, is that the Nüchên immigrants actually settled down to pursue agriculture as their occupation — a change which could not but produce a profound change in the racial composition of this part of China. Unless the Nüchên were born incompetent in the way of agriculture, in which case they might have been driven away economically after the decline of their political influence, I have no reason to doubt that their descendants are largely represented in the later population of Northeastern and part of Central Eastern China — especially Honan, Shantung, and Chihli.

3. *The Mongols*

The Mongol dynasty lasted 88 years. This is the first time that the entire territory of China was in the hands of the You-group. Their contribution to the racial integration of the Chinese people is again quite indeterminable. Their relative influence in different parts of China proper, however, may be inferred in an indirect way.

According to book 81, *History of Yüan*, the 300 candidates for civil service were apportioned as follows:

1. Mongols	75
2. Shê-mu Jen	75
3. Han Jen	75
4. Nan Jen	75

All these terms have a certain ethnical significance. The term Shê-mu Jen occurs very frequently in the History of the Yüan dynasty. The tribesmen from the north were all known to the Chinese by this term at that time. Han Jen indicates those Chinese who had been long in contact with the incoming You-group of the Sung dynasty, while Nan Jen were the members of the We-group who migrated southward during this period.

More significant is the distribution of the number of candidates in different areas:

TABLE 77

Groups	Mongols		Shê-mu Jen		Han Jen		Nan Jen	
Provinces	No.	%	No.	%	No.	%	No.	%
Shantung ⎫ Chihli ⎬ .... Shansi ⎭	34	45.33	28	37.33	42	56.00	..	...
Honan ⎫ N. Kiangsu ⎬ .... Hupeh ⎭	5	6.66	5	6.66	9	12.00	7	9.33
S. Kiangsu ⎫ Chekiang ⎪ Fukien ⎬ .... E. Kwangtung ⎭	5	6.66	11	14.66	..	..	28	37.33
Kiangsi ⎫ Kwangtung ⎬	3	4.00	6	8.00	..	...	22	29.33
Hunan ⎫ Kwangsi ⎬ .... Kweichow ⎭	3	4.00	7	9.33	..	...	18	24.00
Yunnan................	1	1.33	2	2.66	2	2.66	..	...
Szechuan...............	1	1.33	3	4.00	5	6.66	..	...
Shensi..................	5	6.66	3	4.00	5	6.66	..	...
Kansu..................	3	4.00	2	2.66	2	2.66	..	...
Manchuria..............	5	6.66	2	2.66	4	5.33	..	...
Mongolia...............	9	12.00	5	6.66	5	6.66	..	...
Korea..................	1	1.33	1	1.33	1	1.33	..	...
Total...............	75	...	75	...	75	...	75	...

Whatever the actual number of the different elements, I believe the relative percentages represent the relative densities of the different strata of population in this dynasty. What is more interesting than anything else in this table is the status of the Shê-mu Jen. They were found all over China, although their distribution was quite different both from that of the Han Jen and the Nan Jen.

More puzzling, however, is the absence of the Nan Jen from Yunnan where the Han Jen were found. It is probably true that the Han Jen were hybrids between the old Nüchên and the We-group that had been left behind after the Chin K'ang movement. When the Mongols conquered Yunnan,[1] they went there as soldiers. Thus it would seem that although both Nan Jen and Han Jen were of the We-group, the Han Jen were less pure than the Nan Jen; and their lesser purity was mainly due to the influence of the Nüchên blood. I have found, however, no positive evidence showing the frequency of inter-marriage between the Nüchêns and the We-group; neither have I found any explicit taboo. So the previous definitions may be accepted for further discussion without much qualification.

The Mongols, on the other hand, seem to have shown less inclination to inter-breed with the other groups. In the civil law of the Mongol dynasty, I have found this curious exception to the ordinary marriage laws:

50: "Any Han Jen, or Nan Jen who shall marry his step-mother after the death of his father, or the sister-in-law after the death of his brother, shall be subject by law to blows." (*History of Yuan*, book 103.)

Now this is the only one of the sixty-six articles regarding marriage that shows any difference between the Han Jen and Nan Jen on the one hand, and the Mongols and the Shê-mu Jen on the other. The Mongols and the Shê-mu Jen are allowed the full privilege of marrying their step-mother as well as the sister-in-law when there is an opportunity, while the Nan Jen are not encouraged to imitate them. The difference in legal regulation shows that intermarriages between the We-group and the You-group in this period, if existing at all, were hardly a common feature. And we know from history that in the beginning of the Ming dynasty most of the Mongols were expelled to the north of the Great Wall. Even then, however, their impression on the make-up of the Chinese, especially the northern Chinese, is not to be totally denied. This completes the third great northern invasion previous to 1644 A.D.

[1] It is only in this period that Yunnan was incorporated into China proper.

CHAPTER VIII

INTEGRATION OF THE MODERN CHINESE

IF we take the modern Chinese as a vast heterogeneous unit like an organic chemical compound, and analyze it like a chemist into the respective elements which have entered into its formation, we find, on the basis of the previous five chapters, that there are at least ten elements which we can distinguish. They are:

(1) The Descendants of the Yellow Emperor.
(2) The Hsiung-nu group.
(3) The Ch'iang group.
(4) The Hsüen-pei group.
(5) The Khitan group.
(6) The Nüchên group.
(7) The Mongol group.
(8) The Tibeto-Burman-speaking group.
(9) The Shan-speaking group.
(10) The Mon-Khmer-speaking group.

These represent, however, only those which we can treat definitely. Almost equally important are:

(11) The Jungs of the B period.
(12) The Turks of the E period.
(13) The Negritos of an immemorial past.

It is, however, doubtful whether the last three elements have played any appreciable part in the formation of the modern Chinese, although their appearance within the boundary of China proper is out of the question.

It would be interesting, of course, to trace the formative process from the very beginning; but for reasons that I have indicated in the first chapter, I take 722 B.C. as my starting point, when the silk-wearing, city-building, and rice-eating Descendants of the Yellow Emperor were on the eve of developing a civilization in concrete form in the next five hundred years. They represent, in other words, the earliest We-group.

The expansion of this We-group within China proper was mainly in a southward direction as is indicated by the city points (Chapter III). But here a distinction needs to be made between the We-group as an historical concept and the Descendants of the Yellow Emperor as a physical unit. The expansion of the We-group therefore cannot be taken as an index of the expansion of the Descendants of the Yellow Emperor. Since I have treated in detail the expansion of the We-group, my task here is to be limited to tracing the migration of the Descendants of the Yellow Emperor.

Taken by and large, the Descendants of the Yellow Emperor, like the We-group as a whole, show two great movements in historical times: the Yüng Chia drift and the Ching-K'ang drift. But the Yüng-Chia drift represents the Descendants of the Yellow Emperor in a purer form. The reason is that in the period of the first great northern invasion, the Hsiung-nu, the Tungus, and the Ch'iangs, as we have reason to believe (Chapter VII), must have mixed to a certain extent with the Descendants of the Yellow Emperor who had remained in the north since the Yüng Chia drift. As a matter of historical fact, the intermarriage of the Royal House of the Han dynasty with the Zenghis of the Hsiung-nu was a very common practice as a measure of political expediency. For this reason, Mr. Parker has inferred that intermarriage between the Hsiung-nu group and the Descendants of the Yellow Emperor had been in process for a long time along the northern frontier — that is, along the Great Wall. This may be very true. This condition might even be extended far inland as, according to Chiang-T'ung, "several ten thousands" of Hsiung-nu and about five million Ch'iangs are found in northern China in the early D period. There is reason to believe, however, that the mixture could not be very free, since, as Chiang T'ung indicated in his *Memoir*, most of these aliens were in a servile condition. The history of T'ang recorded also that the more artistocratic families of this period were singularly strict in their choice of mates. Social conditions, however, must have changed after the political ascendancy of these intruding groups. While at present we do not have any way of determining even the approximate degree of mixture of races, it is at least safe to conclude that there was a great change in physical type among the inhabitants of northern China in the D period.

If the remaining part of the Descendants of the Yellow Emperor had been mixing with the intruding You-group from the north in this period, it might be interesting to inquire whether the migrating part of the

Descendants of the Yellow Emperor were doing the same thing with the retreating You-group of the south. In this connection, it is necessary to recall that, although the first great southward drift did not take place until the Yüng Chia era, the actual migration began very early. I have found two recorded instances, one showing the intermarriage between the royal house of Ch'in and the "Shu" of Szechuan in the B period, and the other showing that the Chieftain of Yüeh (Kwang-tung) married a girl in Loyang in period C. These serve to show that there was no social taboo on intermarriage between the Descendants of the Yellow Emperor and the southern You-group. If this condition had lasted, the great southern drift that took place in period D must have intensified the process. For intimacy of racial contact is bound to bring about intermarriage; this is true even with widely different types such as the black and the white in America in spite of the strong social aversion. In the case of Eastern Asia, where biological dissimilarity is even less notable than that found in Western Europe, this biological law is bound to have operated. The only question concerning this point is the matter of degree. The Yüng Chia movement, then, not only changed the ethnographical map of North China—it also produced profound changes south of the Yangtze. The Chiang K'ang movement that followed it several centuries later represented no longer the We-group in its earliest form. It was the drift of a kind of alloy, so to speak, tempered and mellowed by a number of new elements. This indicates that previous to 1644 A.D., although the northern intruding groups with the exception of the Mongols seldom crossed the Yangtze, nevertheless the blood of the Hsiung-nu, the Tungus, and the Ch'iang may already have pulsed in Southern China for several centuries.

To sum up: The processes formative of the modern Chinese from 722 B.C. onward consisted in the persistence of the silk-wearing, rice-eating, and city-building Descendants of the Yellow Emperor as the earliest We-group, enlarged by the incorporation of the horse-riding, kumiss-drinking, flesh-eating Hsiung-nus; the yak-driving Ch'iangs; the pig-rearing Tungus and the cattle-stealing Mongols since the beginning of the Christian era; and correlated with the absorption and incorporation of the tattooing Shan-speaking group, the cremating Tibeto-Burman-speaking group and the Kanlan-dwelling Mon-Khmer-speaking group, in the course of the expansion of the We-group south of the Yangtze.

This still leaves a gap of 278 years (1644 A.D.–1922 A.D.). The main new element that has come in to take part in this formative process is that of the Manchus. The Manchus are, however, only a branch of the Tungus, and their addition can be considered merely as a reënforcement of the Tungus group in China proper.

The process, however, has affected different parts of China differently. These various parts thus need individual considerations. The following eighteen tables show the successive appearances of the different ethnographical elements in the different provinces.

TABLE 78

1. KANSU

Periods

B   Occupied by the Descendants of the Yellow Emperor.
C   Intrusion of the Ch'iangs began.
D   The Ch'iang, the Hsiung-nu, and the Tungus, all had capitals here for some time.
E   We-group.
F   Ruled by the Tungus.
G   Invaded by the Mongols.
H   The We-group.

Total Number of Elements

(1) The Descendants of the Yellow Emperor.
(2) The Ch'iangs.
(3) The Hsiung-nu.
(4) The Tungus.
(5) The Mongol.

2. SHENSI

B   Occupied by the Descendants of the Yellow Emperor.
C   Intrusion of the Ch'iangs and the Hsiung-nus began.
D   The Ch'iangs, the Hsiung-nus, the Tungus, and the Mon-Khmer.
E   The We-group.
F   The Second Invasion of the Tungus.
G   Ruled by the Mongols.
H   The We-group.

Total Number of Elements

(1) The Descendants of the Yellow Emperor.
(2) The Ch'iangs.
(3) The Hsiung-nu.
(4) The Tungus.
(5) The Mon-Khmer.
(6) The Mongol.

3. SHANSI

Periods

B   Occupied by the Descendants of the Yellow Emperor.
C   Invasion of the Hsiung-nu began.
D   Invaded by the Hsiung-nu, the Tungus, and the Mon-Khmer.
E   The We-group.
F   The Second Invasion of the Tungus.
G   The Mongol rule.
H   The We-group.

Total Number of Elements

(1) The Descendants of the Yellow Emperor.
(2) The Hsiung-nu.
(3) The Tungus.
(4) The Mon-Khmer.
(5) The Mongol.

4. CHIHLI

B   Occupied by the Descendants of the Yellow Emperor.
C   Invasion of the Hsiung-nu began.
D   The Koreans, the Hsiung-nu, the Tungus, and the Mon-Khmer.
E   The We-group.
F   The Tungus.
G   The Mongol rule.
H   The We-group.

Total Number of Elements

(1) The Descendants of the Yellow Emperor.
(2) The Hsiung-nu.
(3) The Korean.
(4) The Tungus.
(5) The Mon-Khmer.
(6) The Mongol.

TABLE 78 (CONTINUED)

5. SHANTUNG

Periods

B Occupied by the Descendants of the Yellow Emperor.
C The We-group
D The Tungus.
E The We-group.
F The Tungus.
G The Mongol.
H The We-group.

Total Number of Elements

(1) The Descendants of the Yellow Emperor.
(2) The Tungus.
(3) The Mongol.

6. HONAN

B Occupied by the Descendants of the Yellow Emperor.
C The We-group.
D The Tungus, the Mon-Khmer.
E The We-group.
F The Tungus.
G The Mongol.
H The We-group.

Total Number of Elements

(1) The Descendants of the Yellow Emperor.
(2) The Tungus.
(3) The Mon-Khmer.
(4) The Mongol.

7. SZECHUAN

B Occupied by the Shans. (?)
C The We-group.
D The Mon-Khmer, the Tibetans.
E The We-group.
F The We-group.
G The Mongol.
H The We-group.

Total Number of Elements

(1) The Shans.
(2) The We-group of period C (the Descendants of the Yellow Emperor).
(3) The Mon-Khmer.
(4) The Tibeto-Burman.
(5) The Mongol.

8. HUPEH

Periods

B The Descendants of the Yellow Emperor, the Shans.
C The We-group, the Mon-Khmer.
D The Tungus.
E The We-group.
F The We-group.
G The Mongol.
H The We-group.

Total Number of Elements

(1) The Descendants of the Yellow Emperor.
(2) The Shans.
(3) The Mon-Khmer.
(4) The Tungus.
(5) The Mongol.

9. NGANHUI

B The Descendants of the Yellow Emperor.
C The We-group, the Dwarfs.
D The Tungus.
E The We-group.
F The Tungus and the We-group.
G The Mongol.
H The We-group.

Total Number of Elements

(1) The Descendants of the Yellow Emperor.
(2) The Dwarfs.
(3) The Tungus.
(4) The Mongol.

10. KIANGSU

B The Descendants of the Yellow Emperor, the Shans.
C The We-group.
D The We-group.
E The We-group.
F The We-group.
G The Mongol.
H The We-group.

Total Number of Elements

(1) The Descendants of the Yellow Emperor.
(2) The Shans.
(3) The Mongol.

TABLE 78 (Continued)

11. Chekiang

Periods

B   The Descendants of the Yellow Emperor, the Shans.
C   The We-group.
D   The We-group.
E   The We-group.
F   The We-group.
G   The Mongol.
H   The We-group.

Total Number of Elements

(1) The Descendants of the Yellow Emperor.
(2) The Shans.
(3) The Mongol.

12. Kiangsi

B   The Shans, the Mon-Khmer.
C   The We-group (the Descendants of the Yellow Emperor).
D   The We-group.
E   The We-group.
F   The We-group.
G   The Mongol.
H   The We-group.

Total Number of Elements

(1) The Shans.
(2) The Mon-Khmer.
(3) The Descendants of the Yellow Emperor.
(4) The Mongol.

13. Hunan

B   The Mon-Khmer.
C   The We-group (the Descendants of the Yellow Emperor).
D   The We-group.
E   The We-group.
F   The We-group.
G   The Mongol.
H   The We-group.

Total Number of Elements

(1) The Mon-Khmer.
(2) The Descendants of the Yellow Emperor.
(3) The Mongol.

14. Kweichow

Periods

B   The Tibeto-Burman.
C   The Tibeto-Burman.
D   The Mon-Khmer
E
F
G   The Mongol.
H   The We-group.

Total Number of Elements

(1) The Tibeto-Burman.
(2) The Mon-Khmer.
(3) The Mongol.
(4) The We-group of period H.

15. Yunnan

B   The Tibeto-Burman.
C   The We-group.
D   The Mon-Khmer. (?)
E   The Shans.
F   The We-group.
G   The Mongol.
H   The Negroid, the We-group.

Total Number of Elements

(1) The Tibeto-Burman.
(2) The We-group of period C.
(3) The Mon-Khmer.
(4) The Shans.
(5) The We-group of period F.
(6) The Mongol.
(7) The Negroid.

16. Kwangsi

B
C   The Shans.
D   The Mon-Khmer.
E   The We-group.
F   The We-group.
G   The Mongol.
H   The We-group.

Total Number of Elements

(1) The Shans.
(2) The Mon-Khmer.
(3) The We-group of period E.
(4) The Mongol.

TABLE 78 (CONTINUED)

17. KWANGTUNG

Periods

B The Shans.
C The We-group (the Descendants of the Yellow Emperor).
D The Mon-Khmer.
E The We-group.
F The We-group.
G The Mongol.
H The We- group.

Total Number of Elements

(1) The Shans.
(2) The Descendants of the Yellow Emperor.
(3) The Mon-Khmer.
(4) The Mongol.

18. FUKIEN

Periods

B
C The Shans.
D The We-group (the Descendants of the Yellow Emperor).
E The We-group.
F The We-group.
G The Mongol.
H The We-group.

Total Number of Elements

(1) The Shans.
(2) The Descendants of the Yellow Emperor.
(3) The Mongol.

Let it not be supposed for a moment that these elements which have appeared in the different provinces contributed equally to the formation of the population. But there is at least a chance for them to have left some remnants behind, although the size of such remnants cannot be exactly determined now. The number of elements varies from three to eight; the ethnographical complexity in different provinces must also vary accordingly. Shantung seems to retain a more homogeneous population than any other province; next come Honan, Nganhui, Kiangsu, Chekiang, Hunan, and Fukien. If the Mongols, Manchus, and Negroids are left out of consideration, there would be only two strata of population of any importance in each of these provinces, except Honan, which retains three. Thus we have six two-strata provinces: — Shantung, Kiangsu, Nganhui, Chekiang, Hunan, and Fukien. The ages of these provinces, estimated on the basis of city wall-building activity, are respectively as follows:

	Age	Stratum 1	Stratum 2
Kiangsu	1310	Shan	D. Y. E.
Shantung	1180	D. Y. E.	Tungus
Nganhui	1170	Shan	D. Y. E.
Hunan	600	Mon-Khmer	D. Y. E.
Chekiang	450	Shan	D. Y. E.
Fukien	290	Shan	D. Y. E.

In Shantung, then, the Descendants of the Yellow Emperor form the older stratum, while in the other five provinces they are the superficial one. Since Hunan, Chekiang, and Fukien are considerably younger than Kiangsu, Shantung, and Nganhui, we may for the moment consider Kiangsu, Shantung, and Nganhui alone. The physical data given for these provinces in Chapter II are respectively:

	No. of Cases	Cephalic Index	Nasal Index	Stature
Shantung	19	78.21	73.07	1680
Kiangsu	26	85.14	70.21	1661
Nganhui	4	80.86	76.65	1668

Since Nganhui is represented by only four cases, it again has to be eliminated. This leaves only Kiangsu and Shantung for comparison; the one has the Descendants of the Yellow Emperor as the latest stratum, the other has the Tungus as the latest stratum.   If the average indices arrived at represent the later stratum more faithfully, it would show that the Descendants of the Yellow Emperor are strongly round-headed, and decidedly leptorrhinic, while the Tungus are of a long-headed type, also tend to be leptorrhinic, although not so pronouncedly as the Kiangsu type, and are furthermore decidedly taller.

Suppose we describe the Descendants of the Yellow Emperor as the Brachy-Leptorrhinic type, — can this be supported by confirmatory evidence? Chekiang and Fukien, although several hundred years younger than Kiangsu, show the same stratification, and the average indices found for these two provinces are:

	No. of Cases	Cephalic Index	Nasal Index
Chekiang	16	81.85	73.43
Fukien	11	82.53	72.44
Kiangsu	26	85.14	70.21

A remarkable correspondence of these provinces is disclosed in these indices. The most significant point is perhaps the fact that the more round-headed is the average cephalic index, the more closely is it associated with a leptorrhinic nose. The variation may be explained by the different degrees of race mixture. This naturally necessitates the assumption that the Shans are a less round-headed and leptorrhinic type as compared with the Descendants of the Yellow Emperor. The province burdened the most with the Shan-speaking group is Yunnan, but Yunnan is the most complicated province and one for which we have only two measurements available; it is therefore quite impossible to determine what is the most prevalent type there. I do not propose here to discuss the physical type of the Shan-speaking group, which is a problem by itself; but I am willing to lay down the proposition assumed above: that is, the Shans, as found by the Descendants of the Yellow Emperor in southeast China, are less round-headed and leptorrhinic than the decidedly round-headed, leptorrhinic new immigrants.

The case of Kiangsu being to some extent confirmed, the case of Shantung may be considered next. If it is the Tungus element which makes the average indices appear dolichocephalic and leptorrhinic, then Kansu, having had two Tungus occupations in historical times, should show the same tendency. The average indices of twenty cases found by Stein are:

For Cephalic Index...................................... 76.54
For Nasal Index.. 78.20

Thus the dolichocephalic tendency is shown very definitely and even more strongly than in the Shantung average. But the nasal index indicates a somewhat opposite tendency. The Shantung men have on the average a narrower nose than the Kansu men, which implies that there is in Kansu another physical type, also long-headed but platyrrhinic. The strata of population in this province on historical evidence are five in number, and the eldest is the Descendants of the Yellow Emperor, overlaid by the Ch'iangs, the Hsiung-nus, the Tungus, and the Mongol. Several reasons lead me to believe that in Kansu, if they are present at all, the Descendants of the Yellow Emperor as a factor are very insignificant. In the first place, the general trend of the drift of population has been, with the exception of period B, always eastward, southeastward, and southwestward. Seldom has there been a northwestward backwash, so Kansu situated at the extreme northwest corner of China must have poured out its earliest stratum long ago. More concrete is the evidence furnished by Ch'iang-T'ung, who, in his *Memoir*, showed that the earliest We-group was already decreasing before the first great drift took place. This leaves Hsiung-nu, the Ch'iangs, and the Mongols, besides the Tungus for consideration. The presence of the Mongols in any part of China was merely ephemeral, as has been pointed out several times; so it, too, is of no great importance. Of the other two, the Ch'iangs seem to have left a greater impression on the make-up of the population of Kansu than the Hsiung-nus, for, historically, the Hsiung-nus as a definite group disappeared long ago, while the Ch'iangs have persisted up to the present time all over western China and Tibet. The probability is therefore greater on the side of the Ch'iangs, the northern branch of the Tibeto-Burman-speaking group, being responsible for the dolichocephalic-platyrrhinic tendency in Kansu.

So, from the evidences gathered in all these chapters, it may be justifiably concluded that the prevalent type of:

 a. the Descendants of the Yellow Emperor is brachycephalic-leptorrhine;
 b. the Tungus is dolichocephalic-leptorrhine;
 c. the Tibeto-Burman-speaking peoples is dolichocephalic-platyrrhine.

But there are two more types, according to the Chapter, to be accounted for. The dwarf element in Kwangtung can be reasonably explained as a remnant of the old dwarf factor found in Nganhui at the end of the C period. With this element is undoubtedly associated the low-headed type. As for the brachycephalic-platyrrhinic element, I am inclined to attribute it to the Mon-Khmer-speaking group. In both Kwangtung and Kwangsi, for instance, where these elements have been important up to the present, there is this tendency. The average indices for these two provinces are:

	Cephalic Index	Nasal Index
Kwangtung	81.50	86.33
Kwangsi	78.98	82.05

It would, of course, be foolhardy to make any definite line of demarcation in this regard, as linguistic, ethnographical, and biological classifications are widely divergent things and seldom show a complete coincidence. The attempt here is merely to correlate the central types, leaving a wide margin of difference for further research.

Accepting this correlation as a tentative basis, I venture to rank the basic elements of the modern Chinese in their order of importance as such:

I. *The Major Elements:*

Ethnographical or Linguistic Classes: Biological Class
 1. The Descendants of the Yellow Emperor..B. L. (Brachycephalic-Leptorrhine)
 2. The Tungus .... D. L. (Dolichocephalic-Leptorrhine)
 3. The Tibeto-Burman group .... D. P. (Dolichocephalic-Platyrrhine)
 4. The Mon-Khmer group .... B. P. (Brachycephalic-Platyrrhine)
 5. The Shan group.................................... (?)

II. *The Minor Elements:*

 6. The Hsiung-nu....................................... (?)
 7. The Mongols .... (?)
 8. The "Dwarfs"....................................... (?) Low-headed

The geographical centre of the Descendants of the Yellow Emperor is in eastern China; of the Tungus, in the north; of the Tibeto-Burman, in the west; of the Mon-Khmer, in the south, and of the Shans, in the southwest. Interspersed among the five major groups are the Hsiung-nus in the north, the dwarfs in the south, and the Mongols all over China proper, if indeed there are any. This represents the present distribution.

The historical tendency has been for the Tungus to replace the Descendants of the Yellow Emperor and the latter to replace the other three major elements.

It is hard to predict whether this same tendency will continue. But there are reasons for believing that the first has stopped and that the second will be lasting; so in the future one may expect a continued leptorrhinization of the south and a rebrachycephalization of the north, which is indicated by what has already occurred in Chihli. I am, however, prepared to modify my opinion on the basis of further research. The aim of this whole monograph is simply to show the complexity of the problem, and the possible ways of solving it.

APPENDIX

1. The eight different periods are numerically ranked; the following are their numerical equivalents:

A period = 8   B period = 7   C period = 6
D period = 5   E period = 4   F period = 3
G period = 2   H period = 1

2. Half of the referred cases are converted to actual cases of the period to which they are referred; the remaining half are distributed among the older periods in proportion to the length of time as measured by the difference of numerical equivalents of any of the older period and the referring period. The following formulae is used for calculation:

$$X = \frac{Y}{2^{(a-b)+1}}$$

a = the numerical equivalent of any period that is to receive a share of the converted cases.

b = the numerical equivalent of the period of reference.

X = the number of the converted cases due to any of the older periods.

Y = the number of the referred cases of any period.

Thus in Group 1, period H, there are 87 referred cases; suppose we want to find out how many of these are to be converted to period D, the calculation is as the following:

a = 5 (the rank of period D).

b = 1 (the rank of period H).

X, to be calculated.

Y = 87

$$X = \frac{87}{2^{(5-1)+1}} = \frac{87}{2^5} = \frac{87}{32}$$

= 2.71 . . . etc.

3. The doubtful cases are distributed equally among the eight different periods.